Practical Electronics

Volume II

Programming PIC16 Microcontrollers in Assembly and C

(Upgraded to the MPLAB® XC8 PIC® Assembler)

T. VEERAMANIKANDASAMY

Associate Professor
Department of Electronics and Communication Systems
Sri Krishna Arts and Science College
Coimbatore – 641008, India

Practical Electronics
Volume II
Programming PIC16 Microcontrollers in Assembly and C
(Upgraded to the MPLAB® XC8 PIC® Assembler)

Copyright © 2021 T. Veeramanikandasamy

All rights reserved. No part of this publication may be reproduced, distributed, or transmitted in any form or by any means, including photocopying, recording, or other electronic or mechanical methods, without prior written permission of the publisher, except in the case of brief quotations embodied in critical reviews and certain other noncommercial uses permitted by copyright law.

ISBN: 9798453457021 (Paperback)

Cover image by T. Veeramanikandasamy
(Credit: freeimages.com)

Revised Second Edition 2023

About the Author

Dr. T. Veeramanikandasamy is an Associate Professor of Electronics and Communication Systems at Sri Krishna Arts and Science College, Coimbatore, India. He obtained his Doctoral degree in Electronics from Bharathiar University, Coimbatore, India. He has Sixteen years of teaching experience at the undergraduate and postgraduate levels. His current research interests are in Embedded Systems and Nanomaterials Characterization. Five scholars were awarded their M.Phil. degree under his guidance. He has published four books with ISBN and more than 13 research articles in the field of Electronics and Materials Science. He has presented more than seventeen research papers at national/international conferences. He has delivered more than eleven technical lectures in various institutions. He is a Life Member of the Indian Society of Systems for Science and Engineering (ISSE). He holds a certification in Embedded Software Engineer (NSQF-QP ELE/Q1501) received from the Electronics Sector Skills Council of India. He has developed various student enrichment courses on Embedded Systems, Digital System Design using VHDL and Verilog, Digital Signal Processing, Programmable Logic Controller, and IoT with Python.

PREFACE

Laboratory experiments are an essential component of science and engineering education. The purpose of this book is to provide organized experiments and better enable the learners to know the laboratory aspects of Electronics. This book comprises fifty-one laboratory experiments for the **PIC16 Microcontrollers**. This book is designed to help learners to understand the principles of theoretical concepts and give them insight into the design and implementation of software and hardware for the embedded systems. It provides an exhaustive and clear explanation of PIC16 assembly language programming (Upgraded to the MPLAB® XC8 PIC® Assembler (pic-as)) and embedded C programming. Each experiment is set up as a complete module that includes the aim, algorithm, program, circuit diagram, and result. The result section has the sample inputs and outputs in each experiment that helps to verify the experiment easily. The primary audience for this book is undergraduate and postgraduate science and engineering students. Some of the advanced technologies presented in this book are currently used in many sectors like Communication Electronics, Consumer Electronics, Automotive Electronics, Industrial Controls, Medical Electronics and etc.

This book helps to

- Promote experiential learning among the students.
- Give practical or informal knowledge to understand how things work.
- Know the relation between software and hardware in a system.

I hope that you will overlook any errors in this manual and report such to the author at veeramaniks@gmail.com. I will rectify the errors and incorporate your suggestions in the next edition.

- Dr. T. Veeramanikandasamy

CONTENTS

Preface ... iv

PIC16 Microcontrollers Laboratory

1. Introduction to PIC16 Microcontrollers ... 1
2. Pin Diagram of PIC16F877/874 Devices ... 4
3. Mid-range PIC MCUs Instruction Set ... 7
4. Software Development Tools ... 8
5. Addition of Two 8-bit Numbers ... 16
6. Subtraction of Two 8-bit Numbers ... 18
7. Addition of N 8-bit Numbers in an Array ... 20
8. Addition of Two 16-bit Numbers ... 23
9. Subtraction of Two 16-bit Numbers ... 26
10. Multiplication of Two 8-bit numbers ... 29
11. Division of Two 8-bit Numbers ... 32
12. 1's Compliment of an 8-bit Number ... 35
13. 2's Compliment of an 8-bit Number ... 37
14. Largest Number in an Array ... 39
15. Smallest Number in an Array ... 43
16. Descending Order of an Array ... 46
17. Ascending Order of an Array ... 50
18. Block Data Transfer ... 55
19. Fibonacci Series ... 58

20	Binary to ASCII Conversion	61
21	ASCII to Binary Conversion	64
22	Binary to Gray Code Conversion	67
23	Gray Code to Binary Conversion	70
24	4-bit Binary Counter	72
25	Logical Operation - Demorgan's Law	76
26	Square Waveform Generation using Software Delay	80
27	Flashing of LED	85
28	Read Key	87
29	Traffic Light Controller	89
30	Seven Segment Display Interface	93
31	LCD Interface in 4-Bit Mode	96
32	Hex Keyboard Interface	103
33	Solid State Relay Interface	108
34	DC Motor Direction Controller	111
35	Stepper Motor Interface	114
36	Interfacing Proximity Sensor using Interrupt	117
37	Flashing LED using On-chip Timer	121
38	Speed Control of DC Motor using PWM	126
39	Servo Motor Control using PWM	131
40	Frequency Measurement	136
41	Analog to Digital Conversion	141

42	Temperature Monitor using On-chip ADC	145
43	Data Transfer using USART	150
44	Bluetooth Controlled System	155
45	Obstacle Detector using Ultrasonic Sensor	160
46	Sending SMS using GSM Module	165
47	LED ON/OFF Control using GSM Module	170
48	GPS Module Interface	175
49	Motion Detection Alarm using PIR Sensor	180
50	Accelerometer Sensor Interface	183
51	Graphical LCD Interface	190
52	I2C Communication	199
53	Interfacing RTC using I2C Protocol	207
54	SPI Communication	217
55	Interfacing ESP8266 Wi-Fi Module	225

PIC16 MICROCONTROLLERS LABORATORY

1. Introduction to PIC16 Microcontrollers

PIC microcontroller was developed by microchip technology in the year 1993. The term PIC stands for Peripheral Interface Controller. The 8-bit PIC microcontroller uses a Reduced Instruction Set Computer (RISC) architecture that has a separate address bus and data bus. PIC microcontrollers are very popular due to their low cost, wide availability, easy to interface with other peripherals, ease of programming, inbuilt ADC, and serial programming capabilities. PIC microcontrollers offer a wide range of products with core independent peripherals like RAM, flash memory, Timers/Counters, EEPROM, I/O Ports, USART, CCP (Capture/Compare/ PWM module), SSP, Comparator, ADC (Analog to Digital Converter), PSP (Parallel Slave Port), and ICSP (In-Circuit Serial Programming).

The 8-bit PIC microcontrollers have classified into four types based on the internal architecture such as Base Line PIC, Mid-Range PIC, Enhanced Mid-Range PIC, and PIC18. Baseline PIC microcontrollers utilize a 12-bit instruction word and provide the right amount of features and options to minimize expenses. The Baseline can be recognized by their part number structure: 10Fxxx, 12Fxxx, and 16Fxxx. Mid-Range PIC microcontrollers utilize a 14-bit instruction word that is the next tier in performance and has features from the Baseline PIC microcontrollers. The mid-range can be recognized by their part number structure: 10Fxxx, 12Fxxx, and 16Fxxx. The newest family is the enhanced mid-range core that builds upon the best elements of the mid-range core and provides additional performance. The enhanced mid-range can be recognized by their part number structure: 12F1xxx and 16F1xxx. PIC18 family combines the maximum level of performance and integration with an 8-bit architecture. It utilizes a 16-bit instruction word. The high-end devices can be recognized by their part number structure: 18Fxxxx, 18FxxJxx, and 18FxxKxx.

The PIC10F and PIC12F are the cheapest and generally have less memory, smaller pin counts, and fewer peripherals. PIC16F series are the most popular as they have many resource code libraries on the Internet. PIC16F877A is one of the most renowned microcontrollers in the industry. The **PIC16F887, PIC16F18877, and PIC16F1789** microcontrollers seem to be compatible with the PIC16F877, and they have the upgraded peripherals with low-power consumption.

PIC16F877 Microcontroller Core Features:
- High performance RISC CPU with 35 number of instructions
- All instructions are executed in single instruction cycle except for program branches
- Operating speed: DC - 20 MHz clock input with DC - 200ns instruction cycle
- Up to 8K x 14 words of Flash Program Memory
- Up to 368 x 8 bytes of Data Memory (RAM)
- Up to 256 x 8 bytes of EEPROM Data Memory
- Pin out compatible to the PIC16F887, PIC16F18877, PIC16F1789 and PIC16LF1789
- Interrupt capability (up to 14 sources)
- Eight level deep hardware stack
- Direct, indirect and relative addressing modes
- Power-on Reset (POR) and Power-up Timer (PWRT)
- Oscillator Start-up Timer (OST) and Selectable oscillator options

- Watchdog Timer (WDT) with its on-chip RC oscillator for reliable operation
- Programmable code protection and power saving SLEEP mode
- Low power, high speed CMOS Flash/EEPROM technology
- Fully static design with In-Circuit Serial Programming (ICSP) via two pins
- Single 5V In-Circuit Serial Programming capability
- In-Circuit Debugging via two pins
- Processor read/write access to program memory
- Wide operating voltage range 2.0V-5.5V and high sink/source current: 25 mA
- Commercial, Industrial and Extended temperature ranges

PIC16F877 Microcontroller Peripheral Features:
- Timer0: 8-bit timer/counter with 8-bit prescaler
- Timer1: 16-bit timer/counter with prescaler, can be incremented during SLEEP
- Timer2: 8-bit timer/counter with 8-bit period register, prescaler and postscaler
- Two Capture, Compare, PWM modules
    - Capture is 16-bit, max. Resolution is 12.5 ns
    - Compare is 16-bit, max. Resolution is 200 ns
    - PWM, max. Resolution is 10-bit
- 10-bit multi-channel Analog-to-Digital converter
- Synchronous Serial Port (SSP) with SPI (Master mode) and I2C (Master/Slave)
- Universal Synchronous Asynchronous Receiver Transmitter (USART) with 9-bit address detection
- Parallel Slave Port (PSP) 8-bits wide, with external RD, WR and CS controls (40/44-pin only)
- Brown-out detection circuitry for Brown-out Reset (BOR)

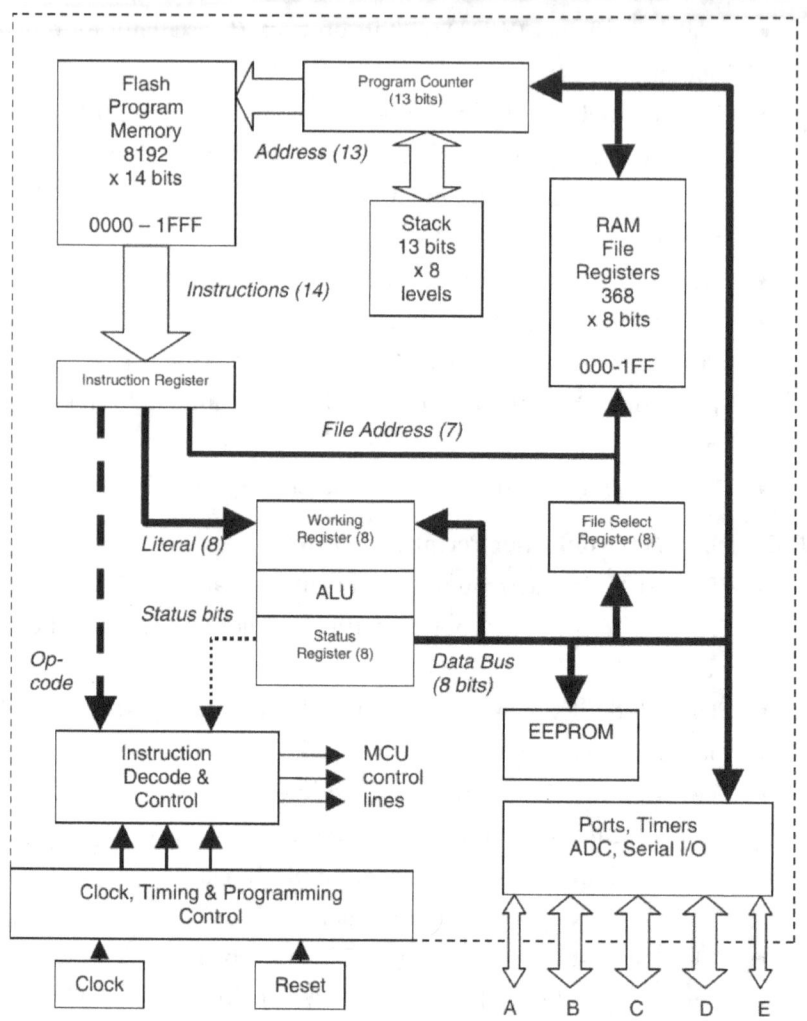

Building Blocks of PIC16F877/874 devices

2. Pin Diagram of PIC16F877/874 devices

The PIC16F877/874 devices can be obtained in four IC packages such as 40-pin PDIP, 44-pin PLCC, 44-pin TQFP, and 44-pin QFN. There are 32 input and output port pins and arranged as five ports: PORTA (5), PORTB (8), PORTC (8), PORTD (8), and PORTE (3). All are operating as digital I/O pins, and most have more than one function, the mode of operation of each is selected by initializing various control registers within the chip.

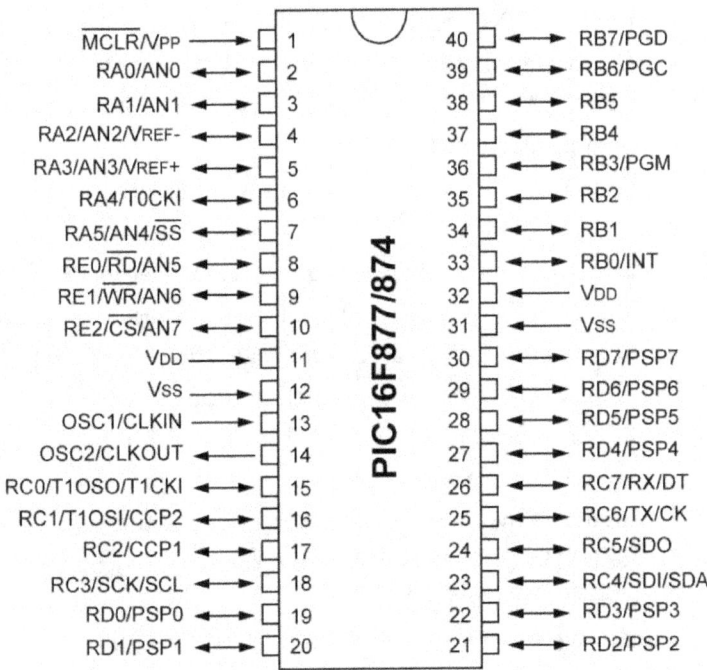

Pin diagram of PIC16F877/874 devices

PIN 1: MCLR: It resets the microcontroller when it is active low.

PIN 2: RA0/AN0: PORTA consists of 6 pins, from pin 2 to pin 7, all of these are bidirectional input/output pins. PORTA0 or this pin can also be used as an analog pin AN0.

PIN 3: RA1/AN1: PORTA1 or this can be the analog input 1.

PIN 4: RA2/AN2/Vref-: PORTA2 or analog input2 or negative analog reference voltage.

PIN 5: RA3/AN3/Vref+: PORTA3 or analog input3 or positive analog reference voltage.

PIN 6: RA4/T0CKI: PORTA4 or the clock input pin of timer0.

PIN 7: RA5/SS/AN4: PORTA5 or analog input 4 or the slave select for the synchronous serial port.

PIN 8: RE0/RD/AN5: PORTE starts from pin 8 to pin 10 and this is also a bidirectional input-output port. PORTE0 or it can be the analog input 5 or read control pin for parallel slave port.

PIN 9:   RE1/WR/AN6: PORTE1 or analog input 6 or write control pin for parallel slave port.

PIN 10:   RE2/CS/A7: PORTE2 or analog input 7 or control select pin for parallel slave port.

PIN 11 and 32: VDD: They should be connected to +5V.

PIN 12 and 31: VSS: They should be connected to GND.

PIN 13: OSC1/CLKIN: A crystal resonator is connected between pin 13 and 14 to provide an external clock to the microcontroller. This pin also acts as an external clock input pin.

PIN 14: OSC2/CLKOUT: This is the oscillator output pin.

PIN 15:   RC0/T1OCO/T1CKI: PORTC consists of 8 pins. It is also a bidirectional input-output port. PORTC0 or it can be the clock input of timer 1 or the oscillator output of timer 2.

PIN 16:   RC1/T1OSI/CCP2: PORTC1 or it can be the oscillator input of timer 1 or CCP 2 pin.

PIN 17:   RC2/CCP1: PORTC2 or it can be the CCP 2 pin.

PIN 18:   RC3/SCK/SCL: PORTC3 or it can be the output for SPI or I2C modes and can be the input/output for synchronous serial clock.

PIN 23:   RC4/SDI/SDA: PORTC4 or it can be the SPI data input pin or data pin of I2C mode.

PIN 24:   RC5/SDO: PORTC5 or it can be the data out of SPI mode.

PIN 25:   RC6/TX/CK: PORTC6 or USART Asynchronous transmit pin or synchronous clock pin.

PIN 26:   RC7/RX/DT: PORTC7 or USART Asynchronous receive pin or synchronous data pin.

PIN 19, 20, 21, 22, 27, 28, 29, and 30: All of these are PORTD pins. It is also a bidirectional input-output port or it can act as the parallel slave port.

PIN 33-40:   All these pins belong to PORTB. RB0 can be used as the external interrupt pin and RB6 and RB7 can be used as in-circuit debugger pins.

	Bits	Pins	Alternate function/s	Bit	Default
Port A	6	RA0–RA5	Analogue inputs Timer0 clock input Serial port slave select input	0,1,2,3,5 4 5	Analogue Input
Port B	8	RB0–RB7	External interrupt Low-voltage programming input Serial programming In-circuit debugging	0 3 6,7 6,7	Digital I/O
Port C	8	RC0–RC7	Timer1 clock input/output Capture/Compare/PWM SPI, I²C synchronous clock/data USART asynchronous clock/data	0,1 1,2 3,4,5 6,7	Digital I/O
Port D	8	RD0–RD7	Parallel slave port data I/O	0–7	Digital I/O
Port E	3	RE0–RE2	Analogue inputs Parallel slave port control bits	0,1,2 0,1,2	Analogue Input

Port Functions of PIC16F877/874 Microcontrollers

3. Mid-range PIC MCUs Instruction Set

All PIC microcontroller instructions execute in one instruction cycle except few conditional branch instructions. There are four oscillator periods in one instruction cycle. Thus, for an oscillator frequency of 4 MHz, the instruction execution time is 1 us. The fetch, decode and execute cycles are pipelined. Therefore, the CPU executes these phases in parallel, so that each instruction executed in one instruction cycle. Each midrange instruction is a 14-bit word opcode that specifies the instruction type, operands and operation of the instruction.

The instruction set is grouped into three basic categories:
- Literal and Control operations
- Bit-oriented operations
- Byte-oriented operations

Mnemonic, Operands		Description	Cycles	14-Bit Instruction Word				Status Affected	Notes
				MSb			LSb		
LITERAL AND CONTROL OPERATIONS									
ADDLW	k	Add literal and W	1	11	111x	kkkk	kkkk	C,DC,Z	
ANDLW	k	AND literal with W	1	11	1001	kkkk	kkkk	Z	
CALL	k	Call subroutine	2	10	0kkk	kkkk	kkkk		
CLRWDT	-	Clear Watchdog Timer	1	00	0000	0110	0100	TO,PD	
GOTO	k	Go to address	2	10	1kkk	kkkk	kkkk		
IORLW	k	Inclusive OR literal with W	1	11	1000	kkkk	kkkk	Z	
MOVLW	k	Move literal to W	1	11	00xx	kkkk	kkkk		
RETFIE	-	Return from interrupt	2	00	0000	0000	1001		
RETLW	k	Return with literal in W	2	11	01xx	kkkk	kkkk		
RETURN	-	Return from Subroutine	2	00	0000	0000	1000		
SLEEP	-	Go into standby mode	1	00	0000	0110	0011	TO,PD	
SUBLW	k	Subtract W from literal	1	11	110x	kkkk	kkkk	C,DC,Z	
XORLW	k	Exclusive OR literal with W	1	11	1010	kkkk	kkkk	Z	

For literal and control operation, 'k' represents eight or eleven-bit constant value.

Mnemonic, Operands		Description	Cycles	14-Bit Instruction Word				Status Affected	Notes
				MSb			LSb		
BIT-ORIENTED FILE REGISTER OPERATIONS									
BCF	f, b	Bit Clear f	1	01	00bb	bfff	ffff		1,2
BSF	f, b	Bit Set f	1	01	01bb	bfff	ffff		1,2
BTFSC	f, b	Bit Test f, Skip if Clear	1 (2)	01	10bb	bfff	ffff		3
BTFSS	f, b	Bit Test f, Skip if Set	1 (2)	01	11bb	bfff	ffff		3

For bit-oriented instructions, 'f' represents a file register designator and 'b' represents a bit field of a file register.

Mnemonic, Operands		Description	Cycles	14-Bit Instruction Word				Status Affected	Notes
				MSb			LSb		
BYTE-ORIENTED FILE REGISTER OPERATIONS									
ADDWF	f, d	Add W and f	1	00	0111	dfff	ffff	C,DC,Z	1,2
ANDWF	f, d	AND W with f	1	00	0101	dfff	ffff	Z	1,2
CLRF	f	Clear f	1	00	0001	1fff	ffff	Z	2
CLRW	-	Clear W	1	00	0001	0xxx	xxxx	Z	
COMF	f, d	Complement f	1	00	1001	dfff	ffff	Z	1,2
DECF	f, d	Decrement f	1	00	0011	dfff	ffff	Z	1,2
DECFSZ	f, d	Decrement f, Skip if 0	1(2)	00	1011	dfff	ffff		1,2,3
INCF	f, d	Increment f	1	00	1010	dfff	ffff	Z	1,2
INCFSZ	f, d	Increment f, Skip if 0	1(2)	00	1111	dfff	ffff		1,2,3
IORWF	f, d	Inclusive OR W with f	1	00	0100	dfff	ffff	Z	1,2
MOVF	f, d	Move f	1	00	1000	dfff	ffff	Z	1,2
MOVWF	f	Move W to f	1	00	0000	1fff	ffff		
NOP	-	No Operation	1	00	0000	0xx0	0000		
RLF	f, d	Rotate Left f through Carry	1	00	1101	dfff	ffff	C	1,2
RRF	f, d	Rotate Right f through Carry	1	00	1100	dfff	ffff	C	1,2
SUBWF	f, d	Subtract W from f	1	00	0010	dfff	ffff	C,DC,Z	1,2
SWAPF	f, d	Swap nibbles in f	1	00	1110	dfff	ffff		1,2
XORWF	f, d	Exclusive OR W with f	1	00	0110	dfff	ffff	Z	1,2

For byte-oriented instructions, 'f' represents a file register designator and 'd' represents a destination designator. If 'd' is zero, the result is placed in the W register. If 'd' is one, the result is placed in the file register.

4. Software Development Tools

Microchip development and debugging tools are used to develop the source code for PIC microcontroller-based embedded systems which include editors, assemblers, compilers, debuggers, simulators, emulators, and device programmers. A typical software development cycle starts with writing an application program using a text editor. This program is then translated into an executable code or HEX code with the help of an assembler or compiler. MPLAB X and Atmel Studio ecosystems provide a variety of embedded design tools. MPLAB X tools are compatible with

Windows, Linux, and macOS operating systems while Atmel Studio tools are compatible with Windows. MPLAB IDE allows writing, debugging, and optimizing PIC microcontroller applications for firmware product designs. MPLAB X IDE having built-in editor and simulators. The MPLAB® XC8 PIC® Assembler tool (pic-as) can be used to write assembly language programs. MPLAB IDE also provides emulator environments to debug the logic of executables.

Compilers for PIC Microcontrollers:

The popular compilers are used to program the PIC microcontrollers are: MPLAB XC8, Mikro C, PIC CCS compiler, and Hi-Tech C compiler. The MPLAB XC8 is the Microchip's official complier. It is free to use and available at Microchip official website.

Getting Started with MPLAB IDE:

The MPLAB IDE desktop contains the following major elements:
- A menu across the top line
- A toolbar below the menu
- A workspace in which various files, windows, and dialogs can be displayed and a status bar at the bottom

A step by step procedure for creating a new project with MPLAB X IDE:

1. Double click on MPLAB X IDE icon (*Version v6.05*)
   (If you have project(s) in project window, Go to File menu → Close all projects)

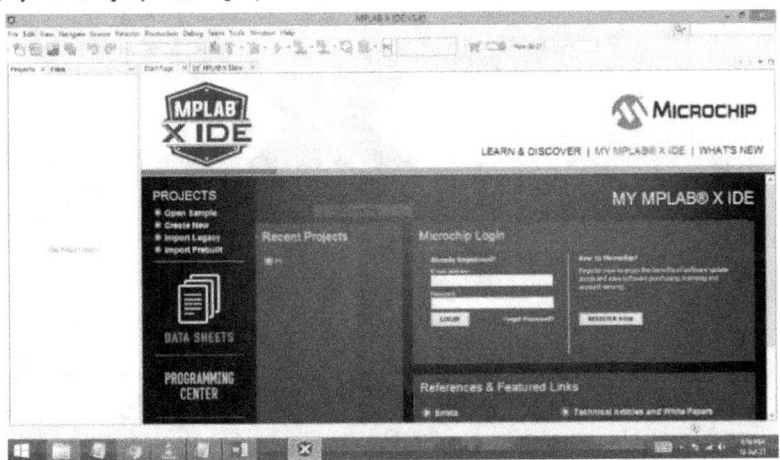

2. To create new project in MPLAB X IDE
   File → New project

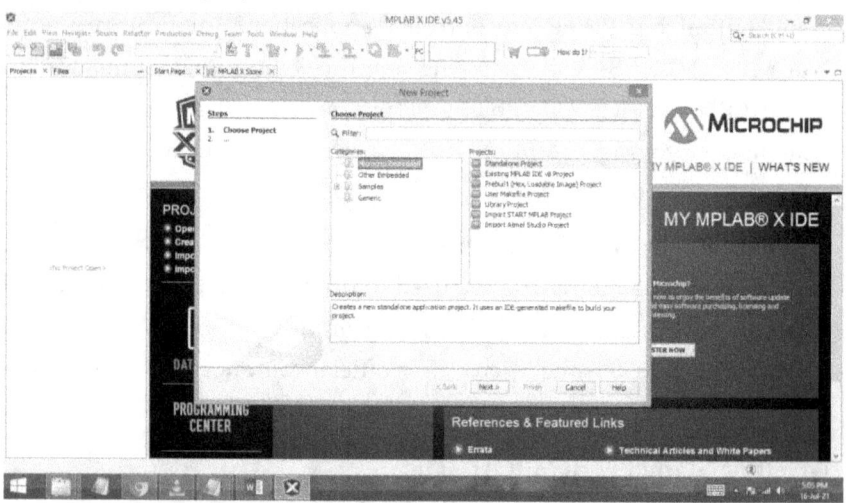

   Categories: Microchip Embedded
   Projects: Standalone project / any other options

3. Select Device
   Family: Midrange PIC
   Device: PIC16F877A
   Tool: Simulator / PICkit3 / PICkit4

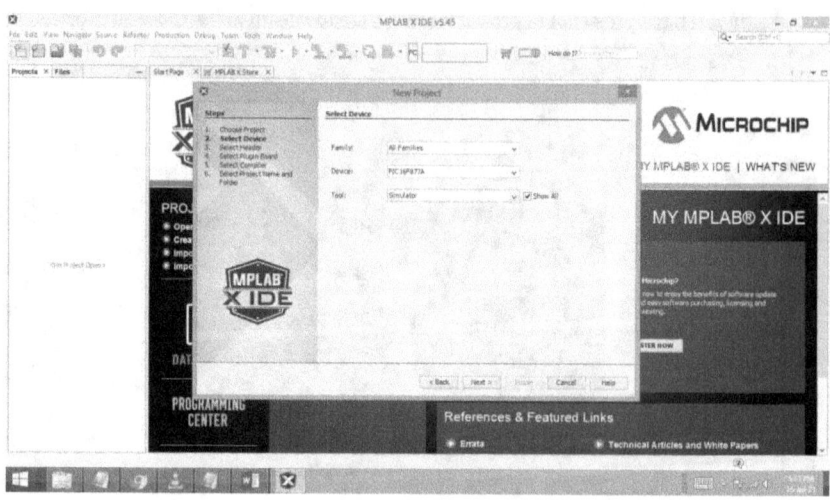

4. Select Compiler

   For ASM CODE: pic-as (version number) like pic-as (v2.40)

   For C CODE: xc8 (version number) like XC8 (v2.40)

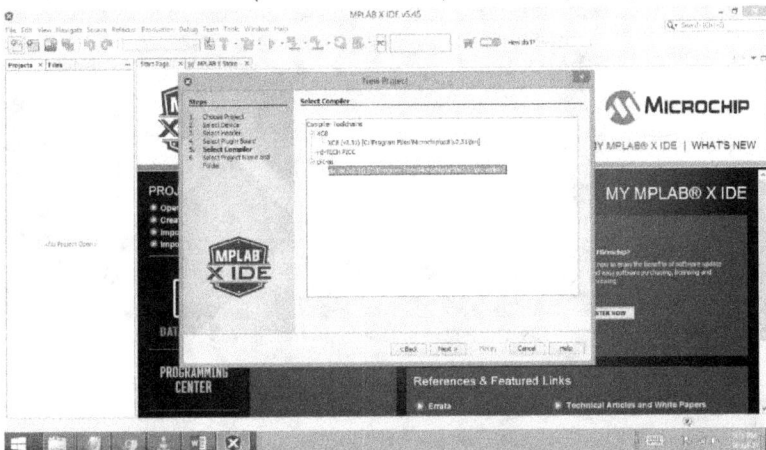

5. Select Project Name and Folder

   Project Name: ******

   Project Location: *******

   Project Folder: *******

   Check set as main project

   Encoding: ******** (ISO-8859-1)

   Finish

6. To create a source file, go to File menu and click on new file

   Categories:

   For Assembly Language Program, choose Assembler

   For C Program, choose C

   For Python, choose Python and so on.

   File Types:

   Choose the file with proper extension (.asm / .s / .inc)

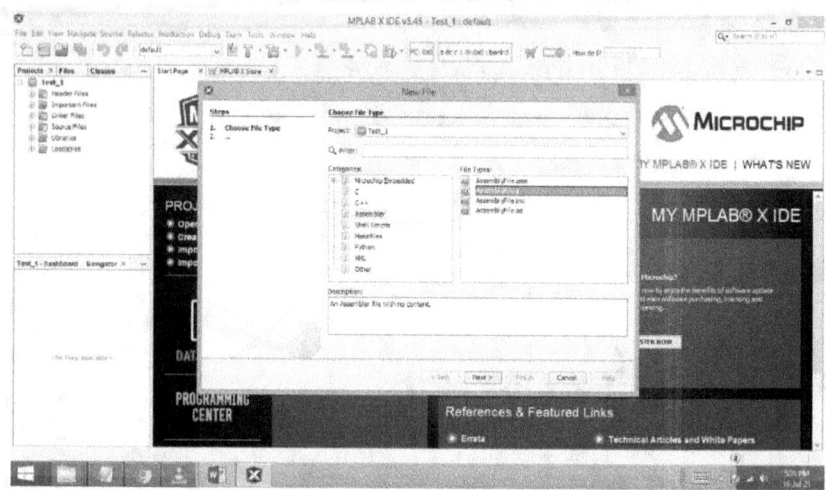

7. Set the file name (Test_1.s) and location. Click on Finish.

   Add the source file (Test_1.s) to the project.

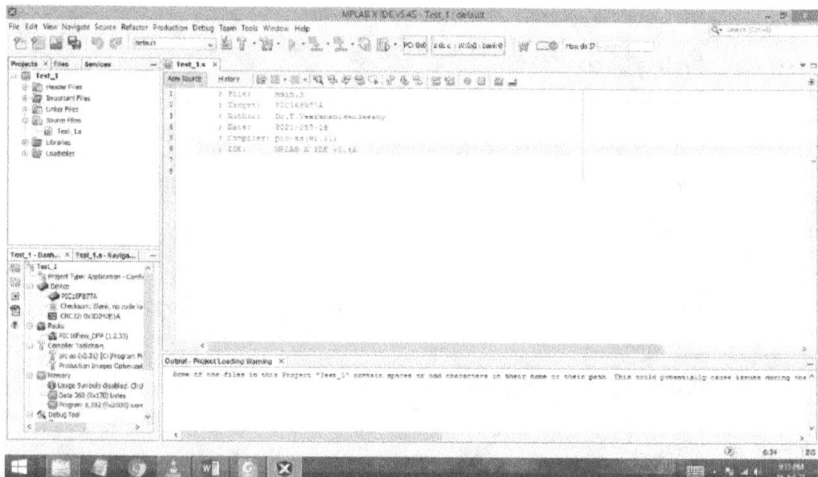

8. Go to Production menu and select "Set Configuration Bits"

Field:	HS	// LP up to about 200kHz, XT up to about 4MHz, HS up to 20MHz.
WDTE:	OFF	// Watch dog timer
PWRTE:	OFF	// PWRT delay (72 ms) allows VDD to rise to an acceptable level. The Power-up Timer should always be enabled when Brown-out Reset is enabled.

BOREN:	OFF	// On-chip Brown-out Reset circuitry places the device into reset when the device voltage falls below a trip point.
LVP:	OFF	// If you using PGD and PGC for ICSP, LVP is OFF If LVP is ON, PGM has to be used for programming
CPD:	OFF	// Data EEPROM code protection off
WRT:	OFF	// Flash memory write protection off
CP:	OFF	// Flash memory code protection off

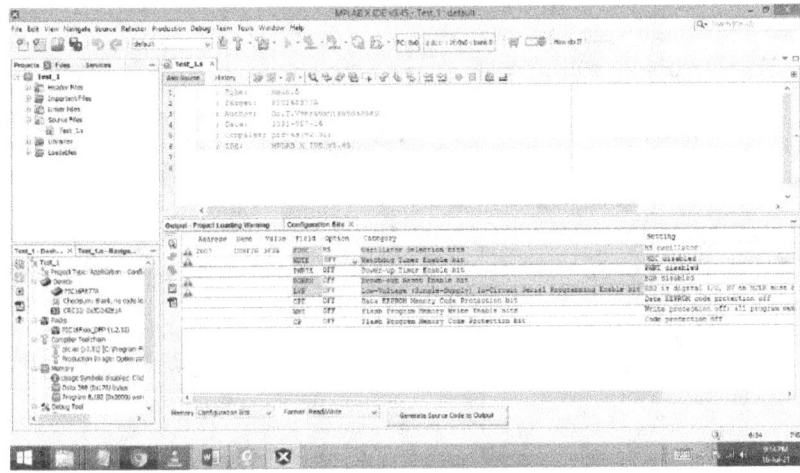

Click on Generate Source Code to output.

Copy the codes and paste it in .s editor file.

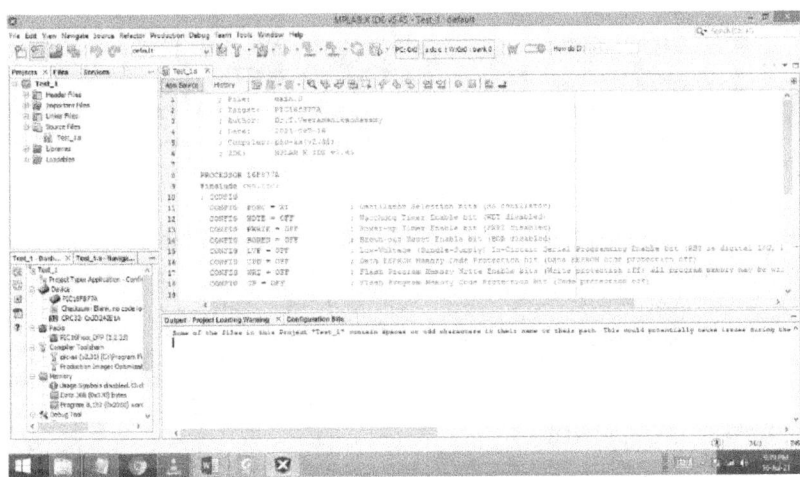

9. Create your program in editor after the *config* lines.

    ; File   : main.S

    ; Target   : PIC16F877A

```asm
; Author        : Dr.T.Veeramanikandasamy
; Date          : 2023-01-28
; Compiler      : pic-as(v2.40)
; IDE           : MPLAB X IDE v6.05

#include <xc.inc>
    CONFIG  FOSC = HS          ; Device Configurations
    CONFIG  WDTE = OFF
    CONFIG  PWRTE = OFF
    CONFIG  BOREN = OFF
    CONFIG  LVP = OFF
    CONFIG  CPD = OFF
    CONFIG  WRT = OFF
    CONFIG  CP = OFF

    PSECT reset_Vec, class=CODE, delta=2    ; Initialization code at 00h
reset_Vec:
    goto main
    PSECT int_Vec, class=CODE, delta=2      ; interrupt code at 04h
int_Vec:
    retfie

    PSECT code, abs            ; main code starts at 50h
    org 50h
main:
    C1 equ 0x25                ; 0x25 assigned to C1
    C2 equ 0x26                ; 0x26 assigned to C2
    C3 equ 0x27                ; 0x27 assigned to C3
    banksel TRISB              ; Select Bank 1 to access TRISB register
    movlw 0b00000000
    movwf TRISB
    banksel PORTB              ; Select Bank 0 to access PORTB register
again:
    movlw 0xff                 ; Write 0xff to the PORTB
    movwf PORTB
    call delay                 ; Call delay function
    movlw 0x00                 ; Write 0x00 to the PORTB
    movwf PORTB
    call delay                 ; Call delay function
    goto again                 ; Repeat the main task
delay:                         ; 1 second delay
    movlw 6
```

```
            movwf C1
            movlw 24
            movwf C2
            movlw 167
            movwf C3
loop:
            decfsz C3,1
            goto loop
            decfsz C2,1
            goto loop
            decfsz C1,1
            goto loop
            return
            END reset_Vec
```

10. Go to Production menu → Build Main Project /

    Click on Build Project icon

    The result of build process will be available on output window.
    like **BUILD SUCCESSFUL**

11. For simulation: Go to Debug menu → Debug Main Project /
    Click on the Debug icon appearing on the Toolbar.

    Pause and Reset

    To view the output: Go to Window → Debugging →

    Variables. Choose the respective registers to see the program output or Choose the SFRs in memory view.

12. Press F7/F8 for single step execution and watch the Variables/SFRs to verify the program sequence.

5. ADDITION OF TWO 8-BIT NUMBERS

Aim:

Write an assembly language program to perform the addition of two 8-bit numbers in the PIC16F877A/887 Microcontroller. Verify the result using the simulator.

Software Used:
- IDE: MPLAB X IDE v6.05
- PIC Assembler: pic-as (v2.40)

Algorithm:
1. Initialize the memory location for the first operand in 0x30 and second operand in 0x31.
2. Initialize the PORTB and PORTD as output ports for storing the sum and carry of addition result; Clear both the registers.
3. Move the first operand to the WREG.
4. Add WREG with the second operand and store the sum in WREG.
5. Move the sum value to PORTB.
6. Check the STATUS register for the carry; skip the next step if the carry flag is clear.
7. Increment PORTD (increment carry value).
8. Halt.

Program:
```
#include <xc.inc>
  CONFIG  FOSC = HS           ; Device Configurations
  CONFIG  WDTE = OFF
  CONFIG  PWRTE = OFF
  CONFIG  BOREN = OFF
  CONFIG  LVP = OFF
  CONFIG  CPD = OFF
  CONFIG  WRT = OFF
```

```
CONFIG  CP = OFF

PSECT reset_Vec, class=CODE, delta=2        ; Initialization code at 00h
reset_Vec:
    goto main
PSECT int_Vec, class=CODE, delta=2          ; interrupt code at 04h
int_Vec:
    retfie
PSECT code, abs              ; main code starts at 50h
org 50h
main:
; Enter the inputs at 0x30 & 0x31; result will be at PORTB and PORTD
    X1      equ     30h
    X2      equ     31h
    banksel         TRISB       ; Select Bank1
    CLRF            TRISB       ; Initialize PORTB as output
    CLRF            TRISD       ; Initialize PORTD as output
    banksel         PORTB       ; Select Bank 0
    CLRF            PORTB       ; Clear PORT8B (sum)
    CLRF            PORTD       ; Clear PORTD (carry)
    MOVF            X1, W       ; Move X1 value to WREG
    ADDWF           X2, W       ; Add WREG with X2 and hold the sum in WREG
    MOVWF           PORTB       ; Move the sum to PORTB
    BTFSC           STATUS, 0   ; If no carry, skip the next statement
    INCF            PORTD, F    ; Increment PORTD
    GOTO            $           ; Halt
END reset_Vec
```

Experimental Result:

Input Data		Result	
Memory location	Operand	Memory location	Operand
X1 (0x30)	64 H	PORTB	16 H (sum)

| X2 (0x31) | B2 H | PORTD | 01 H (carry) |

Calculation:

I/O	in HEX		in Binary	
Operand 1	64 H		0110	0100
Operand 2	B2 H		1011	0010
Result (carry & sum)	116 H	1	0001	0110

Conclusion:

Thus the PIC16F877A assembly language program for the addition of two 8-bit numbers has been executed and verified the result.

6. SUBTRACTION OF TWO 8-BIT NUMBERS

Aim:

Write an assembly language program to perform the subtraction of two 8-bit numbers in the PIC16F877A/887 Microcontroller. Verify the result using the simulator.

Software Used:
- IDE: MPLAB X IDE v6.05
- PIC Assembler: pic-as (v2.40)

Algorithm:
1. Initialize the memory location for the first operand in 0x30 and second operand in 0x31.
2. Initialize the PORTB and PORTD as output ports for storing difference and borrow of subtraction result, respectively.
3. Move the first operand to the WREG.
4. Subtract the WREG from the second operand and store the difference in WREG.
5. Move the difference value to PORTB.

6. Check the STATUS register for the carry/borrow; skip the next step if the carry flag is set.
7. Increment PORTD (increment borrow value).
8. Halt.

Program:

```
#include <xc.inc>
    CONFIG  FOSC = HS           ; Device Configurations
    CONFIG  WDTE = OFF
    CONFIG  PWRTE = OFF
    CONFIG  BOREN = OFF
    CONFIG  LVP = OFF
    CONFIG  CPD = OFF
    CONFIG  WRT = OFF
    CONFIG  CP = OFF


PSECT reset_Vec, class=CODE, delta=2    ; Initialization code at 00h
reset_Vec:
    goto main
PSECT int_Vec, class=CODE, delta=2      ; interrupt code at 04h
int_Vec:
    retfie
PSECT code, abs                         ; main code starts at 50h
org 50h
main:
; Enter the inputs at 0x30 & 0x31; result will be at PORTB and PORTD
    X1      equ     30h
    X2      equ     31h
    banksel         TRISB       ; Select Bank1
    CLRF            TRISB       ; Initialize PORTB as output
    CLRF            TRISD       ; Initialize PORTD as output
    banksel         PORTB       ; Select Bank 0
    CLRF            PORTB       ; Clear PORTB (Diff.)
    CLRF            PORTD       ; Clear PORTD (Borrow)
```

MOVF	X1, W	; Move X1 value to WREG
SUBWF	X2, W	; Subtract WREG from X2 and hold the Diff. in WREG
MOVWF	PORTB	; Move the Diff. to PORTB
BTFSS	STATUS, 0	; If carry/borrow, skip the next statement
INCF	PORTD, F	; Increment PORTD
GOTO	$	; Halt

END reset_Vec

Experimental Result:

Input Data		Result	
Memory location	Operand	Memory location	Operand
X1 (0x30)	64 H	PORTB	4E H (Diff)
X2 (0x31)	B2 H	PORTD	00 H (Borrow)

Note: B2h − 64h = 4Eh

Calculation:

I/O	in HEX	in Binary		
Operand 1	64 H		0110	0100
Operand 2	B2 H		1011	0010
Result (Diff & Brw)	4E H	0	0100	1110

Conclusion:

Thus the PIC16F877A assembly language program for the subtraction of two 8-bit numbers has been executed and verified the result.

7. ADDITION OF N 8-BIT NUMBERS IN AN ARRAY

Aim:

Write an assembly language program to perform the addition of N 8-bit numbers in an array using the PIC16F877A/887 Microcontroller. Verify the result using the simulator.

Software Used:
- IDE: MPLAB X IDE v6.05
- PIC Assembler: pic-as (v2.40)

Algorithm:
1. Clear Carry register.
2. Initialize the memory location of input data in FSR; FSR points 30H.
3. Move the first data of an array (number of array elements) to Count register.
4. Clear WREG which will hold the sum of addition.
5. Increment FSR.
6. Add the WREG value with the content of FSR and hold the sum in WREG.
7. Test the STATUS register for the carry; skip the next step if carry is not set.
8. Increment the carry register.
9. Decrement the count register; skip the next step if it is zero.
10. Go to step 5.
11. Move the WREG value (Sum) to PORTB.
12. Move the Carry register value to PORTD.
13. Halt.

Program:
```
#include <xc.inc>
  CONFIG  FOSC = HS          ; Device Configurations
  CONFIG  WDTE = OFF
  CONFIG  PWRTE = OFF
  CONFIG  BOREN = OFF
  CONFIG  LVP = OFF
  CONFIG  CPD = OFF
  CONFIG  WRT = OFF
  CONFIG  CP = OFF

PSECT reset_Vec, class=CODE, delta=2   ; Initialization code at 00h
```

```
reset_Vec:
    goto main
PSECT int_Vec, class=CODE, delta=2      ; interrupt code at 04h
int_Vec:
    retfie
PSECT code, abs                          ; main code starts at 50h
org 50h
main:
; Enter the inputs from 0x30 (first location should be the count value of an array); result will
; be at PORTB and PORTD
IP      equ     0x30            ; Enter the Input Data Count and Data
Count   equ     0x40            ; Temp register for Count
    BANKSEL     TRISB           ; Select Bank1
    CLRF        TRISB           ; Initialize PORTB as output
    CLRF        TRISD           ; Initialize PORTD as output
    BANKSEL     PORTB           ; Select Bank 0
    CLRF        PORTB           ; Clear sum register
    CLRF        PORTD           ; Clear Carry register
    MOVLW       IP              ; 1st address of input data to FSR
    MOVWF       FSR
    MOVF        IP, W           ; Move array count to WREG
    MOVWF       Count
    MOVLW       0x00            ; Clear WREG
Again:
    INCF        FSR, 1          ; Increment the data pointer
    ADDWF       INDF, 0         ; Add WREG with the value of data pointer
                                ; and hold the sum in WREG
    MOVWF       PORTB           ; Move the sum to PORTB
    BTFSC       STATUS, 0       ; Check the carry, skip the next
                                ; instruction if it is clear
    INCF        PORTD, 1        ; Increment carry register
    DECFSZ      Count, 1        ; Decrement count register, skip the next
                                ; instruction if it is zero
    GOTO        Again
```

```
        GOTO        $              ; Halt
        END reset_Vec
```

Experimental Result:

Input Data		Result	
Memory location	Operand	Memory location	Operand
30	04 H*	PORTB	03 H (sum)
31	16 H	PORTD	01 H (carry)
32	42 H		
33	73 H		
34	38 H		

Number of array elements

Calculation:

I/O	in HEX
Count	04 H
Operand 1	16 H
Operand 2	42 H
Operand 3	73 H
Operand 4	38 H
Result	103 H

Conclusion:

Thus the PIC16F877A assembly language program for the addition of N 8-bit numbers in an array has been executed and verified the result.

8. ADDITION OF TWO 16-BIT NUMBERS

Aim:

Write an assembly language program to perform the addition of two 16-bit binary numbers using the PIC16F877A/887 Microcontroller. Verify the result using the simulator.

Software Used:
- IDE: MPLAB X IDE v6.05
- PIC Assembler: pic-as (v2.40)

Algorithm:
1. Set PORTB, PORTD, and PORTC as output ports.
2. Clear Carry register.
3. Move the LSBs (X1) of the first operand to the WREG.
4. Add the WREG with the LSBs (Y1) of the second operand and hold the sum in WREG.
5. Move the WREG value to PORTB.
6. Test the Carry flag in the STATUS register; skip the next step if the Carry flag is clear.
7. Increment MSB 8-bits (X2) of operand 1.
8. Move the MSBs (X2) of operand 1 to the WREG.
9. Add the WREG with the MSBs (Y2) of the second operand and hold the sum in WREG.
10. Move the WREG value to PORTD.
11. Test the Carry flag in the STATUS register; skip the next step if the Carry flag is clear.
12. Increment the Carry register.
13. Move the value of the Carry register to PORTC.
14. Halt.

Program:
```
#include <xc.inc>
 CONFIG  FOSC = HS           ; Device Configurations
 CONFIG  WDTE = OFF
 CONFIG  PWRTE = OFF
 CONFIG  BOREN = OFF
 CONFIG  LVP = OFF
 CONFIG  CPD = OFF
 CONFIG  WRT = OFF
 CONFIG  CP = OFF
```

```
PSECT reset_Vec, class=CODE, delta=2   ; Initialization code at 00h
reset_Vec:
    goto main
PSECT int_Vec, class=CODE, delta=2     ; interrupt code at 04h
int_Vec:
    retfie
PSECT code, abs                        ; main code starts at 50h
org 50h
main:
; Enter the inputs from 0x30; result will be at PORTC, PORTD and PORTB
    X1  EQU     0x30            ; Defining a list of named constants
    X2  EQU     0x31
    Y1  EQU     0x32
    Y2  EQU     0x33

    BANKSEL   TRISB         ; Select Bank1
    CLRF      TRISB         ; Initialize PORTB as output
    CLRF      TRISD         ; Initialize PORTD as output
    CLRF      TRISC         ; Initialize PORTD as output
    BANKSEL   PORTB         ; Select Bank 0
    CLRF      PORTC         ; Clear Carry register
    MOVF      X1, W         ; Move LSBs of operand 1 to WREG
    ADDWF     Y1, 0         ; Add WREG with LSBs of operand 2
                            ; and hold the sum in WREG
    MOVWF     PORTB         ; Move the LSBs of result to PORTB
    BTFSC     STATUS, 0     ; Check the carry, skip the next
                            ; instruction if the carry is clear
    INCF      X2, F         ; Increment the MSBs of operand 1
    MOVF      X2, W         ; Move X2 to WREG
    ADDWF     Y2, 0         ; Add the WREG with MSBs of operand 2
                            ; and hold the sum in WREG
    MOVWF     PORTD         ; Move the WREG to PORTD
    BTFSC     STATUS, 0     ; Check the carry, skip the next
                            ; instruction if the carry is clear
```

```
        INCF        PORTC, F    ; Increment Carry register
        GOTO        $           ; Halt
END reset_Vec
```

Experimental Result:

Input Data		Result	
Memory location	Operand	Memory location	Operand
30	A3 H (LSB)	PORTB	DF H (LSB)
31	81 H (MSB)	PORTD	13 H (MSB)
32	3C H (LSB)	PORTC	01 H (carry)
33	92 H (MSB)		

Calculation:

I/O	in HEX		in Binary				
Operand 1	81A3 H			1000	0001	1010	0011
Operand 2	923C H			1001	0010	0011	1100
Result (C & S)	113DF H		1	0001	0011	1101	1111

Conclusion:

Thus the PIC16F877A assembly language program for the addition of two 16-bit numbers has been executed and verified the result.

9. SUBTRACTION OF TWO 16-BIT NUMBERS

Aim:

Write an assembly language program to perform the subtraction of two 16-bit binary numbers using the PIC16F877A/887 Microcontroller. Verify the result using the simulator.

Software Used:
- IDE: MPLAB X IDE v6.05
- PIC Assembler: pic-as (v2.40)

Algorithm:
1. Set PORTB, PORTD, and PORTC as output ports.
2. Clear borrow registers.
3. Move the LSBs (Y1) of the second operand to the WREG.
4. Subtract the WREG from the LSBs (X1) of the first operand and hold the Difference in WREG.
5. Move the WREG value to PORTB.
6. Test the Carry flag in the STATUS register; skip the next step if the Carry flag is set.
7. Decrement MSBs (Y2) of the second operand.
8. Move the MSBs (Y2) of the second operand to the WREG.
9. Subtract the WREG from the MSBs (X2) of the first operand and hold the Difference in WREG.
10. Move the WREG value to PORTD.
11. Clear WREG.
12. Test the Carry flag in the STATUS register; skip the next step if the Carry flag is set.
13. Increment the borrow register and store the result to WREG.
14. Move the WREG to PORTC.
15. Halt.

Program:
```
#include <xc.inc>
  CONFIG  FOSC = HS           ; Device Configurations
  CONFIG  WDTE = OFF
  CONFIG  PWRTE = OFF
  CONFIG  BOREN = OFF
  CONFIG  LVP = OFF
  CONFIG  CPD = OFF
  CONFIG  WRT = OFF
  CONFIG  CP = OFF

PSECT reset_Vec, class=CODE, delta=2   ; Initialization code at 00h
reset_Vec:
```

```
    goto main
PSECT int_Vec, class=CODE, delta=2    ; interrupt code at 04h
int_Vec:
    retfie
PSECT code, abs              ; main code starts at 50h
org 50h
main:
; Enter the inputs from 0x30; result will be at PORTC, PORTD and PORTB
    X1      EQU     0x30         ; Defining a list of named constants
    X2      EQU     0x31
    Y1      EQU     0x32
    Y2      EQU     0x33
    borrow  EQU     0x34

    BANKSEL   TRISB          ; Select Bank1
    CLRF      TRISB          ; Initialize PORTB as output
    CLRF      TRISD          ; Initialize PORTD as output
    CLRF      TRISC          ; Initialize PORTD as output
    BANKSEL   PORTB          ; Select Bank 0
    CLRF      borrow         ; Clear borrow register
    MOVF      Y1, W          ; Move LSBs of operand 2 to WREG
    SUBWF     X1, 0          ; Subtract WREG from X1
                             ; and hold the Diff. in WREG
    MOVWF     PORTB          ; Move the LSBs (8-bits) of result to PORTB
    BTFSS     STATUS, 0      ; If carry/borrow, skip the next statement
    DECF      Y2, F          ; Increment PORTD
    MOVF      Y2, W          ; Move array count to WREG
    SUBWF     X2, 0          ; Subtract WREG from X2
                             ; and hold the Diff. in WREG
    MOVWF     PORTD          ; Move the MSBs (8-bits) of result to PORTD
    MOVLW     0x00
    BTFSS     STATUS, 0      ; Check the carry, skip the next
                             ; instruction if the carry is set
    INCF      borrow, 0      ; Move the MSBs (8-bits) of result to PORTD
```

```
            MOVWF      PORTC       ; Move the borrow to PORTC
            GOTO       $           ; Halt
END reset_Vec
```

Experimental Result:

Input Data		Result	
Memory location	Operand	Memory location	Operand
30	A5 H (LSB)	PORT B	73 H (LSB)
31	87 H (MSB)	PORT D	24 H (MSB)
32	32 H (LSB)	PORT C	00 H
33	63 H (MSB)		

Calculation:

I/O	in HEX		in Binary			
Minuend	87A5 H		1000	0111	1010	0101
Subtrahend	6332 H		0110	0011	0011	0010
Result (Difference)	2473 H		0010	0100	0111	0011

Conclusion:

Thus the PIC16F877A assembly language program for the subtraction of two 16-bit numbers has been executed and verified the result.

10. MULTIPLICATION OF TWO 8-BIT NUMBERS

Aim:

Write an assembly language program to perform the multiplication of two 8-bit binary numbers using the PIC16F877A/887 Microcontroller. Verify the result using the simulator.

Software Used:
- IDE: MPLAB X IDE v6.05
- PIC Assembler: pic-as (v2.40)

Algorithm:
1. Set PORTB and PORTD as output ports.
2. Clear Carry register.
3. Clear WREG.
4. Add the WREG with Multiplier and store the sum in WREG.
5. Test the STATUS register for the carry; skip the next step if it is clear.
6. Increment Carry register.
7. Decrement the Multiplicand; skip the next step if it is zero.
8. Go to step 4.
9. Move the WREG (Product-LSB) to PORTB.
10. Move the Carry register (Product-MSB) to PORTD.
11. Halt

Program:
```
#include <xc.inc>
  CONFIG  FOSC = HS          ; Device Configurations
  CONFIG  WDTE = OFF
  CONFIG  PWRTE = OFF
  CONFIG  BOREN = OFF
  CONFIG  LVP = OFF
  CONFIG  CPD = OFF
  CONFIG  WRT = OFF
  CONFIG  CP = OFF


PSECT reset_Vec, class=CODE, delta=2   ; Initialization code at 00h
reset_Vec:
   goto main


PSECT int_Vec, class=CODE, delta=2     ; interrupt code at 04h
int_Vec:
```

```
        retfie

PSECT code, abs              ; main code starts at 50h
org 50h
main:
; Enter the inputs at 0x30 & 0x31; result will be at PORTD and PORTB
Multiplicand    equ 0x30     ; Initializing Constants
Multiplier      equ 0x31
Carry           equ 0x40

        BANKSEL   TRISB          ; Select Bank1
        CLRF      TRISB          ; Initialize PORTB as output
        CLRF      TRISD          ; Initialize PORTD as output
        BANKSEL   PORTB          ; Select Bank 0
        CLRF      Carry          ; Clear Carry register
        MOVLW     0x00           ; Clear WREG

Again:
        ADDWF     Multiplier, 0  ; Add WREG with multiplier and store
                                 ; the sum in WREG
        BTFSC     STATUS, 0      ; Check the carry, skip the next
                                 ; instruction if it is clear
        INCF      Carry, 1       ; Increment carry register
        DECFSZ    Multiplicand, 1 ; Decrement multiplicand value; skip
                                 ; the next instruction if it is zero
        GOTO      Again          ; Goto Again
        MOVWF     PORTB          ; Move the sum to PORTB
        MOVF      Carry, W       ; Move the carry to PORTD
        MOVWF     PORTD
        GOTO      $              ; Halt
END reset_Vec
```

Experimental Result:

Input Data		Result	
Memory location	Operand	Memory location	Operand
30	06 H	PORTB	18 H (Product-LSB)
31	04 H	PORTD	00 H (Product-MSB)

Calculation:

I/O	in HEX
Multiplicand	06 H
Multiplier	04 H
Product 18H	Multiplicand x Multiplier 06H x 04H
Product (LSB)	18 H
Product (MSB)	00 H

Conclusion:

Thus the PIC16F877A assembly language program for the multiplication of two 8-bit numbers has been executed and verified the result.

11. DIVISION OF TWO 8-BIT NUMBERS

Aim:

Write an assembly language program to perform the division of two 8-bit binary numbers using the PIC16F877A/887 Microcontroller. Verify the result using the simulator.

Software Used:
- IDE: MPLAB X IDE v6.05
- PIC Assembler: pic-as (v2.40)

Algorithm:
1. Set PORTB and PORTD as output ports.
2. Clear the Quotient register.
3. Move Divisor value to WREG.
4. Subtract WREG from Dividend register and store the result in the Dividend register.
5. Increment the Quotient register.
6. Test the STATUS register for the carry flag; skip the next step if the carry flag is clear.
7. Go to step 4.
8. Decrement the Quotient register.
9. Add WREG with Dividend register and hold the result in WREG.
10. Move WREG (Remainder) to PORTD.
11. Move Quotient value to PORTB.
12. Halt

Program:
```
#include <xc.inc>
  CONFIG  FOSC = HS          ; Device Configurations
  CONFIG  WDTE = OFF
  CONFIG  PWRTE = OFF
  CONFIG  BOREN = OFF
  CONFIG  LVP = OFF
  CONFIG  CPD = OFF
  CONFIG  WRT = OFF
  CONFIG  CP = OFF


PSECT reset_Vec, class=CODE, delta=2   ; Initialization code at 00h
reset_Vec:
   goto main


PSECT int_Vec, class=CODE, delta=2    ; interrupt code at 04h
int_Vec:
   retfie
```

```
PSECT code, abs              ; main code starts at 50h
org 50h
main:
; Enter the inputs at 0x30 & 0x31; result will be at PORTD and PORTB
Dividend       equ 0x30      ; Inputs at 0x30 & 0x31
Divisor        equ 0x31
Quotient       equ 0x40

    BANKSEL    TRISB         ; Select Bank1
    CLRF       TRISB         ; Initialize PORTB as output
    CLRF       TRISD         ; Initialize PORTD as output
    BANKSEL    PORTB         ; Select Bank 0

    CLRF       Quotient      ; Clear Carry register
    MOVF       Divisor, W    ; Move divisor to WREG
Again:
    SUBWF      Dividend, 1   ; Subtract WREG from dividend and
                             ; store the result in dividend itself.
    INCF       Quotient, 1   ; Increment Quotient
    BTFSC      STATUS, 0     ; Check the carry, skip the next
                             ; instruction if it is clear
    GOTO       Again         ; Go to Again
    DECF       Quotient, 1   ; Decrement Quotient
    ADDWF      Dividend, 0   ; Add WREG with dividend and hold
                             ; the result in WREG
    MOVWF      PORTD         ; Move the remainder to PORTD
    MOVF       Quotient, W   ; Move the Quotient to PORTB
    MOVWF      PORTB
    GOTO       $             ; Halt
END reset_Vec
```

Experimental Result:

Input Data		Result	
Memory location	Operand	Memory location	Operand
30	19 H	PORTB	08 H (Quotient)
31	03 H	PORTD	01 H (Remainder)

Calculation:

I/O	in HEX
Dividend	19 H
Divisor	03 H
Quotient	Dividend / Divisor 19H / 03H
Remainder	01 H
Quotient	08 H

Conclusion:

Thus the PIC16F877A assembly language program for the division of two 8-bit numbers has been executed and verified the result.

12. 1'S COMPLIMENT OF AN 8-BIT NUMBER

Aim:

Write an assembly language program to perform the 1's compliment of an 8-bit number using the PIC16F877A/887 Microcontroller. Verify the result using the simulator.

Software Used:

- o   IDE: MPLAB X IDE v6.05
- o   PIC Assembler: pic-as (v2.40)

Algorithm:
1. Set PORTB as output port.
2. Complement the input data and hold it in the WREG.
3. Store the WREG value in PORTB.
4. Halt

Program:
```
#include <xc.inc>
  CONFIG  FOSC = HS          ; Device Configurations
  CONFIG  WDTE = OFF
  CONFIG  PWRTE = OFF
  CONFIG  BOREN = OFF
  CONFIG  LVP = OFF
  CONFIG  CPD = OFF
  CONFIG  WRT = OFF
  CONFIG  CP = OFF


PSECT reset_Vec, class=CODE, delta=2   ; Initialization code at 00h
reset_Vec:
   goto main
PSECT int_Vec, class=CODE, delta=2     ; interrupt code at 04h
int_Vec:
    retfie
PSECT code, abs                 ; main code starts at 50h
org 50h
main:
; Enter the inputs at 0x30; result will be at PORTB
   X      equ     0x30          ; Get the input at 0x30
    BANKSEL    TRISB            ; Select Bank1
    CLRF       TRISB            ; Initialize PORTB as output
    BANKSEL    PORTB            ; Select Bank 0

    COMF       X, 0             ; Complement the value of X register
                                ; and hold the result in WREG.
```

```
    MOVWF      PORTB        ; Move the WREG to PORTB
    GOTO       $            ; Halt
END reset_Vec
```

Experimental Result:

Input Data		Result	
Memory location	Operand	Memory location	Operand
30	75 H	PORTB	8A H

Calculation:

I/O	in HEX	in Binary	
Operand	75 H	0111	0101
Result	8A H	1000	1010

Conclusion:

Thus the PIC16F877A assembly language program for the 1's compliment of an 8-bit number has been executed and verified the result.

13.	2'S COMPLIMENT OF AN 8-BIT NUMBER

Aim:

Write an assembly language program to perform the 2's compliment of an 8-bit number using the PIC16F877A/887 Microcontroller. Verify the result using the simulator.

Software Used:
- o   IDE: MPLAB X IDE v6.05
- o   PIC Assembler: pic-as (v2.40)

Algorithm:
1. Set PORTB as an output port.

2. Complement the input data and hold it in X register.
3. Move literal value 0x01 to the WREG.
4. Add WREG with X register and hold the result in WREG.
5. Store the WREG value in PORTB.
6. Halt

Program:
#include <xc.inc>
  CONFIG FOSC = HS   ; Device Configurations
  CONFIG WDTE = OFF
  CONFIG PWRTE = OFF
  CONFIG BOREN = OFF
  CONFIG LVP = OFF
  CONFIG CPD = OFF
  CONFIG WRT = OFF
  CONFIG CP = OFF

PSECT reset_Vec, class=CODE, delta=2 ; Initialization code at 00h
reset_Vec:
    goto main
PSECT int_Vec, class=CODE, delta=2   ; interrupt code at 04h
int_Vec:
    retfie
PSECT code, abs   ; main code starts at 50h
org 50h
main:
; Enter the inputs at 0x30; result will be at PORTB
    X   equ   0x30   ; Get the input at 0x30
    BANKSEL TRISB   ; Select Bank1
    CLRF   TRISB   ; Initialize PORTB as output
    BANKSEL PORTB   ; Select Bank 0
    COMF   X, 1   ; Complement the value of X register
                                   ; and hold the result in WREG.
    MOVLW   0x01   ; Move literal value 0x01 to WREG

ADDWF	X, 0	; Add WREG with X register and hold
		; the result in WREG
MOVWF	PORTB	; Move WREG to PORTB
GOTO	$	; Go to start

END reset_Vec

Experimental Result:

Input Data		Result	
Memory location	Operand	Memory location	Operand
30	75 H	PORTB	8B H

Calculation:

I/O	in HEX	in Binary	
Operand	75 H	0111	0101
1's complement		1000	1010
Add 01H		0000	0001
Result	8B H	1000	1011

Conclusion:

Thus the PIC16F877A assembly language program for the 2's compliment of an 8-bit number has been executed and verified the result.

14. LARGEST NUMBER IN AN ARRAY

Aim:

Write an assembly language program to find the largest number from an array of N 8-bit numbers using the PIC16F877A/887 Microcontroller and verify the result using the simulator.

Software Used:

- o IDE: MPLAB X IDE v6.05
- o PIC Assembler: pic-as (v2.40)

Algorithm:
1. Set PORTB as an output port.
2. Move the literal value 0x30 to WREG.
3. Move the WREG to FSR (Memory Pointer).
4. Move the content pointed by the FSR to the WREG.
5. Move the WREG to the Count register.
6. Increment FSR (The memory pointer).
7. Move the content pointed by the FSR to the WREG.
8. Decrement the Count register.
9. Move the WREG to the Temp register.
10. Increment FSR (The memory pointer).
11. Subtract the WREG from the content of memory pointer and hold the result in WREG.
12. Test the STATUS register for the carry flag, skip the next step if the carry flag is clear.
13. Go to step 18.
14. Move the Temp register value to the WREG.
15. Decrement Counter register, skip the next step if it is zero.
16. Go to step 9.
17. Go to step 21.
18. Move the content pointed by the FSR to the WREG.
19. Decrement Counter register, skip the next step if it is zero.
20. Go to step 9.
21. Move the WREG to the PORTB.
22. Halt

Program:
```
#include <xc.inc>
  CONFIG  FOSC = HS         ; Device Configurations
  CONFIG  WDTE = OFF
  CONFIG  PWRTE = OFF
  CONFIG  BOREN = OFF
  CONFIG  LVP = OFF
  CONFIG  CPD = OFF
```

```
CONFIG  WRT = OFF
CONFIG  CP = OFF


PSECT reset_Vec, class=CODE, delta=2   ; Initialization code at 00h
reset_Vec:
    goto main
PSECT int_Vec, class=CODE, delta=2     ; interrupt code at 04h
int_Vec:
    retfie
PSECT code, abs                        ; main code starts at 50h
org 50h
main:
; Enter the inputs from 0x30 (first location should be the count value of an array); result will be at PORTB
    Array equ 0x30
    Count equ 0x40
    Temp equ 0x41
    BANKSEL   TRISB          ; Select Bank1
    CLRF      TRISB          ; Initialize PORTB as output
    BANKSEL   PORTB          ; Select Bank 0

    MOVLW     Array          ; Move 0x30 to WREG
    MOVWF     FSR            ; Load memory pointer by 0x30
    MOVF      INDF, W        ; Move content of 0x30 to WREG
    MOVWF     Count          ; Move WREG to Count Register
    INCF      FSR            ; Increment memory pointer
    MOVF      INDF, W        ; Move the content of memory to WREG
    DECF      Count          ; Decrement Count register
Again:
    MOVWF     Temp           ; Move WREG to Temp register
    INCF      FSR            ; Increment memory pointer
    SUBWF     INDF, 0        ; Subtract WREG from the memory and
                             ; hold the result in WREG
    BTFSC     STATUS, 0      ; Test the STATUS register for Carry;
```

		; skip the next instruction if it is clear
GOTO	Next	; Go to next
MOVF	Temp, W	; Move Temp value to WREG
DECFSZ	Count	; Decrement Count register; skip the
		; next instruction if it is zero
GOTO	Again	; Go to Again
GOTO	Result	; Go to Result
Next:		
MOVF	INDF, W	; Move memory to WREG
DECFSZ	Count	; Decrement Count register; skip the
		; next instruction if it is zero
GOTO	Again	; Go to Again
Result:		
MOVWF	PORTB	; Move WREG to PORTB
GOTO	$	; Go to start
END reset_Vec		

Experimental Result:

Input Data		Result	
Memory location	Operand	Memory location	Operand
30	04 H*	PORTB	CD H
31	56 H		
32	92 H		
33	13 H		
34	CD H		

* *Number of array elements*

Conclusion:

Thus the PIC16F877A assembly language program to find the largest element in an array of N 8-bit numbers has been executed and verified the result.

15. SMALLEST NUMBER IN AN ARRAY

Aim:

Write an assembly language program to find the smallest number from an array of N 8-bit numbers using the PIC16F877A/887 Microcontroller and verify the output. Verify the result using the simulator.

Software Used:
- IDE: MPLAB X IDE v6.05
- PIC Assembler: pic-as (v2.40)

Algorithm:
1. Set PORTB as an output port.
2. Move the literal value 0x30 to WREG.
3. Move the WREG to FSR (The Memory Pointer).
4. Move the content pointed by the FSR to the WREG.
5. Move the WREG to the Count register.
6. Increment FSR (The Memory pointer).
7. Move the content pointed by the FSR to the WREG.
8. Decrement the Count register.
9. Move the WREG to the Temp register.
10. Increment FSR (The Memory pointer).
11. Subtract the WREG from the content of memory pointer and hold the result in WREG.
12. Test the STATUS register for the carry flag, skip the next step if the carry flag is set.
13. Go to step 18.
14. Move the Temp register value to the WREG.
15. Decrement the Counter register, skip the next step if it is zero.
16. Go to step 9.
17. Go to step 12.
18. Move the content pointed by the FSR to the WREG.
19. Decrement the Counter register, skip the next step if it is zero.

20. Go to step 9.
21. Move the WREG to the PORTB.
22. Halt

Program:
```
#include <xc.inc>
  CONFIG  FOSC = HS         ; Device Configurations
  CONFIG  WDTE = OFF
  CONFIG  PWRTE = OFF
  CONFIG  BOREN = OFF
  CONFIG  LVP = OFF
  CONFIG  CPD = OFF
  CONFIG  WRT = OFF
  CONFIG  CP = OFF


PSECT reset_Vec, class=CODE, delta=2   ; Initialization code at 00h
reset_Vec:
    goto main


PSECT int_Vec, class=CODE, delta=2     ; interrupt code at 04h
int_Vec:
     retfie


PSECT code, abs              ; main code starts at 50h
org 50h
main:
; Enter the inputs from 0x30 (first location should be the count value of an array); result will be at PORTB
    Array equ 0x30
    Count equ 0x40
    Temp equ 0x41
    BANKSEL    TRISB         ; Select Bank1
    CLRF       TRISB         ; Initialize PORTB as output
    BANKSEL    PORTB         ; Select Bank 0
```

MOVLW	Array	; Move 0x30 to WREG
MOVWF	FSR	; Load memory pointer by 0x30
MOVF	INDF, W	; Move content of 0x30 to WREG
MOVWF	Count	; Move WREG to Count Register
INCF	FSR	; Increment memory pointer
MOVF	INDF, W	; Move the content of memory to WREG
DECF	Count	; Decrement Count register

Again:
MOVWF	Temp	; Move WREG to Temp register
INCF	FSR	; Increment memory pointer
SUBWF	INDF, 0	; Subtract WREG from the memory and
		; hold the result in WREG
BTFSS	STATUS, 0	; Test the STATUS register for Carry;
		; skip the next instruction if it is clear
GOTO	Next	; Go to next
MOVF	Temp, W	; Move Temp value to WREG
DECFSZ	Count	; Decrement Count register; skip the
		; next instruction if it is zero
GOTO	Again	; Go to Again
GOTO	Result	; Go to Result

Next:
MOVF	INDF, W	; Move memory to WREG
DECFSZ	Count	; Decrement Count register; skip the
		; next instruction if it is zero
GOTO	Again	; Go to Again

Result:
MOVWF	PORTB	; Move WREG to PORTB
GOTO	$	; Go to start

END reset_Vec

Experimental Result:

Input Data		Result	
Memory location	Operand	Memory location	Operand
30	04 H*	PORTB	13 H
31	56 H		
32	92 H		
33	13 H		
34	CD H		

Number of array elements

Conclusion:

Thus the PIC16F877A assembly language program to find the smallest element in an array of N 8-bit numbers has been executed and verified the result.

16. DESCENDING ORDER OF AN ARRAY

Aim:

Write an assembly language program to sort an array of 8-bit binary numbers in descending order using the PIC16F877A/887 Microcontroller and verify the result using the simulator.

Software Used:
- IDE: MPLAB X IDE v6.05
- PIC Assembler: pic-as (v2.40)

Algorithm:
1. Move the literal value 0x30 to WREG.
2. Move the WREG to FSR (Memory Pointer).
3. Move the content pointed by the FSR to the WREG.
4. Move the WREG to the Count1 register.
5. Decrement the Count1 register.

6. Move the WREG to the Count2 register.
7. Decrement the Count2 register.
8. Increment FSR (The memory pointer).
9. Move the content pointed by the FSR to the WREG.
10. Increment FSR (The memory pointer).
11. Subtract the WREG from the content of memory location pointed by FSR and hold the result in WREG.
12. Test the STATUS register for the carry flag; skip the next step if the carry flag is set.
13. Go to step 27.
14. Move the content pointed by the FSR to the WREG.
15. Move the WREG to the Temp register1.
16. Decrement FSR (The memory pointer).
17. Move the content pointed by the FSR to the WREG.
18. Move the WREG to the Temp register2.
19. Move the content of the Temp1 register to the WREG.
20. Move the WREG to the location pointed by the FSR.
21. Increment FSR (The memory pointer).
22. Move the content of Temp2 register to the WREG.
23. Move the WREG to the location pointed by the FSR.
24. Decrement Counter2 register; skip the next step if it is zero.
25. Go to step 9.
26. Go to step 29.
27. Decrement Counter2 register; skip the next step if it is zero.
28. Go to step 9.
29. Move the literal value 0x30 to WREG.
30. Move the WREG to FSR (Memory Pointer).
31. Move the content pointed by the FSR to the WREG.
32. Move the WREG to the Count2 register.
33. Decrement the Count2 register.
34. Increment FSR (The memory pointer).
35. Decrement Counter1 register; skip the next step if it is zero.
36. Go to step 9.
37. Halt

Program:

```
#include <xc.inc>
  CONFIG  FOSC = HS          ; Device Configurations
  CONFIG  WDTE = OFF
  CONFIG  PWRTE = OFF
  CONFIG  BOREN = OFF
  CONFIG  LVP = OFF
  CONFIG  CPD = OFF
  CONFIG  WRT = OFF
  CONFIG  CP = OFF

PSECT reset_Vec, class=CODE, delta=2   ; Initialization code at 00h
reset_Vec:
   goto main
PSECT int_Vec, class=CODE, delta=2     ; interrupt code at 04h
int_Vec:
   retfie
PSECT code, abs                        ; main code starts at 50h
org 50h
main:
; Enter the inputs from 0x30 (first location should be the count value of an array); result will be at the same locations
   Array equ 0x30
   Count1 equ 0x40
   Count2 equ 0x41
   Temp1 equ 0x42
   Temp2 equ 0x43


        MOVLW     Array         ; Move 0x30 to WREG
        MOVWF     FSR           ; Load memory pointer by 0x30
        MOVF      INDF, W       ; Move the content of 0x30 to WREG
        MOVWF     Count1        ; Move WREG to Count1 Register
        DECF      Count1, F     ; Decrement Count1 register
        MOVWF     Count2        ; Move WREG to Count2 Register
```

DECF	Count2, F	; Decrement Count2 register	
INCF	FSR, F	; Increment memory pointer	

Again:
MOVF	INDF, W	; Move the content of memory to WREG
INCF	FSR, F	; Increment memory pointer
SUBWF	INDF, 0	; Subtract WREG from the memory and
		; hold the result in WREG
BTFSS	STATUS, 0	; Test the STATUS register for Carry;
		; skip the next instruction if it is clear
GOTO	Next	; Go to next
MOVF	INDF, W	; Move the content of memory to WREG
MOVWF	Temp1	; Move the WREG to Temp1 register
DECF	FSR, F	; Decrement memory pointer
MOVF	INDF, W	; Move the content of memory to WREG
MOVWF	Temp2	; Move the WREG to Temp2 register
MOVF	Temp1, W	; Move Temp1 register to the WREG
MOVWF	INDF	; Move the WREG to the location
		; pointed by FSR
INCF	FSR, F	; Increment memory pointer
MOVF	Temp2, W	; Move Temp2 register to the WREG
MOVWF	INDF	; Move the WREG to the location
		; pointed by FSR
DECFSZ	Count2	; Decrement Count Register; skip the
		; next instruction if it is zero
GOTO	Again	; Go to Again
GOTO	Outer	; Go to Outer

Next:
DECFSZ	Count2	; Decrement Count Register; skip the
		; next instruction if it is zero
GOTO	Again	; Go to Again

Outer:
MOVLW	Array	; Move 0x30 to WREG
MOVWF	FSR	; Move the WREG to the FSR

MOVF	INDF, W	; Move the content of 0x30 to WREG
MOVWF	Count2	; Move WREG to Count Register
DECF	Count2, F	; Decrement Count Register
INCF	FSR, F	; Increment memory pointer
DECFSZ	Count1	; Decrement Count Register; skip the
		; next instruction if it is zero
GOTO	Again	; Go to Again
GOTO	$	; Go to start

END reset_Vec

Experimental Result:

Before Execution		After Execution	
Memory location	Operand	Memory location	Operand
30	04 H*	30	04 H*
31	56 H	31	C9 H
32	92 H	32	92 H
33	14 H	33	56 H
34	C9 H	34	14 H

* Number of array elements

Conclusion:

Thus the PIC16F877A assembly language program for sorting numbers of an array in descending order has been executed and verified the result.

17. ASCENDING ORDER OF AN ARRAY

Aim:

Write an assembly language program to sort an array of 8-bit binary numbers in ascending order using the PIC16F877A/887 Microcontroller and verify the result. Verify the result using the simulator.

Software Used:
- IDE: MPLAB X IDE v6.05
- PIC Assembler: pic-as (v2.40)

Algorithm:
1. Move the literal value 0x30 to WREG.
2. Move the WREG to FSR (Memory Pointer).
3. Move the content pointed by the FSR to the WREG.
4. Move the WREG to the Count1 register.
5. Decrement the Count1 register.
6. Move the WREG to the Count2 register.
7. Decrement the Count2 register.
8. Increment FSR (The memory pointer).
9. Move the content pointed by the FSR to the WREG.
10. Increment FSR (The memory pointer).
11. Subtract the WREG from the content of memory location pointed by FSR and hold the result in WREG.
12. Test the STATUS register for the carry flag; skip the next step if the carry flag is clear.
13. Go to step 27.
14. Move the content pointed by the FSR to the WREG.
15. Move the WREG to the Temp register1.
16. Decrement FSR (The memory pointer).
17. Move the content pointed by the FSR to the WREG.
18. Move the WREG to the Temp register2.
19. Move the content of the Temp1 register to the WREG.
20. Move the WREG to the location pointed by the FSR.
21. Increment FSR (The memory pointer).
22. Move the content of Temp2 register to the WREG.
23. Move the WREG to the location pointed by the FSR.
24. Decrement Counter2 register; skip the next step if it is zero.
25. Go to step 9.
26. Go to step 29.
27. Decrement Counter2 register; skip the next step if it is zero.

28. Go to step 9.
29. Move the literal value 0x30 to WREG.
30. Move the WREG to FSR (Memory Pointer).
31. Move the content pointed by the FSR to the WREG.
32. Move the WREG to the Count2 register.
33. Decrement the Count2 register.
34. Increment FSR (The memory pointer).
35. Decrement Counter1 register; skip the next step if it is zero.
36. Go to step 9.
37. Halt

Program:

```
#include <xc.inc>
  CONFIG  FOSC = HS           ; Device Configurations
  CONFIG  WDTE = OFF
  CONFIG  PWRTE = OFF
  CONFIG  BOREN = OFF
  CONFIG  LVP = OFF
  CONFIG  CPD = OFF
  CONFIG  WRT = OFF
  CONFIG  CP = OFF


PSECT reset_Vec, class=CODE, delta=2   ; Initialization code at 00h
reset_Vec:
   goto main
PSECT int_Vec, class=CODE, delta=2     ; interrupt code at 04h
int_Vec:
   retfie
PSECT code, abs                        ; main code starts at 50h
org 50h
main:
; Enter the inputs from 0x30 (first location should be the count value of an array); result will be at the same locations
   Array equ 0x30
```

```
Count1 equ 0x40
Count2 equ 0x41
Temp1 equ 0x42
Temp2 equ 0x43

        MOVLW    Array         ; Move 0x30 to WREG
        MOVWF    FSR           ; Load memory pointer by 0x30
        MOVF     INDF, W       ; Move the content of 0x30 to WREG
        MOVWF    Count1        ; Move WREG to Count1 Register
        DECF     Count1, F     ; Decrement Count1 register
        MOVWF    Count2        ; Move WREG to Count2 Register
        DECF     Count2, F     ; Decrement Count2 register
        INCF     FSR, F        ; Increment memory pointer
Again:
        MOVF     INDF, W       ; Move the content of memory to WREG
        INCF     FSR, F        ; Increment memory pointer
        SUBWF    INDF, 0       ; Subtract WREG from the memory and
                               ; hold the result in WREG
        BTFSC    STATUS, 0     ; Test the STATUS register for Carry;
                               ; skip the next instruction if it is clear
        GOTO     Next          ; Go to next
        MOVF     INDF, W       ; Move the content of memory to WREG
        MOVWF    Temp1         ; Move the WREG to Temp1 register
        DECF     FSR, F        ; Decrement memory pointer
        MOVF     INDF, W       ; Move the content of memory to WREG
        MOVWF    Temp2         ; Move the WREG to Temp2 register
        MOVF     Temp1, W      ; Move Temp1 register to the WREG
        MOVWF    INDF          ; Move the WREG to the location
                               ; pointed by FSR
        INCF     FSR, F        ; Increment memory pointer
        MOVF     Temp2, W      ; Move Temp2 register to the WREG
        MOVWF    INDF          ; Move the WREG to the location
                               ; pointed by FSR
        DECFSZ   Count2        ; Decrement Count Register; skip the
```

| | GOTO | Again | ; Go to Again |
| | GOTO | Outer | ; Go to Outer |

Next:
	DECFSZ	Count2	; Decrement Count Register; skip the
			; next instruction if it is zero
	GOTO	Again	; Go to Again

Outer:
	MOVLW	Array	; Move 0x30 to WREG
	MOVWF	FSR	; Move the WREG to the FSR
	MOVF	INDF, W	; Move the content of 0x30 to WREG
	MOVWF	Count2	; Move WREG to Count Register
	DECF	Count2, F	; Decrement Count Register
	INCF	FSR, F	; Increment memory pointer
	DECFSZ	Count1	; Decrement Count Register; skip the
			; next instruction if it is zero
	GOTO	Again	; Go to Again
	GOTO	$	; Go to start

END reset_Vec

Experimental Result:

Before Execution		After Execution	
Memory location	Operand	Memory location	Operand
30	04 H*	30	04 H*
31	56 H	31	14 H
32	92 H	32	56 H
33	14 H	33	92 H
34	C9 H	34	C9 H

* *Number of array elements*

Conclusion:

Thus the PIC16F877A assembly language program for sorting numbers of an array in ascending order has been executed and verified the result.

18. BLOCK DATA TRANSFER

Aim:

Write an assembly language program to transfer N bytes of data from one memory to another memory block using the PIC16F877A/887 Microcontroller. Verify the result using the simulator.

Software Used:
- IDE: MPLAB X IDE v6.05
- PIC Assembler: pic-as (v2.40)

Algorithm:
1. Move the starting address of source block (0x30) to WREG.
2. Move the WREG to the Temp1 register.
3. Move the starting address of destination block (0x40) to WREG.
4. Move the WREG to the Temp2 register.
5. Move the Temp1 register to the WREG.
6. Move the WREG to the FSR.
7. Move the content pointed by FSR to the WREG.
8. Move the WREG to the Data1 register.
9. Increment the memory pointer (FSR).
10. Move the FSR to the WREG.
11. Move the WREG to the Temp1 register.
12. Move the Temp2 register to the WREG.
13. Move the WREG to the FSR.
14. Move the Data1 register to the WREG.
15. Move the WREG to the location pointer by the FSR.
16. Increment the memory pointer (FSR).
17. Move the FSR to the WREG.
18. Move the WREG to the Temp2 register.
19. Decrement the Count register; skip the next instruction if it is zero.
20. Go to step 5.
21. Halt

Program:
```
#include <xc.inc>
  CONFIG FOSC = HS        ; Device Configurations
  CONFIG WDTE = OFF
  CONFIG PWRTE = OFF
  CONFIG BOREN = OFF
  CONFIG LVP = OFF
  CONFIG CPD = OFF
  CONFIG WRT = OFF
  CONFIG CP = OFF


PSECT reset_Vec, class=CODE, delta=2   ; Initialization code at 00h
reset_Vec:
   goto main
PSECT int_Vec, class=CODE, delta=2     ; interrupt code at 04h
int_Vec:
   retfie
PSECT code, abs                        ; main code starts at 50h
org 50h
main:
; Inputs at 0x20 (no of data in a block) and starting address of source block at 0x30; starting address of destination block at 0x40
   Count equ 0x20
   Block1 equ 0x30
   Block2 equ 0x40
   Temp1 equ 0x21
   Temp2 equ 0x22
   Data1 equ 0x23


   MOVLW   Block1     ; Move 0x30 to WREG
   MOVWF   Temp1      ; Move the WREG to the Temp1 register
   MOVLW   Block2     ; Move 0x30 to WREG
   MOVWF   Temp2      ; Move the WREG to the Temp2 register
```

Again:
```
    MOVF    Temp1, W    ; Move the Temp1 register to the WREG
    MOVWF   FSR         ; Move the WREG to the FSR
    MOVF    INDF, W     ; Move content of 0x30 to WREG
    MOVWF   Data1       ; Move the WREG to the Data1 register
    INCF    FSR, F      ; Increment FSR
    MOVF    FSR, W      ; Move the FSR to the WREG
    MOVWF   Temp1       ; Move the WREG to the Temp1 register
    MOVF    Temp2, W    ; Move the Temp2 register to the WREG
    MOVWF   FSR         ; Move the WREG to the FSR
    MOVF    Data1, W    ; Move the Data1 register to the WREG
    MOVWF   INDF        ; Move the WREG to the memory
                        ; location pointed by FSR
    INCF    FSR, F      ; Increment FSR
    MOVF    FSR, W      ; Move the FSR to the WREG
    MOVWF   Temp2       ; Move the WREG to the Temp2 register
    DECFSZ  Count       ; Decrement Count Register, skip the
                        ; next instruction if it is zero
    GOTO    Again       ; Go to Again
    GOTO    $           ; Go to start
    END reset_Vec
```

Experimental Result:

Before Execution		After Execution	
Memory location	Operand	Memory location	Operand
20	05 H*	20	00 H
30	54 H	40	54 H
31	23 H	41	23 H
32	A4 H	42	A4 H
33	49 H	43	49 H
34	B7 H	44	B7 H

* Number of elements in Source block to be transferred

Conclusion:

Thus the PIC16F877A assembly language program for block data transfer has been executed and verified the result.

19. FIBONACCI SERIES

Aim:

Write an assembly language program to find N elements of the Fibonacci series in 8-bit binary using the PIC16F877A/887 Microcontroller. Verify the result using the simulator.

Software Used:
- o   IDE: MPLAB X IDE v6.05
- o   PIC Assembler: pic-as (v2.40)

Algorithm:
1. Move the literal value 0x00 to the WREG.
2. Move the WREG to the Temp1 register (first value of series).
3. Move the literal value 0x01 to the WREG.
4. Move the WREG to the Temp2 register (2nd value of series).
5. Move the starting address of output (Series) to the WREG.
6. Move the WREG to the FSR.
7. Move the Temp1 register to the WREG.
8. Move the WREG to the location pointed by FSR.
9. Decrement the Count register.
10. Increment the FSR.
11. Move the Temp2 register to the WREG.
12. Move the WREG to the location pointed by FSR.
13. Decrement the Count register.
14. Increment the FSR.
15. Add the WREG with the Temp1 register and store the result in the WREG.

16. Move the next value of series to the memory.
17. Move the Temp2 register value to the WREG.
18. Move the WREG to the Temp1 register.
19. Move the content pointed by the FSR to the WREG.
20. Move the WREG to the Temp2 register.
21. Increment the memory pointer.
22. Decrement the Count register; skip the next instruction if it is zero.
23. Go to step 7.
24. Half

Program:

```
#include <xc.inc>
    CONFIG  FOSC = HS          ; Device Configurations
    CONFIG  WDTE = OFF
    CONFIG  PWRTE = OFF
    CONFIG  BOREN = OFF
    CONFIG  LVP = OFF
    CONFIG  CPD = OFF
    CONFIG  WRT = OFF
    CONFIG  CP = OFF


PSECT reset_Vec, class=CODE, delta=2   ; Initialization code at 00h
reset_Vec:
    goto main
PSECT int_Vec, class=CODE, delta=2     ; interrupt code at 04h
int_Vec:
    retfie
PSECT code, abs                ; main code starts at 50h
org 50h
main:
; Input at 0x30 (no of data in a series); result will be from 0x40
    Count equ 0x30
    Series equ 0x40
    Temp1 equ 0x31
```

```
Temp2    equ    0x32
         MOVLW  0x00         ; Move 0x30 to WREG
         MOVWF  Temp1        ; Move the WREG to the Temp1 register
         MOVLW  0x01         ; Move 0x30 to WREG
         MOVWF  Temp2        ; Move the WREG to the Temp1 register
         MOVLW  Series       ; Move the starting address of output to
                             ; the WREG
         MOVWF  FSR          ; Move the WREG to FSR
         MOVF   Temp1, W     ; Move the Temp1 register to the WREG
         MOVWF  INDF         ; Move the WREG to the location
                             ; pointed by the FSR
         DECF   Count, F     ; Decrement the Count register
         INCF   FSR, F       ; Increment the memory pointer
         MOVF   Temp2, W     ; Move the Temp2 register to the WREG
         MOVWF  INDF         ; Move the WREG to the location
                             ; pointed by the FSR
         DECF   Count, F     ; Decrement the Count register
         INCF   FSR, F       ; Increment the memory pointer
Again:
         ADDWF  Temp1, 0     ; Add the WREG with Temp1 register
                             ; and hold the result in the WREG
         MOVWF  INDF         ; Move the WREG to the location
                             ; pointed by the FSR
         MOVF   Temp2, W     ; Move the Temp2 register to the WREG
         MOVWF  Temp1        ; Move the WREG to the Temp1 register
         MOVF   INDF, W      ; Move the content pointed by FSR to
                             ; the WREG
         MOVWF  Temp2        ; Move the WREG to the Temp2 register
         INCF   FSR, F       ; Increment memory pointer
         DECFSZ Count        ; Decrement the Count register; skip the
                             ; next instruction if it is zero
         GOTO   Again        ; Go to Again
         GOTO   $            ; Go to start
END reset_Vec
```

Experimental Result:

Before Execution		After Execution	
Memory location	Operand	Memory location	Operand
30	0A H	40	00 H
		41	01 H
		42	01 H
		43	02 H
		44	03 H
		45	05 H
		46	08 H
		47	0D H
		48	15 H
		49	22 H

Conclusion:

Thus the PIC16F877A assembly language program for Fibonacci series has been executed and verified the result.

20. BINARY TO ASCII CONVERSION

Aim:

Write an assembly language program to convert a binary number into its equivalent ASCII number using the PIC16F877A/887 Microcontroller. Verify the result using the simulator.

Software Used:
- IDE: MPLAB X IDE v6.05
- PIC Assembler: pic-as (v2.40)

Algorithm:
1. Define the file registers to hold the value of Binary and ASCII.

2. Move the literal value 0x0A to the WREG.
3. Subtract the WREG from the Binary register and hold the result in the WREG.
4. Move the WREG to the Temp register.
5. Test the carry flag in the STATUS register; skip the next instruction if the carry flag is set.
6. Go to step 11.
7. Move the literal value 0x41 to the WREG.
8. Add the WREG with the Temp register and hold the result in the WREG.
9. Move the WREG value to the ASCII register.
10. Halt
11. Move the literal value 0x30 to the WREG.
12. Add the WREG with the Binary register and hold the result in the ASCII register.
13. Halt

Program:

```
#include <xc.inc>
  CONFIG  FOSC = HS           ; Device Configurations
  CONFIG  WDTE = OFF
  CONFIG  PWRTE = OFF
  CONFIG  BOREN = OFF
  CONFIG  LVP = OFF
  CONFIG  CPD = OFF
  CONFIG  WRT = OFF
  CONFIG  CP = OFF


PSECT reset_Vec, class=CODE, delta=2   ; Initialization code at 00h
reset_Vec:
   goto main
PSECT int_Vec, class=CODE, delta=2     ; interrupt code at 04h
int_Vec:
   retfie
```

```
PSECT code, abs              ; main code starts at 50h
org 50h
main:
; Enter the input at 0x30; result will be at 0x31
    Binary equ 0x30
    ASCII equ 0x31
    Temp equ 0x32
    MOVLW   0x0A         ; Move 0x30 to WREG
    SUBWF   Binary, 0    ; Subtract the WREG from the binary
                         ; value and hold the result in the WREG.
    MOVWF   Temp         ; Move the WREG to the Temp register
    BTFSS   STATUS, 0    ; Test the carry in STATUS register; skip
                         ; the next instruction if the carry is clear
    GOTO    Next         ; Go to Next
    MOVLW   0x41         ; Move the literal value 0x41 to WREG
    ADDWF   Temp, 0      ; Add the WREG with the Temp register
                         ; and hold the result in the WREG.
    MOVWF   ASCII        ; Move the WREG to the ASCII register
    GOTO    $            ; Halt
Next:
    MOVLW   0x30         ; Move the literal value 0x30 to WREG
    ADDWF   Binary, 0    ; Add the WREG with the Binary
                         ; register and hold the result in WREG.
    MOVWF   ASCII        ; Move the WREG to the ASCII register
    GOTO    $            ; Halt
END reset_Vec
```

Experimental Result:

Before Execution		After Execution	
Memory location	Operand	Memory location	Operand
30	05 H (Binary)	30	05 H (Binary)
31	-	31	35 H (ASCII)

Before Execution		After Execution	
Memory location	Operand	Memory location	Operand
30	0E H (Binary)	30	0E H (Binary)
31	-	31	45 H (ASCII)

Calculation:

Step	Binary Number	ASCII Number
1	05 H	05 – 0A (Carry will set) 05 + 30 = 35 H
2	0E H	0E – 0A = 04 H (No carry) 04 + 41 = 45 H

Conclusion:

Thus the PIC16F877A assembly language program for the binary to ASCII conversion has been executed and verified the result.

21. ASCII TO BINARY CONVERSION

Aim:

Write an assembly language program to convert an ASCII number into its equivalent binary number using the PIC16F877A/887 Microcontroller. Verify the result using the simulator.

Software Used:
- IDE: MPLAB X IDE v6.05
- PIC Assembler: pic-as (v2.40)

Algorithm:
1. Define the file registers to hold the value of ASCII and Binary.
2. Move the literal value 0x30 to the WREG.
3. Subtract the WREG from the ASCII register and hold the result in WREG.

4. Move the WREG to the Temp register.
5. Load WREG by 0x30.
6. Subtract the WREG from the Temp register and hold the result in WREG.
7. Test carry flag in STATUS register; skip the next step if it is set.
8. Go to step 13.
9. Load WREG by 0x07.
10. Subtract the WREG from the Temp register and hold the result in WREG.
11. Move WREG to the Binary register.
12. Halt.
13. Move the Temp register to the WREG.
14. Move WREG to the Binary register.
15. Halt.

Program:
```
#include <xc.inc>
  CONFIG  FOSC = HS          ; Device Configurations
  CONFIG  WDTE = OFF
  CONFIG  PWRTE = OFF
  CONFIG  BOREN = OFF
  CONFIG  LVP = OFF
  CONFIG  CPD = OFF
  CONFIG  WRT = OFF
  CONFIG  CP = OFF


PSECT reset_Vec, class=CODE, delta=2   ; Initialization code at 00h
reset_Vec:
   goto main
PSECT int_Vec, class=CODE, delta=2     ; interrupt code at 04h
int_Vec:
   retfie
PSECT code, abs              ; main code starts at 50h
org 50h
```

main:
; Enter the input at 0x40; result will be at 0x41
    ASCII equ 0x40
    Binary equ 0x41
    Temp equ 0x50

MOVLW	0x30	; Move the literal value 0x30 to WREG.
SUBWF	ASCII, 0	; Subtract the WREG from the ASCII
		; register and hold the result in WREG.
MOVWF	Temp	; Move the WREG to the Temp register
MOVLW	0x0A	; Move 0x30 to WREG
SUBWF	Temp, 0	; Subtract the WREG from the Temp
		; register and hold the result in WREG
BTFSS	STATUS, 0	; Test the Carry flag; skip the next
		; instruction if the carry flag is set
GOTO	Next	; Go to Next
MOVLW	0x07	; Move the literal value 0x07 to WREG
SUBWF	Temp, 0	; Subtract the WREG from the Temp
		; register and hold the result in WREG
MOVWF	Binary	; Move the WREG to the Binary register
GOTO	$	; Halt

Next:
MOVF	Temp, W	; Move the Temp register to the WREG
MOVWF	Binary	; Move the WREG to the Binary register
GOTO	$	; Halt

END reset_Vec

Experimental Result:

Before Execution		After Execution	
Memory location	Operand	Memory location	Operand
40	37 H	40	37 H
41	-	41	07 H

Before Execution		After Execution	
Memory location	Operand	Memory location	Operand
40	44 H	40	44 H
41	-	41	0D H

Calculation:

Step	Binary Number	ASCII Number
1	37 H	37H – 30H = 07H 07H – 0AH (Carry will set) = 07H is ASCII number
2	44 H	44H – 30H = 14 H 14H – 0AH (No carry) 14H – 07H = 0D H is ASCII number

Conclusion:

Thus the PIC16F877A assembly language program for an ASCII number to the binary number conversion has been executed and verified the result.

22. BINARY TO GRAY CODE CONVERSION

Aim:

Write an assembly language program to convert Binary code into Gray code using the PIC16F877A/887 Microcontroller. Verify the result using the simulator.

Software Used:
- IDE: MPLAB X IDE v6.05
- PIC Assembler: pic-as (v2.40)

Algorithm:
1. Move the input binary value to the WREG.
2. Move the WREG to the Temp register.

3. Clear the carry flag in the STATUS register.
4. Rotate Temp register right with carry and hold the result in the WREG.
5. XOR the WREG with the content of the Binary register and hold the result in the WREG.
6. Move the WREG to the Gray register.
7. Halt

Program:

```
#include <xc.inc>
  CONFIG  FOSC = HS          ; Device Configurations
  CONFIG  WDTE = OFF
  CONFIG  PWRTE = OFF
  CONFIG  BOREN = OFF
  CONFIG  LVP = OFF
  CONFIG  CPD = OFF
  CONFIG  WRT = OFF
  CONFIG  CP = OFF


PSECT reset_Vec, class=CODE, delta=2   ; Initialization code at 00h
reset_Vec:
    goto main
PSECT int_Vec, class=CODE, delta=2     ; interrupt code at 04h
int_Vec:
    retfie
PSECT code, abs                ; main code starts at 50h
org 50h
main:
; Enter the input at 0x30; result will be at 0x31
    Binary equ 0x30
    Gray equ 0x31
    Temp equ 0x40
    MOVF       Binary, W       ; Move the Binary register to the WREG
    MOVWF      Temp            ; Move the WREG to the Temp register
```

```
BCF     STATUS, 0   ; Clear carry flag
RRF     Temp, 0     ; Rotate right the Temp register with
                    ; carry and hold the result in the WREG
XORWF   Binary, 0   ; XOR the WREG with the Binary
                    ; register and hold the result in WREG
MOVWF   Gray        ; Move the WREG to the Gray register
GOTO    $           ; Halt
END reset_Vec
```

Calculation:

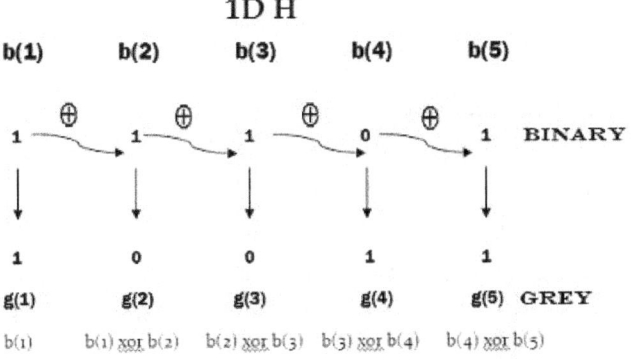

Experimental Result:

Before Execution		After Execution	
Memory location	Operand	Memory location	Operand
30	1D H	30	1D H
31	-	31	13 H

Conclusion:

Thus the PIC16F877A assembly language program for the binary to gray code conversion has been executed and verified the result.

23. GRAY CODE TO BINARY CONVERSION

Aim:

Write an assembly language program to convert Grey code into Binary number using the PIC16F877A/887 Microcontroller. Verify the result using the simulator.

Software Used:
- IDE: MPLAB X IDE v6.05
- PIC Assembler: pic-as (v2.40)

Algorithm:
1. Move the input Gray value to the WREG.
2. Move the WREG to the Temp register.
3. Move the literal value 0x07 to the WREG.
4. Move the WREG to the Count register.
5. Clear the carry flag in the STATUS register.
6. Rotate Temp register right with carry and hold the result in the WREG.
7. XOR the WREG with the content of Gray register and hold the result in the WREG.
8. Move the WREG to the Temp register.
9. Decrement the Count register; skip the next step if it is zero.
10. Go to step 5.
11. Move the WREG to the Binary register.
12. Halt

Program:
```
#include <xc.inc>
  CONFIG  FOSC = HS          ; Device Configurations
  CONFIG  WDTE = OFF
  CONFIG  PWRTE = OFF
  CONFIG  BOREN = OFF
```

```
CONFIG LVP = OFF
CONFIG CPD = OFF
CONFIG WRT = OFF
CONFIG CP = OFF


PSECT reset_Vec, class=CODE, delta=2   ; Initialization code at 00h
reset_Vec:
  goto main
PSECT int_Vec, class=CODE, delta=2     ; interrupt code at 04h
int_Vec:
  retfie
PSECT code, abs                        ; main code starts at 50h
org 50h
main:
; Enter the input at 0x30; result will be at 0x31
    Gray equ 0x30
    Binary equ 0x31
    Temp equ 0x40
    Count equ 0x41

    MOVF    Gray, W      ; Move Gray register to the WREG
    MOVWF   Temp         ; Move the WREG to the Temp register
    MOVLW   0x07         ; Move literal value 0x07 to the WREG
    MOVWF   Count        ; Move the WREG to the Count register
Again:
    BCF     STATUS, 0    ; Clear Carry flag
    RRF     Temp, 0      ; Rotate Temp register right and hold
                         ; the result in the WREG
    XORWF   Gray, 0      ; XOR the WREG with the Gray register
                         ; and hold the result in the WREG
    MOVWF   Temp         ; Move the WREG to the Temp register
    DECFSZ  Count        ; Decrement the Count register; skip the
                         ; next instruction if it is zero
    GOTO    Again        ; Go to Again
```

```
MOVWF    Binary      ; Move the WREG to the Binary register
GOTO     $           ; Halt
END reset_Vec
```

Experimental Result:

Before Execution		After Execution	
Memory location	Operand	Memory location	Operand
30	13 H	30	13 H
31	-	31	1D H

Calculation:

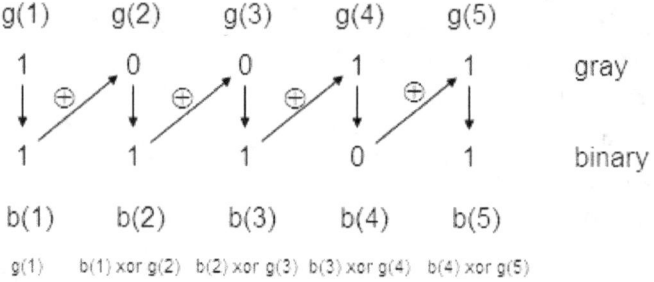

Conclusion:

Thus the PIC16F877A assembly language program for the gray code to binary number conversion has been executed and verified the result.

| 24. | 4-BIT BINARY COUNTER |

Aim:

Build an embedded system for a 4-bit binary counter using a PIC16F877A/887 Microcontroller and assembly language program. Verify its output.

Hardware and Software Used:
- PIC16F877A/887 Microcontroller Development Board
- MPLAB X IDE (v6.05) with pic-as (v2.40)

Algorithm:
1. Make PORTD as an output port and clear it.
2. Clear Digit Carry flag.
3. Call delay.
4. Set RD0.
5. Test Digit Carry; skip the next step if it is set.
6. Jump to step 3.
7. Jump to step 1.

Delay Subroutine:
1. Initialize the counter1 value.
2. Initialize the counter2 value.
3. Initialize the counter3 value.
4. Decrement the counter3; skip the next statement if the counter 3 is zero.
5. Go to step 4.
6. Decrement the counter2, skip the next statement if the counter 2 is zero.
7. Go to step 3.
8. Decrement the counter1, skip the next statement if the counter 1 is zero.
9. Go to step 2.
10. Return to the main program.

Program:
```
#include <xc.inc>
  CONFIG  FOSC = HS         ; Device Configurations
  CONFIG  WDTE = OFF
  CONFIG  PWRTE = OFF
  CONFIG  BOREN = OFF
  CONFIG  LVP = OFF
```

```
CONFIG  CPD = OFF
CONFIG  WRT = OFF
CONFIG  CP = OFF
PSECT reset_Vec, class=CODE, delta=2   ; Initialization code at 00h
reset_Vec:
  goto main
PSECT int_Vec, class=CODE, delta=2     ; interrupt code at 04h
int_Vec:
  retfie
PSECT code, abs                        ; main code starts at 50h
org 50h
main:
    d1     EQU 0x30
    d2     EQU 0x31
    d3     EQU 0x32
    BANKSEL   TRISD           ; Bank1 selection for TRISD
    MOVLW     0x00            ; All bits in PORTD are output
    MOVWF     TRISD
    BANKSEL   PORTD           ; Bank0 selection for PORTD
    MOVWF     PORTD           ; Count Value set to 00h
    BCF       STATUS, 1       ; Clear Digit Carry (DC)
Next:
    CALL      Delay           ; Call time delay
    MOVLW     0x01            ; Setting increment
    ADDWF     PORTD, F        ; Increment counter
    BTFSS     STATUS, 1       ; if DC is set, skip the next instruction
    GOTO      Next            ; Go to Next label
    GOTO      main            ; Go to main label

Delay:
    MOVLW     0x02            ; Count1 = 02h
    MOVWF     d1
    MOVLW     0xFF            ; Count2 = ffh
    MOVWF     d2
```

MOVLW	0xFF		; Count3 = ffh
MOVWF	d3		
DECFSZ	d3, F		; Decrement d3 register; skip the next
			; instruction if it is zero
GOTO	$-1		
DECFSZ	d2, F		; Decrement d2 register; skip the next
			; instruction if it is zero
GOTO	$-5		
DECFSZ	d1, F		; Decrement d1 register; skip the next
			; instruction if it is zero
GOTO	$-9		
RETURN			; Return to the main function
END reset_Vec			

Experimental Result:

Counting means incrementing or decrementing the values of an operator, with respect to its previous state value. This particular counter is implemented with PIC16F877A/887 Microcontroller. It can start counts from 0000 to 1111.

RD3	RD2	RD1	RD0
0	0	0	0
0	0	0	1
0	0	1	0
0	0	1	1
0	1	0	0
0	1	0	1
0	1	1	0
0	1	1	1
1	0	0	0
1	0	0	1
1	0	1	0
1	0	1	1
1	1	0	0
1	1	0	1
1	1	1	0
1	1	1	1

Circuit Diagram:

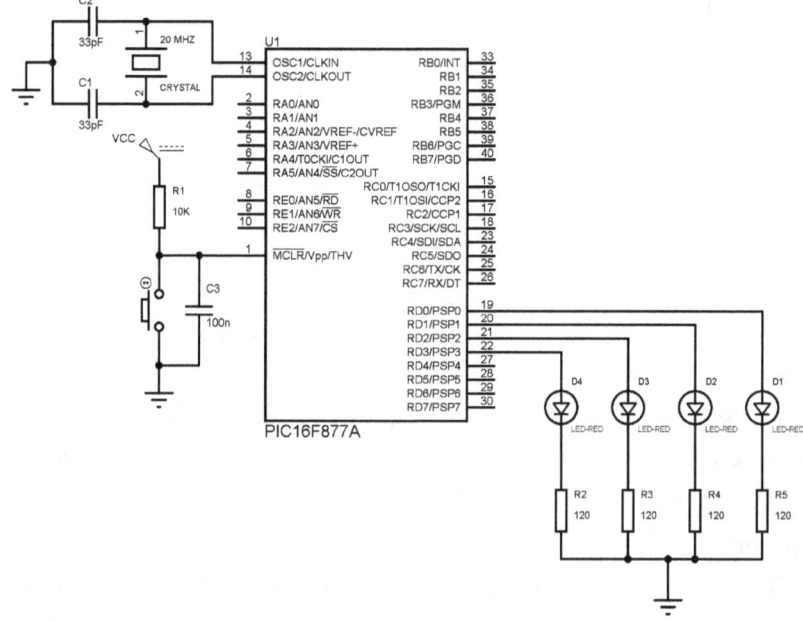

Conclusion:

Thus the PIC16F877A assembly language program for the 4-bit binary counter has been executed and verified the result.

---

25. LOGICAL OPERATION - DEMORGAN's LAW

Aim:

Write an assembly language program to verify the Demorgan's Law using the PIC16F877A/887 Microcontroller.

Software Used:

- MPLAB X IDE (v6.05) with pic-as (v2.40)

Theory:

De Morgan's laws are commonly written as:

$$\overline{A+B} \equiv \overline{A} \cdot \overline{B},$$

and

$$\overline{A \cdot B} \equiv \overline{A} + \overline{B}$$

where,
- . is a logical AND
- + is a logical OR

Algorithm:

Verification of Demorgan's First Law
1. The declaration of variables using udata. We can see these variables in the watch window while debugging the program.
2. Call Fun_LHS function.
3. Call Fun_RHS function.
4. Stop executing program sequences.

Fun_LHS subroutine:
1. Get A1 value at WREG.
2. Logically OR WREG with B1 register and hold the result in WREG.
3. Move the WREG value to the Temp register.
4. Complement Temp register.
5. Move Temp register to the LHS register.
6. Return

Fun_LHS subroutine:
1. Complement A1 and move it to WREG.
2. Move WREG to the Temp register.
3. Complement B1 and move it to WREG.
4. Logically AND WREG with Temp register and hold result in WREG.
5. Move WREG to the RHS register.
6. Return

Program:

```
#include <xc.inc>
  CONFIG  FOSC = HS          ; Device Configurations
  CONFIG  WDTE = OFF
  CONFIG  PWRTE = OFF
  CONFIG  BOREN = OFF
  CONFIG  LVP = OFF
  CONFIG  CPD = OFF
  CONFIG  WRT = OFF
  CONFIG  CP = OFF

PSECT reset_Vec, class=CODE, delta=2   ; Initialization code at 00h
reset_Vec:
   goto main
PSECT int_Vec, class=CODE, delta=2     ; interrupt code at 04h
int_Vec:
   retfie
PSECT code, abs              ; main code starts at 50h
org 50h
main:
; Enter the inputs at 0x30; result will be at 0x32
    A1    EQU 0x30
    B1    EQU 0x31
    LHS   EQU 0x32
    RHS   EQU 0x33
    Temp  EQU 0x34
    CALL      Fun_LHS         ; Call the Fun_LHS subroutine
    CALL      Fun_RHS         ; Call the Fun_LHS subroutine
    GOTO      $               ; Halt

Fun_LHS:
    MOVF      A1, W           ; Move A1 Register to the WREG
    IORWF     B1, W           ; OR the WREG with B1 register and
                              ; hold the result in WREG
```

MOVWF	Temp		; Move the WREG to the Temp register
COMF	Temp, W		; Compliment the Temp register and
			; hold the result in WREG
MOVWF	LHS		; Move the WREG to the LHS register
RETURN			; Return to the main function

Fun_RHS:
```
    COMF    A1, W       ; Complement A1 register and move the
                        ; result to the WREG
    MOVWF   Temp        ; Move the WREG to the Temp register
    COMF    B1, W       ; Complement B1 register and move the
                        ; result to the WREG
    ANDWF   Temp, W     ; AND the WREG with the Temp
                        ; register and hold the result in WREG
    MOVWF   RHS         ; Move the WREG to the RHS register
    RETURN              ; Return to the main function
END reset_Vec
```

Experimental Result:

Before Execution		After Execution	
Memory location	Operand	Memory location	Operand
30H (A1)	24 H	32H (LHS)	93 H
31H (B1)	68 H	33H (RHS)	93 H

Calculation:

Step	Formula Elements	Output Value
LHS	$A + B$	24H **OR** 68H = 6CH
	$\overline{A + B}$	Complement of 6CH = 93H
RHS	$\overline{A}$	Complement of 24H = DBH
	$\overline{B}$	Complement of 68H = 97H
	$\overline{A} . \overline{B}$	DBH **AND** 93H = 93H

Conclusion:

Thus the PIC16F877A assembly language program for the verification of Demorgan's law has been executed and verified the result.

26. SQUARE WAVEFORM GENERATION USING SOFTWARE DELAY

Aim:

Build an embedded system with PIC16F877A/887 Microcontroller to generate 500 Hz square wave signal using software delay and verify its output. Use assembly language program

Hardware and Software Used:
- PIC16F877A Microcontroller Development Board and CRO.
- MPLAB X IDE (v6.05) with pic-as (v2.40)

Theory:

Time delay generation is one of the important concepts dealing with the Microcontrollers and it is used in almost all microcontroller applications.

There are two ways to generate a time delay
- Time delay using software
- Time delay using an on-chip timer

The following factors should be considered during the calculation of time delay using software
- External crystal oscillator connected to the MCU.
- To calculate the machine cycle or instruction cycle of the system.
- Number of machine cycles for each instruction.

Crystal oscillator: The frequency of the crystal connected to the PIC16F877A/887 Microcontroller can vary from 4 MHz to 20 MHz, depending on the chip.

Instruction cycle: CPU executing an instruction takes a certain number of clock cycles.

In PIC16F8xx, one instruction cycle takes 4 oscillator periods. The clock input (from OSC1) is internally divided by four to generate four non-overlapping Quadrature clocks, namely Q1, Q2, Q3, and Q4. The program counter (PC) is incremented every Q1, and the instruction is fetched from the program memory and latched into the instruction register in Q4. The instruction is decoded and executed during the following Q1 through Q4. Because of pipeline operation, all instructions are single cycle, except for any program branches.

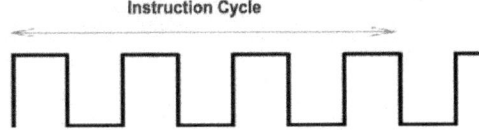

Instruction Cycle

Calculating the instruction cycle of PIC16F8xx for the following crystals:

4 MHz: 4 MHz/4 = 1 MHz
Instruction cycle = 1/1 MHz = 1 us [us=microsecond]

20 MHz: 20 MHz/4 = 5 MHz
Instruction cycle = 1/5 MHz = 0.2 us

Instructions – Execution time for 20 MHz:

Label	Instructions	Instruction Cycle	No. of times to be executed	Total Execution Time	
Delay:	MOVLW D'07'	1	1	= 1*1*0.2µS	= 0.2 µS
	MOVWF A1	1	1	= 1*1*0.2µS	= 0.2 µS
back2:	MOVLW D'237'	1	7	= 1*7*0.2µS	=1.4 µS
	MOVWF A2	1	7	= 1*7*0.2µS	=1.4 µS
Back1:	DECFSZ B1, 1	1 / 2	236 x 7 1 x 7	=1*236*7*0.2µS =330.4 µS = 1*7*0.2µS =1.4 µS	
	GOTO Back1	2	236 x 7	= 2*236*7*0.2µS =660.8µS	
	DECFSZ A1, 1	1 / 2	6 1	= 1*6*0.2µS = 1.2 µS =2*1*0.2µS = 0.4 µS	
	GOTO Back2	2	6	= 2*6*0.2µS	= 2.4 µS
	RETURN	2	1	= 2*1*0.2µS	= 0.4 µS

Time delay = (0.2 + 0.2 + 1.4 + 1.4 + 330.4 + 1.4 + 660.8 + 1.2 + 0.4 + 2.4 + 0.4) µS = 1000.2 µS = ~ 1 mS

Algorithm:

Main Program:
1. Configure PORTD0 as an output port and clear it.
2. Call Delay subroutine.
3. Set PORTD0.
4. Call Delay subroutine.
5. Go to step 1.

Delay Subroutine:
1. Load outer loop count value in the A1 register.
2. Load inner loop count value in the B1 register.
3. Decrement B1 register; skip the next step if it is zero.
4. Go to step 3.
5. Decrement A1 register; skip the next step if it is zero.
6. Go to step 2.
7. Return to the main program.

Program:

```
#include <xc.inc>
  CONFIG  FOSC = HS          ; Device Configurations
  CONFIG  WDTE = OFF
  CONFIG  PWRTE = OFF
  CONFIG  BOREN = OFF
  CONFIG  LVP = OFF
  CONFIG  CPD = OFF
  CONFIG  WRT = OFF
  CONFIG  CP = OFF


PSECT reset_Vec, class=CODE, delta=2   ; Initialization code at 00h
reset_Vec:
   goto main
PSECT int_Vec, class=CODE, delta=2     ; interrupt code at 04h
```

```
int_Vec:
    retfie
PSECT code, abs              ; main code starts at 50h
org 50h
main:
    A1  EQU 0x30
    B1  EQU 0x31
    BANKSEL   TRISD          ; Bank1 selection for TRISD
    BCF       TRISD, 0       ; RD0 in PORTD is output
    BANKSEL   PORTD          ; Bank0 selection for PORTD

    BCF       PORTD, 0       ; Clear RD0
    call      Delay          ; Call delay subroutine
    BSF       PORTD, 0       ; Set RD1
    call      Delay          ; Call delay subroutine
    GOTO      main           ; Halt

Delay:
    MOVLW     7              ; Outer loop count D'7' at WREG
    MOVWF     A1             ; Move the WREG to A1 register
Back2:
    MOVLW     237            ; Inner loop count D'237' at WREG
    MOVWF     B1             ; Move the WREG to B1 register
Back1:
    DECFSZ B1, 1             ; Decrement B1 register; skip the next
                             ; instruction if it is zero
    GOTO Back1               ; Go to Back1
    DECFSZ A1, 1             ; Decrement B1 register; skip the next
                             ; instruction if it is zero
    GOTO Back2               ; Go to Back2
    RETURN                   ; Return from subroutine
END reset_Vec
```

Calculation:

Frequency of square wave:

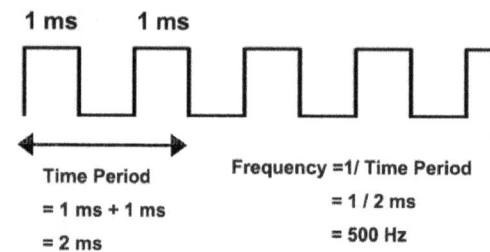

Time Period
= 1 ms + 1 ms
= 2 ms

Frequency =1/ Time Period
= 1 / 2 ms
= 500 Hz

Circuit Diagram:

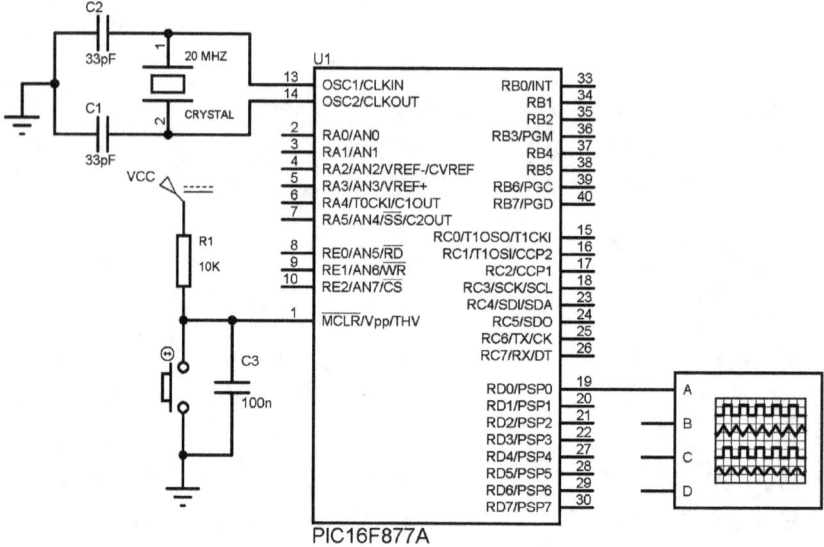

Experimental Result:

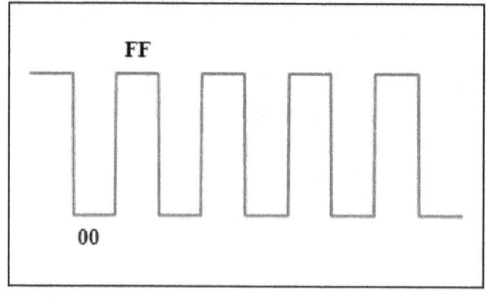

Conclusion:

Thus the PIC16F877A assembly language program for generating a 50 Hz square waveform has been executed and verified the result in Oscilloscope.

27. FLASHING OF LED

Aim:
Build an embedded system to flash an LED using a PIC16F877A/887 Microcontroller and Embedded C Program. Verify its output.

Hardware and Software Used:
- PIC16F877A Microcontroller Development Board, LED and resistor.
- MPLAB X IDE v6.05 & Compiler XC8 v2.40

Algorithm:
1. Set PORTD0 (RD0) as an output port using TRISD Register ('1' for input & '0' for output).
2. Clear RD0.
3. Call delay function for 500 ms.
4. Set RD0.
5. Call delay function for 500 ms.
6. Repeat steps from 2.

Program:
```c
#pragma config FOSC = HS, WDTE = OFF, PWRTE = OFF, BOREN = OFF, LVP = OFF, CPD = OFF, WRT = OFF, CP = OFF
#include <xc.h>
#define _XTAL_FREQ    20000000
void main() {
    TRISD0 = 0;              // Set PORTD0 (RD0) as output port
    while (1)
    {
```

```
    RDO = 0;                  // Clear RD0
    __delay_ms(500);          // 500 ms delay using built-in function
    RDO = 1;                  // Set RD0
    __delay_ms(500);          // 500 ms delay using built-in function
  }
}
```

Circuit Diagram:

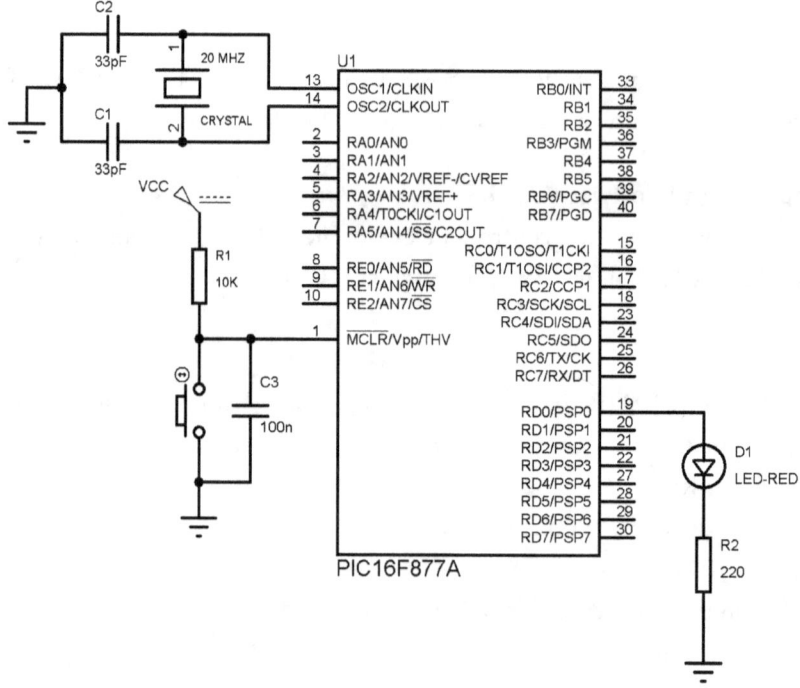

Experimental Result:

The LED connected to RD0 is flashing at regular time interval (500 ms + 500 ms).

Conclusion:

Thus the Embedded C Program for flashing of LED has been executed and verified the output using the PIC16F877A Microcontroller.

28. READ KEY

Aim:

Write an Embedded C Program to read a key and toggle the output LED using the PIC16F877A/887 Microcontroller.

Hardware and Software Used:
- PIC16F877A Microcontroller Development Board, Pushbutton, LED and resistor.
- MPLAB X IDE v6.05 & Compiler XC8 v2.40

Theory:

The pushbutton is a type of switch to turn the circuit on or off. Here the pushbutton is connected to the input port PORTC0 (RC0) and it is connected to a pull-up resistor. The RC0 gets VCC potential when the switch is not pressed. The RC0 is grounded when the switch is pressed. An LED is connected to PORTD0 (RD0) which will toggle the state for every key-press.

Algorithm:
1. Initialize the PORTC0 as input port and PORTD0 as output port using TRISC and TRISD registers. Clear RD0.
2. Execute the 'if' block if the key is pressed.
3. Make a delay of 50 ms for key debounce.
4. Continue the steps if the key is still pressed.
5. Toggle the RD0.
6. Wait for the switch release.
7. Repeat the sequence from step 2.

Program:
```
#pragma config FOSC = HS, WDTE = OFF, PWRTE = OFF, BOREN = OFF, LVP = OFF, CPD = OFF, WRT = OFF, CP = OFF
#include <xc.h>
#define _XTAL_FREQ 20000000
```

```c
void main()              // Main Function
{
  TRISC0 = 1;            // PORTC0 is configured as input port
  TRISD0 = 0;            // PORTD0 is configured as output port
  RD0 = 0;               // Clear PORTD0
  while (1) {            // Forever loop
    if(RC0 == 0)         // If the switch is pressed
    {
      __delay_ms(50);    // Debounce Delay
      if(RC0 == 0)       // If the switch is still pressed
      {
        RD0 = ~ RD0;     // Toggle LED
        while(RC0 == 0); // Wait for release
      }
}}}
```

Circuit Diagram:

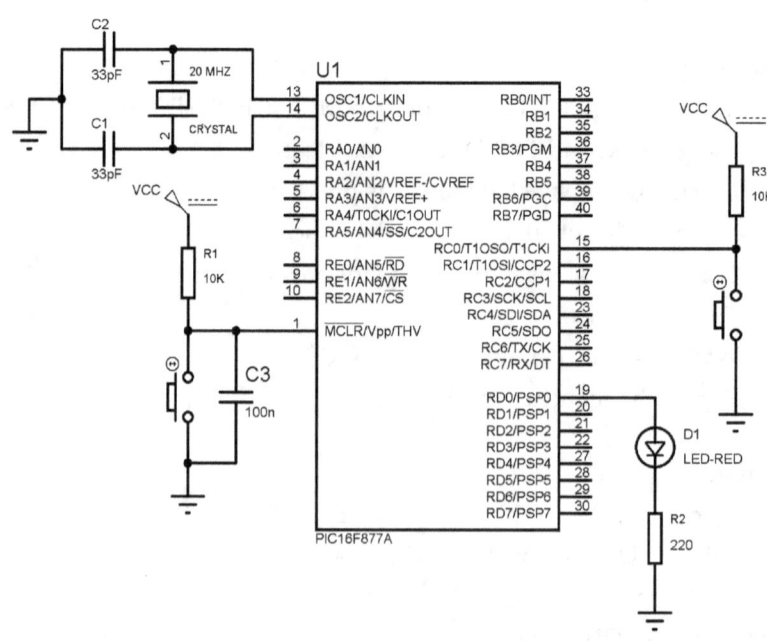

Conclusion:

Thus the Embedded C Program for read key and toggle the output LED has been executed and verified the output using the PIC16F877A Microcontroller.

29. TRAFFIC LIGHT CONTROLLER

Aim:
Design a traffic light controller using the PIC16F877A/887 Microcontroller.

Hardware and Software Used:
- PIC16F877A Microcontroller Development Board, LEDs and resistors
- MPLAB X IDE v6.05 & Compiler XC8 v2.40

Theory:
The traffic light arrangement of the proposed traffic light system is shown in the below figure.

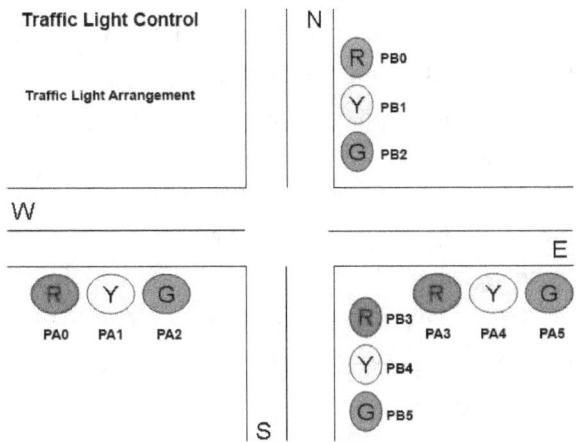

The traffic light sequence for the traffic light controller is described as follows,

1) Allow traffic from W to E and E to W transition for 20 seconds.

2) Give transition time of 4 seconds (Yellow bulbs ON)
3) Allow traffic from N to S and S to N for 20 seconds
4) Give transition time of 4 seconds (Yellow bulbs ON)
5) Repeat the process.

South			North			East			West			HEX
Green	Yellow	Red	Green	Yellow	Red	Green	Yellow	Red	Green	Yellow	Red	RD/RB
RD5	RD4	RD3	RD2	RD1	RD0	RB5	RB4	RB3	RB2	RB1	RB0	
0	0	1	0	0	1	1	0	0	1	0	0	09/24
Delay for 6 seconds													
0	1	0	0	1	0	0	1	0	0	1	0	12/12
Delay for 2 seconds													
1	0	0	1	0	0	0	0	1	0	0	1	24/09
Delay for 6 seconds													
0	1	0	0	1	0	0	1	0	0	1	0	12/12
Delay for 2 seconds													

Algorithm:
1. The digital values of traffic light sequence for PORTB and PORTD are initialized as array elements with static int constant type.
2. Configure the PORTB and PORTD as output ports and clear it.
3. Send the PB_Val[0] element to PORTB.
4. Send the PD_Val[0] element to PORTD.
5. Make 5000 ms delay.
6. Send the PB_Val[1] element to PORTB.
7. Send the PD_Val[1] element to PORTD.
8. Make 1000 ms delay.
9. Send the PB_Val[2] element to PORTB.
10. Send the PD_Val[2] element to PORTD.
11. Make 5000 ms delay.
12. Send the PB_Val[3] element to PORTB.
13. Send the PD_Val[3] element to PORTD.
14. Make 1000 ms delay.
15. Repeat the steps from step 3.

Program:

```c
#pragma config FOSC = HS, WDTE = OFF, PWRTE = OFF, BOREN = OFF, LVP = OFF, CPD = OFF, WRT = OFF, CP = OFF
#include <xc.h>
#define _XTAL_FREQ 20000000

void main()
{
    static int const PB_Val[4] = {0x24,0x12,0x09,0x12};
    static int const PD_Val[4] = {0x09,0x12,0x24,0x12};
    TRISB = 0x00;                   // set PORTB as output
    TRISD = 0x00;                   // set PORTD as output
    PORTB = 0x00;                   // Clear PORTB
    PORTD = 0x00;                   // Clear PORTD
    while (1)
    {
        PORTB = PB_Val[0];          // 0x24 to PORTB
        PORTD = PD_Val[0];          // 0x09 to PORTD
        __delay_ms(5000);           // Delay for 5 sec
        PORTB = PB_Val[1];          // 0x12 to PORTB
        PORTD = PD_Val[1];          // 0x12 to PORTD
        __delay_ms(1000);           // Delay for 1 sec
        PORTB = PB_Val[2];          // 0x09 to PORTB
        PORTD = PD_Val[2];          // 0x24 to PORTD
        __delay_ms(5000);           // Delay for 5 sec
        PORTB = PB_Val[3];          // 0x12 to PORTB
        PORTD = PD_Val[3];          // 0x12 to PORTD
        __delay_ms(1000);           // Delay for 1 sec
    }
}
```

Circuit Diagram:

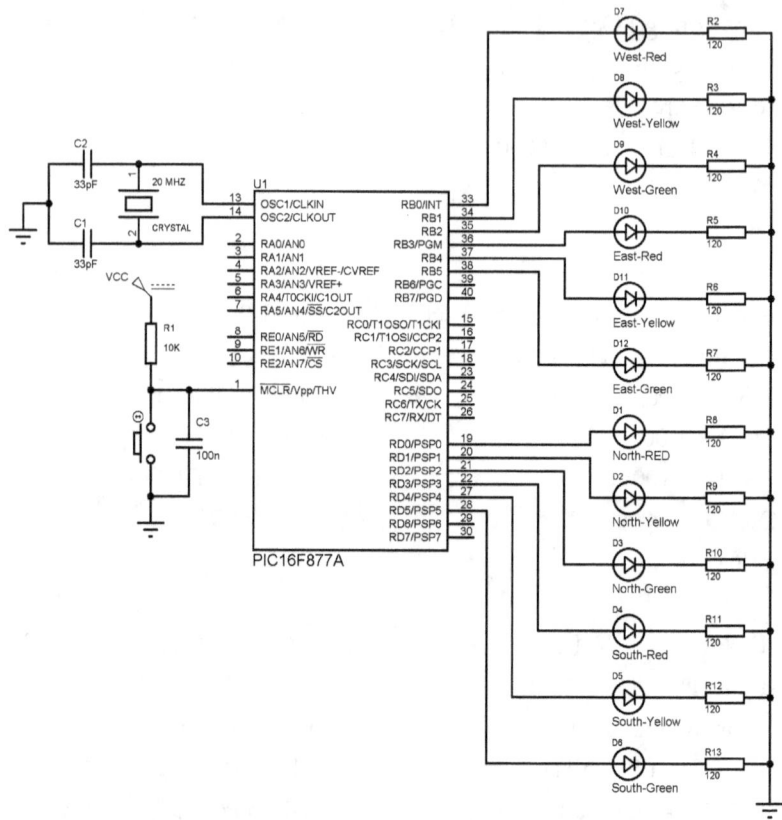

Experimental - Inputs:

PORTD	PORTB
09H	24H
12H	12H
24H	09H
12H	12H

Conclusion:

Thus the traffic control system has been designed and verified its output using the PIC16F877A Microcontroller.

30. SEVEN SEGMENT DISPLAY INTERFACE

Aim:
Write an Embedded C Program to interface 2-digits seven segment LED display with PIC16F877A/887 Microcontroller and do seconds counting from 00 to 59 on the display.

Hardware and Software Used:
- PIC16F877A Microcontroller Development Board, CA seven segment display units, NPN transistors and resistors
- MPLAB X IDE v6.05 & Compiler XC8 v2.40

Theory:
A seven-segment display is an electronic device used to display numbers and some alphabets. It has seven LED segments. The seven-segment display comes with two different configurations. They are the common anode and a common cathode. There is a common terminal in the seven-segment display. In the Common Cathode (CC) device, the cathode terminal of all seven segments is connected to a common terminal. It should be connected to the Ground of power source while operating the display.

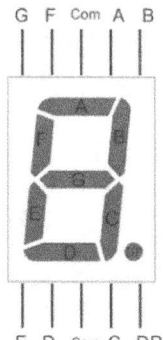

In the Common Anode (CA) device, anode terminal of all seven segments is connected to a common terminal. It should be connected to the positive of the power source while operating the display. Display codes are the HEX numbers that will be given to the segment to display a character. Below is a table with display codes of digits from 0 to 9 for the CA display.

The multiplexing technique is used for operating more than one seven-segment displays. Only one segment is working at a time and the switching between the segments is made faster to display the character on all modules. For seconds counter, the two seven-segments are used. In the circuit diagram, PORTB and PORTD are configured as output ports. PORTD provides the segment code input to the display and PORTB provides a selection input to the display.

Number To display	H	G	F	E	D	C	B	A	HEX
0	1	1	0	0	0	0	0	0	0xC0
1	1	1	1	1	1	0	0	1	0xF9
2	1	0	1	0	0	1	0	0	0xA4
3	1	0	1	1	0	0	0	0	0xB0
4	1	0	0	1	1	0	0	1	0x99
5	1	0	0	1	0	0	1	0	0x92
6	1	0	0	0	0	0	1	0	0x82
7	1	1	1	1	1	0	0	0	0xF8
8	1	0	0	0	0	0	0	0	0x80
9	1	0	0	1	0	0	0	0	0x90

Algorithm:
1. Initialize the seven-segment digit codes for common anode.
2. Configure PORTB and PORTD as output ports using TRIS registers.
3. Clear the PORTB and PORTD.
4. Initialize the variables i, j, and k as integer and clear i and j.
5. Create a for loop with the target value of 100 (a to f).
    a. Select digit 0 by setting RB1=1.
    b. Send the segment code to PORTD which is indexed by 'i'.
    c. Make 5 ms delay.
    d. Select digit 1 by setting RB0=1.
    e. Send the segment code to PORTD which is indexed by 'j'.
    f. Make 5 ms delay.
6. Increment 'i'.
7. If 'i' value is equal to 10, i=0, j++.
8. If 'j' value is equal to 6, j=0.
9. Repeat the steps from step 5.

Program:

```c
#pragma config FOSC = HS, WDTE = OFF, PWRTE = OFF, BOREN = OFF, LVP = OFF, CPD = OFF, WRT = OFF, CP = OFF
#include <xc.h>
#define _XTAL_FREQ 20000000

void main()
{
    static int const Segment_Code[10] = {0xc0, 0xf9, 0xa4, 0xb0, 0x99, 0x92, 0x83, 0xf8, 0x80, 0x98};
    TRISB = 0x00;               // set PORTB as output
    TRISD = 0x00;               // set PORTD as output
    PORTB = 0x00;               // Clear PORTB
    PORTD = 0x00;               // Clear PORTD
    int i=0,j=0,k;

    while (1)
    {
        for (k=0; k<100; k++)
        {
        RB0=0; RB1=1;           //select LSB digit
        PORTD = Segment_Code[i]; //Send the segment code indexed by i to PORTD
        __delay_ms(5);          //buffer delay time for 5 ms
        RB0=1; RB1=0;           //select LSB digit
        PORTD = Segment_Code[j]; //Send the segment code indexed by j to PORTD
        __delay_ms(5);          // buffer delay time for 5 ms
        }
        i++;                    // increment the digit0 value
        if (i==10) {            // if digit0 is >9
        i=0;                    // digit0 index is cleared and digit1
                                // index is increment by 1
        j++;
        }
        if(j==6)                // if digit1 index is >5, clear digit1 index
        {
```

```
        j=0;
    }
}}
```

Circuit Diagram:

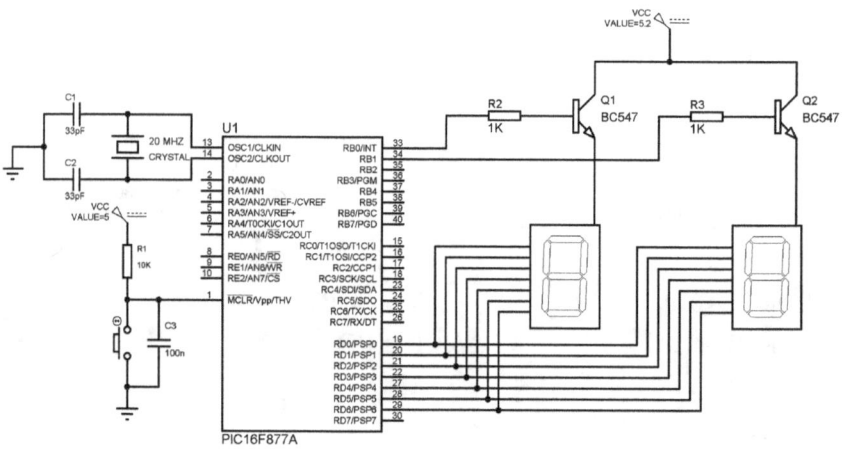

Conclusion:

Thus the Embedded C Program for seconds counter has been executed and verified the output using the PIC16F877A Microcontroller and seven segment displays.

31.	**LCD INTERFACE IN 4-BIT MODE**

Aim:

Write an Embedded C Program to interface 16x2 LCD with PIC16F877A/887 Microcontroller and display the characters on the LCD screen.

Hardware and Software Used:

- o   PIC16F877A Microcontroller Development Board and 16x2 LCD
- o   MPLAB X IDE v6.05 & Compiler XC8 v2.40

Theory:

16×2 LCD is an output device which displays any data or information. The name 16x2 LCD means 16 characters can be displays in 2 lines. The ability of LCD is to display numbers, characters and special characters. To display characters on the LCD, the ASCII value of the character should be sent to the data register. To configure an LCD, the command words should be sent to the command register of LCD.

LCD Pin description:

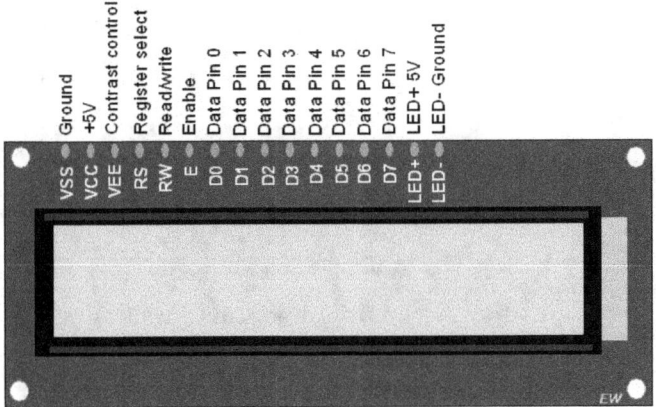

- **Vss/GND, Vdd, VE & +Ve**
    - Supply +5V to Vdd(pin2) and +Ve (pin15)
    - Connect Ground to Vss (pin1) and backlight cathode (pin16)
    - VE is used to control the contrast of the LCD screen.
- **RS, Register select**
    - There are two important registers in the LCD. One is a data register and the other is the command register.
    - If data is sent to data register the data is considered as data to be displayed on the LCD. If the command is sent to the command register which configures the LCD.
    * If RS=0, the command register is selected
    * If RS=1, the data register is selected
- **R/W, Read/Write**

It is an input pin that allows the user to read data from the LCD or write data into the LCD.

* To write data to LCD connect R/W pin to GND
* To read data from LCD connect R/W pin to VCC

S. No	HEX Value	Command to LCD
1	0x01	Clear Display Screen
2	0x30	Function set: 8-bit, 1 Line, 5x7 Dots
3	0x38	Function set: 8-bit, 2 Line, 5x7 Dots
4	0x20	Function set: 4-bit, 1 Line, 5x7 Dots
5	0x28	Function set: 4-bit, 2 Line, 5x7 Dots
6	0x06	Entry Mode
7	0x08	Display off, Cursor off
8	0x0E	Display on, Cursor on
9	0x0C	Display on, Cursor off
10	0x0F	Display on, Cursor blinking
11	0x18	Shift entire display left
12	0x1C	Shift entire display right
13	0x10	Move cursor left by one character
14	0x14	Move cursor right by one character
15	0x80	Force cursor to beginning of first row
16	0xC0	Force cursor to beginning of second row

Algorithm:

Here the16x2 LCD is interfaced with PIC16F877A/887 in 4-bit mode.
Only RS, E, D4, D6, D7 and D8 pins of LCD will be used for the interfacing. (RW pin is grounded)

Main File:
1. RD2 and RD3 are defined as RS and EN respectively.
2. RD4, RD5, RD6, and RD7 are defined as data bus of LCD.
3. Include the header file "lcd4bit_head.h".

4. main () function
   1) Initialize int variable 'i'.
   2) Make PORTD as output ports using TRIS registers.
   3) Call the lcd_init() function to initialize the LCD in 4-bit mode.
   4) Call lcd_cmd () function to send 0x80 command to LCD (Keep cursor at first row first column).
   5) Call lcd_display() function to send the characters to display ("Interfacing LCD").
   6) Call lcd_cmd () function to send 0xC0 command to LCD (Keep cursor at second row first column).
   7) Call lcd_display() function to send the characters to display ("Interfacing LCD").
   8) Make 3000 ms delay to hold the screen.
   9) Clear LCD screen.
   10) Repeat the steps from step 4.

Header file:
1. Lcd_WriteBit() function
    i. Write the LSB of argument value to RD4-RD7.
2. lcd_cmd () function
    i. Make RS pin low, RS=0 (CMD register).
    ii. Send Higher Nibble of argument value to Lcd_WriteBit().
    iii. Give High to Low pulse to Enable (E).
    iv. Make RS pin low, RS=0 (CMD register).
    v. Send Lower Nibble of argument value to Lcd_WriteBit().
    vi. Give High to Low pulse to Enable (E).
3. lcd_data () function
    i. Make RS pin low, RS=1 (DAT register).
    ii. Send Higher Nibble of argument value to Lcd_WriteBit().
    iii. Give High to Low pulse to Enable (E).
    iv. Make RS pin low, RS=1 (DAT register).
    v. Send Lower Nibble of argument value to Lcd_WriteBit().
    vi. Give High to Low pulse to Enable (E).
4. lcd_display () function

i. If the null character coming from the function argument.
   ii. Call lcd_data () function to write character on LCD screen.
   iii. Make 10 ms delay.
   iv. Increment argument variable.
5. lcd_init() function
   Call lcd_cmd() function to write the command 0x02 to LCD.
   Call lcd_cmd() function to write the command 0x28 to LCD.
   Call lcd_cmd() function to write the command 0x0C to LCD.
   Call lcd_cmd() function to write the command 0x06 to LCD.
   Call lcd_cmd() function to write the command 0x01 to LCD.

Program:

//Main file:

```c
#pragma config FOSC = HS, WDTE = OFF, PWRTE = OFF, BOREN = OFF, LVP = OFF, CPD = OFF, WRT = OFF, CP = OFF
#include <xc.h>
#define _XTAL_FREQ 20000000
#define RS      RD2         // RD2 is named as RS
#define EN      RD3         // RD3 is named as EN
#define D4      RD4         // 4-bit mode (RD4-D4, RD5-D5
#define D5      RD5         // RD6-D6, RD7-D7)
#define D6      RD6
#define D7      RD7
#include "lcd4bit_head.h"   // Include header file - lcd4bit_head.h

void main() {                          // Main function
    TRISD = 0x00;                      // set PORT D as output ports
    lcd_init ();                       // Call lcd_init() function
    while (1) {                        // Forever loop
        lcd_cmd(0x80);                 // cursor position at 0th addr of line1
        lcd_display("Interfacing LCD");// Call lcd_display() function
        lcd_cmd(0xC0);                 // cursor position at 0th addr of line2
        lcd_display("With PIC16F MCU");// Call lcd_display() function
        __delay_ms(3000);              // Make 3000 ms delay time
```

```c
        lcd_cmd(0x01);                          // clear the screen
    }
}
```

//Header file: lcd4bit_head.h

```c
void Lcd_WriteBit(unsigned char bt) {    //write the nibble on 4-bit data bus of LCD
    if(bt & 1)
        D4 = 1;
    else
        D4 = 0;
    if(bt & 2)
        D5 = 1;
    else
        D5 = 0;
    if(bt & 4)
        D6 = 1;
    else
        D6 = 0;
    if(bt & 8)
        D7 = 1;
    else
        D7 = 0;
}


void lcd_cmd(unsigned char CMD) {          // Definition of lcd_cmd() function
    RS = 0;                                // Make RS pin low to select CMD reg.
    Lcd_WriteBit((CMD >> 4) & 0x0FU);      // Send Higher Nibble of CMD
    EN = 1;                                // Give High to Low pulse to Enable (E)
    __delay_ms(2);
    EN = 0;
    __delay_ms(5);
    RS = 0;
    Lcd_WriteBit(CMD & 0x0FU);             // Send Lower Nibble of CMD
    EN = 1;                                // Give High to Low pulse to Enable (E)
```

```c
    __delay_ms(2);
    EN = 0;
    __delay_ms(5);
}

void lcd_data(unsigned char DAT) {        // Definition of lcd_data() function
    RS = 1;                                // Make RS pin high to select data reg.
    Lcd_WriteBit((DAT >> 4) & 0x0FU);      // Send Higher Nibble of data
    EN = 1;                                // Give High to Low pulse to Enable (E)
    __delay_ms(2);
    EN = 0;
    __delay_ms(5);
    RS = 1;
    Lcd_WriteBit(DAT & 0x0FU);             // Send Lower Nibble of data
    EN = 1;                                // Give High to Low pulse to Enable (E)
    __delay_ms(2);
    EN = 0;
    __delay_ms(5);
}

void lcd_display( unsigned char *x){      // Definition of lcd_display () function
    while(*x!=0x0) {                       // Condition is true until null character
    lcd_data(*x);                          // Send a character to LCD screen
    __delay_ms(10);                        // Make 10 ms delay
    x++;                                   // Increment pointer variable
    }
}

void lcd_init () {
    lcd_cmd(0x02); __delay_ms(12);         // 16X2 LCD in 4-bit mode
    lcd_cmd(0x28); __delay_ms(12);         // 2 lines, 5X7 dots in 4-bit mode
    lcd_cmd(0x0C); __delay_ms(12);         // Display ON Cursor OFF
    lcd_cmd(0x06); __delay_ms(12);         // Auto Increment cursor
    lcd_cmd(0x01); __delay_ms(12);         // Clear Display
}
```

Circuit Diagram:

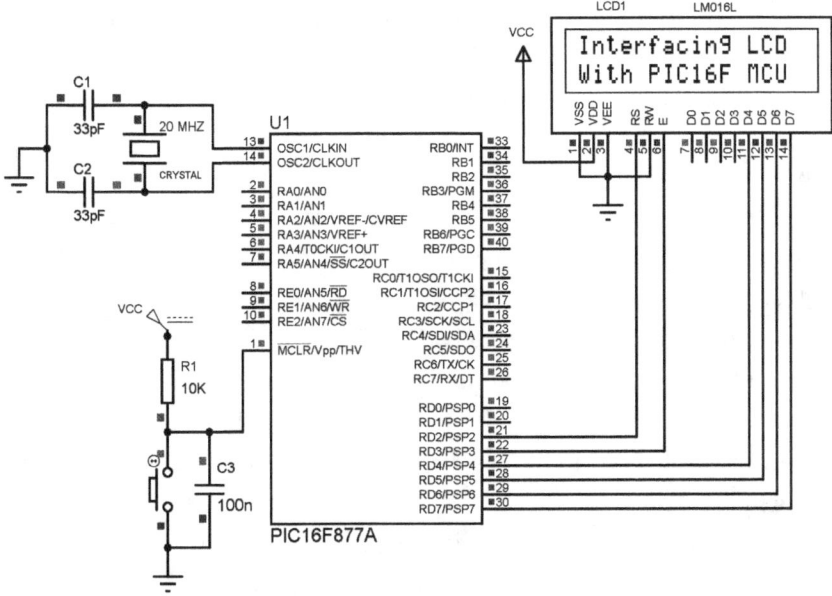

Experimental Output:

Display on LCD Screen	
Line 1	Interfacing LCD
Line 2	With PIC16F MCU

Conclusion:

Thus the 16x2 LCD has been interfaced with PIC16F877A Microcontroller in 4-bit mode and the characters are displayed on the LCD screen.

32. HEX KEYBOARD INTERFACE

Aim:

Write an Embedded C Program to interface Hex keyboard with PIC16F877A Microcontroller and display the pressed key number on the seven segment display module.

Hardware and Software Used:
- PIC16F877A Microcontroller Development Board, Hex key board and CA Seven segment display unit
- MPLAB X IDE v6.05 & Compiler XC8 v2.40

Theory:

Hex keyboard is a collection of 16 keys arranged in the form of a 4×4 matrix. Typically, a hex keyboard has keys representing numbers 0, 1, 2, 3, 4, 5, 6, 7, 8, 9, and letters A, B, C, D, *, and #. The hex keyboard has 8 communication lines namely R1, R2, R3, R4 and C1, C2, C3, and C4 representing the rows and columns respectively. When a particular key is pressed the corresponding row and column to which the terminals of the key are connected (shorted). The diagram of a typical hex keypad is shown in the figure below.

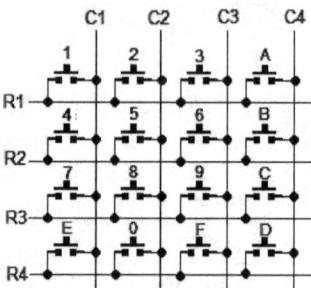

The column scanning method is used to identify the pressed key. In this method, a particular row is kept low whereas other rows are high. The logic status of each column line is scanned. If a particular column is found low, which means the key comes in between that column and row is short (pressed).

Algorithm:
Main Program:
1. Configure the LSB 4-bits of PORTB are output ports and MSB 4-bits of PORTB are input ports using the TRIS register.
2. Configure PORTC as an output port using the TRIS register.
3. Clear the PORTC.
4. Set key value as 0xff.

5. Call Read_Key() function and store the return value in segment (PORTC) variable.
6. Make 200 ms delay
7. Repeat steps from step 5.

Subroutine: Read_Key()
1. Scan ROW1 of the keyboard by clearing r1 and setting r2, r3, and r4.
   If c1 is clear, return 0x8E to display F.
   If c2 is clear, return 0x86 to display E.
   If c3 is clear, return 0xA1 to display D.
   If c4 is clear, return 0xC6 to display C.
2. Scan ROW2 of the keyboard by clearing r2 and setting r1, r3, and r4.
   If c1 is clear, return 0x83 to display B.
   If c2 is clear, return 0x88 to display A.
   If c3 is clear, return 0x90 to display 9.
   If c4 is clear, return 0x80 to display 8.
3. Scan ROW3 of the keyboard by clearing r3 and setting r1, r2, and r4.
   If c1 is clear, return 0xF8 to display 7.
   If c2 is clear, return 0x82 to display 6.
   If c3 is clear, return 0x92 to display 5.
   If c4 is clear, return 0x99 to display 4.
4. Scan ROW4 of the keyboard by clearing r4 and setting r1, r2, and r3.
   If c1 is clear, return 0xB0 to display 3.
   If c2 is clear, return 0xA4 to display 2.
   If c3 is clear, return 0xF9 to display 1.
   If c4 is clear, return 0xC0 to display 0.

Program:

```
#pragma config FOSC = XT, WDTE = OFF, PWRTE = OFF, BOREN = OFF, LVP = OFF, CPD = OFF, WRT = OFF, CP = OFF
#include <xc.h>
#define _XTAL_FREQ 20000000
#define r1  RB0             // RB0-RB3 connected with r1 to r4
#define r2  RB1
#define r3  RB2
```

```c
#define r4  RB3
#define c1  RB4            // RB4-RB7 connected with c1 to c4
#define c2  RB5
#define c3  RB6
#define c4  RB7
#define segment PORTC      // PORTC is connected with 7 segment
int key;                   // Global declaration
int Read_Key(void);        // Function declaration
// C    D    E    F        // Keys position at HEX keyboard
// 8    9    A    B
// 4    5    6    7
// 0    1    2    3

void main(void) {          // Main function
    TRISB = 0xF0;          // RB7-RB4 are input ports and
                           // PB3-RB0 are output ports
    TRISC = 0x00;          // PORTC as output port
    PORTC = 0x00;          // Clear PORTC
    key = 0xff;            // Assume no key pressed
    while(1)  {
        segment = Read_Key();  // Read the pressed key and move it to
                               // the seven segment display
        __delay_ms(200);       // Make 200 ms delay
    }
}

// Scan all the keys in the HEX keypad and detect the pressed key that will be return to the main function
int Read_Key(void) {
r1=0; r2=1; r3=1; r4=1; __delay_ms(10);         // Scan r1 of keyboard
if (c1==0){__delay_ms(200); while(c1==0); return 0x8e;}      //f
if (c2==0){__delay_ms(200); while(c2==0); return 0x86;}      //e
if (c3==0){__delay_ms(200); while(c3==0); return 0xa1;}      //d
if (c4==0){__delay_ms(200); while(c4==0); return 0xc6;}      //c

r1=1; r2=0; r3=1; r4=1; __delay_ms(10);         // Scan r2 of keyboard
```

```
if (c1==0){__delay_ms(200); while(c1==0); return 0x83;}     //b
if (c2==0){__delay_ms(200); while(c2==0); return 0x88;}     //a
if (c3==0){__delay_ms(200); while(c3==0); return 0x90;}     //9
if (c4==0){__delay_ms(200); while(c4==0); return 0x80;}     //8

r1=1; r2=1; r3=0; r4=1; __delay_ms(10);        // Scan r3 of keyboard
if (c1==0){__delay_ms(200); while(c1==0); return 0xf8;}     //7
if (c2==0){__delay_ms(200); while(c2==0); return 0x82;}     //6
if (c3==0){__delay_ms(200); while(c3==0); return 0x92;}     //5
if (c4==0){__delay_ms(200); while(c4==0); return 0x99;}     //4

r1=1; r2=1; r3=1; r4=0; __delay_ms(10);        // Scan r4 of keyboard
if (c1==0){__delay_ms(200); while(c1==0); return 0xb0;}     //3
if (c2==0){__delay_ms(200); while(c2==0); return 0xa4;}     //2
if (c3==0){__delay_ms(200); while(c3==0); return 0xf9;}     //1
if (c4==0){__delay_ms(200); while(c4==0); return 0xc0;}     //0
return (key);
}
```

Circuit Diagram:

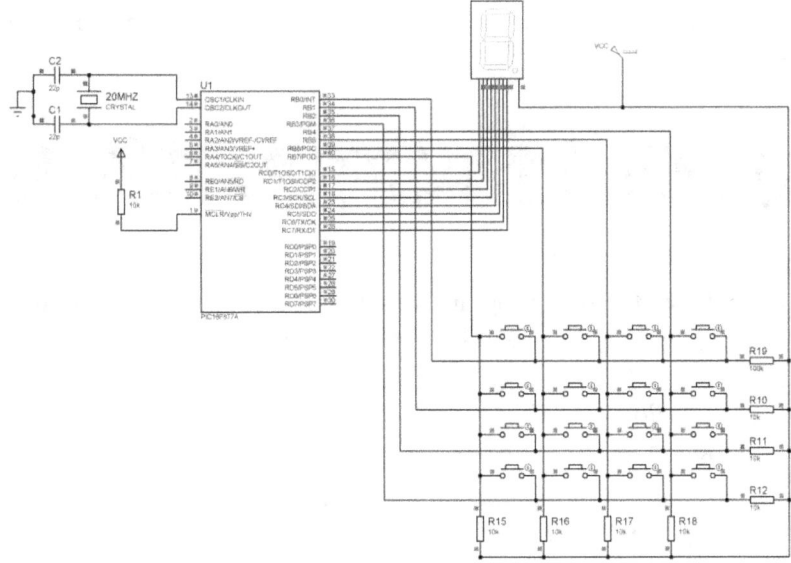

Experimental Output:

Name of the Key pressed	Character on the 7 segment display
0	0
1	1
2	2
3	3
4	4
5	5
6	6
7	7
8	8
9	9
A	A
B	B
C	C
D	D
E	E
F	F

Conclusion:

Thus the HEX keyboard has been interfaced with PIC16F877A Microcontroller and displayed the pressed key number on the seven segment display.

33. SOLID STATE RELAY INTERFACE

Aim:

Write an Embedded C Program to interface solid state relay with PIC16F877A/887 Microcontroller.

Hardware and Software Used:
- PIC16F877A Microcontroller Development Board, MOC3021, BT136 TRIAC, NPN transistor, Lamp, Pushbutton and resistors
- MPLAB X IDE v6.05 & Compiler XC8 v2.40

Theory:

A solid-state relay is a non-contact switch fully composed of the semiconductor element. It is an equivalent for electromechanical relay and can be used to control electrical loads without the use of moving parts.

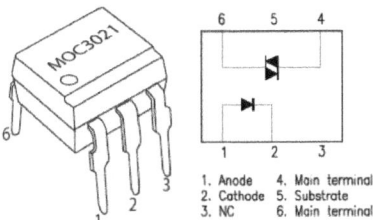

1. Anode   4. Main terminal
2. Cathode 5. Substrate
3. NC   6. Main terminal

It can drive the high-current load with a small control signal. Solid-state relay has many advantages over electromagnetic relays such as no contact, no spark, fast switching speed, high reliability, long life, anti-interference ability, and small size.

Algorithm:

1. Initialize the PORTD7 as input port and PORTC0 as output port using TRISD and TRISC registers. (0 for output; 1 for input).
2. Clear RC0.
3. Check whether the key (RD7) is pressed or not; continue the next step if the key is pressed.
4. Make a delay of 50 ms for key debounce.
5. Check whether the key is still pressed or not; continue the next step if the key is pressed.
6. Toggle the state of RC0 (Relay).
7. Wait for the switch release.
8. Repeat the steps from step 3.

Program:

```
#pragma config FOSC = HS, WDTE = OFF, PWRTE = OFF, BOREN = OFF,
LVP = OFF, CPD = OFF, WRT = OFF, CP = OFF
#include <xc.h>
#define _XTAL_FREQ 20000000
#define Key RD7
#define Relay RC0
```

```c
void main()              // Main Function
{
   TRISD7 = 1;           // PORTD7 is configured as input port
   TRISC0 = 0;           // PORTC0 is configured as output port
   Relay = 0;            // Clear RC0
   while (1)             // Forever loop
   {
   if(Key == 0)          // If the switch is pressed
   {
      __delay_ms(50);    // Debounce Delay
      if(Key == 0)       // If the switch is still pressed
        {
         Relay = ~ Relay;  // Toggle Solid state relay
         while(Key == 0);  // Wait for release
        }
   }
  }
}
```

Circuit Diagram:

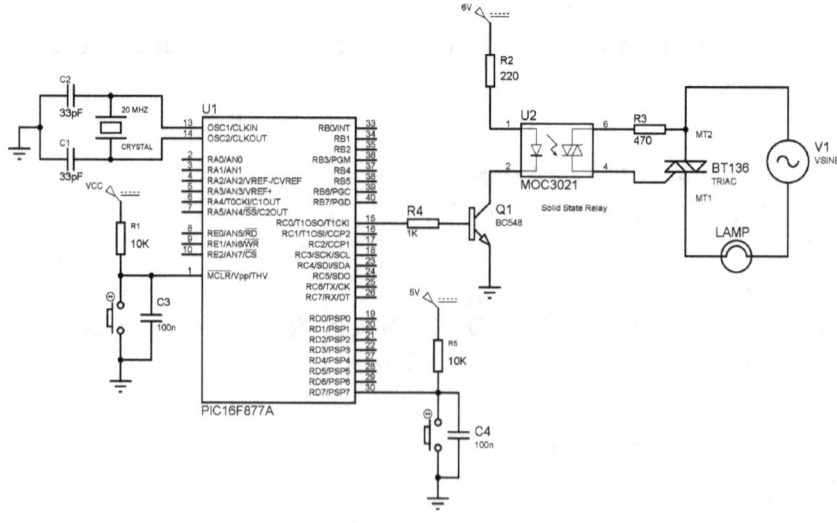

110

Conclusion:

Thus the solid state relay has been interfaced with PIC16F877A Microcontroller and toggled the solid state relay output for every key press.

34. DC MOTOR DIRECTION CONTROLLER

Aim:
Write and execute an Embedded C Program to control the direction of rotation of a DC motor using PIC16F877A/887 Microcontroller.

Hardware and Software Used:
- PIC16F877A Microcontroller Development Board, DC motor, NPN transistors, Diodes and resistors
- MPLAB X IDE v6.05 & Compiler XC8 v2.40

Algorithm:
1. Initialize the PORTD6 and PORTD7 are input ports.
2. Initialize the PORTC as an output port.
3. Clear the direction control inputs (OUT1 and OUT2).
4. Check whether the switch A is pressed or not; continue the next step if switch A is pressed.
5. Make a delay of 50 ms for key debounce.
6. Check whether the switch A is still pressed or not; continue the next step if switch A is pressed.
7. Set OUT1 and Clear OUT2.
8. Wait for the switch A release.
9. Check whether the switch B is pressed or not; continue the next step if switch B is pressed.
10. Make a delay of 50 ms for key debounce.
11. Check whether the switch B is still pressed or not; continue the next step if switch B is pressed.
12. Clear OUT1 and Set OUT2.

13. Wait for the switch B release.
14. Repeat the steps from step 4.

Program:

```c
#pragma config FOSC = HS, WDTE = OFF, PWRTE = OFF, BOREN = OFF, LVP = OFF, CPD = OFF, WRT = OFF, CP = OFF
#include <xc.h>
#define _XTAL_FREQ 20000000

#define SW_A RD6
#define SW_B RD7
#define OUT1 RC0
#define OUT2 RC1

void main()                // Main Function
{
   TRISD = 0xC0;           // PORTD6&7 are configured as input ports
   TRISC = 0x00;           // PORTC is configured as output port
   OUT1 = 0;               // Clear output to stop motor
   OUT2 = 0;

while (1)                  // Forever loop
  {
  if(SW_A == 0)            // If the switch is pressed
  {
   __delay_ms(50);         // Debounce Delay
   if(SW_A == 0)           // If the switch is still pressed
    {
     OUT1 = 1;             // Motor rotates Anti-clock wise
     OUT2 = 0;
     while(SW_A == 0);     // Wait for release
    }
  }
```

```c
    if(SW_B == 0)                  // If the switch is pressed
    {
     __delay_ms(50);               // Debounce Delay
     if(SW_B == 0)                 // If the switch is still pressed
       {
        OUT1 = 0;                  // Motor rotates Anti-clock wise
        OUT2 = 1;
        while(SW_B == 0);          // Wait for release
       }
    }
   }
  }
```

Circuit Diagram:

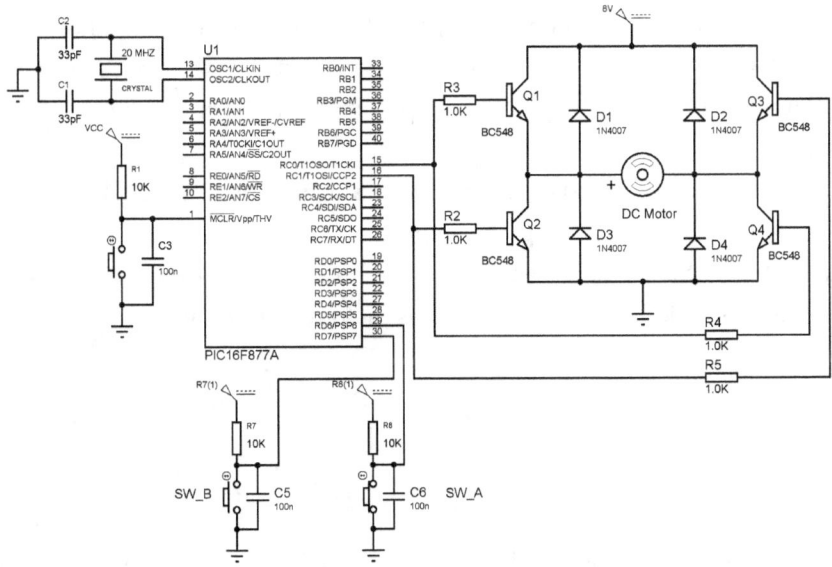

Conclusion:

Thus the DC motor has been interfaced with PIC16F877A Microcontroller using H-bridge and controlled the direction of rotation of the motor.

35. STEPPER MOTOR INTERFACE

Aim:

Write an Embedded C Program to interface stepper motor with PIC16F877A/887 Microcontroller and rotate the stepper motor for 360-degree clock-wise as well as 360-degree anti clock-wise.

Hardware and Software Used:
- PIC16F877A Microcontroller Development Board, Stepper motor and Motor driver
- MPLAB X IDE v6.05 & Compiler XC8 v2.40

Theory:

Stepper motor is a brushless, synchronous DC electric motor, which divides the full rotation into a number of equal steps. It is also known as Step Motor. For example, in the case of a 200 step motor, one complete rotation (360°) is divided into 200 steps, which means one step is equal to 1.8°.

There are two types of stepper motors: Unipolar and Bipolar. Due to the ease of operation unipolar stepper motor is most widely used. A unipolar motor contains center-tapped windings. The center connection of the coils is tied together and used as the power terminal.

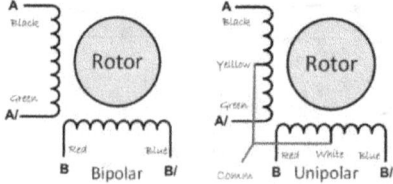

A standard motor will have the step angle of 1.8 degrees, then the number of steps required to complete one revolution will be

Steps per Revolution = 360⁰ / Step Angle
                     = 360⁰/1.8⁰ = 200

Stepper motors can be driven in three different patterns or sequences. Namely,

Wave Step sequence: The motor is operated with only one phase energized at a time. It is the 4 step sequence.

Full Step Sequence: The motor is operated with two phases energized at a time. It is the 4 step sequence. In Full Step Drive method, two coils are energized at a time. Thus, here two adjacent coils are excited at a time. It is the 4 step sequence.

Step	A	B	A/	B/	Hex Value
1	1	1	0	0	0x0C
2	0	1	1	0	0x06
3	0	0	1	1	0x03
4	1	0	0	1	0x09

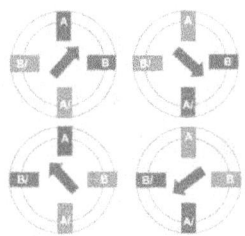

Half Step Sequence: In this method, coils are energized alternatively. Thus it rotates with half step angle. It is the 8 step sequence.

Stepper motor Connector:

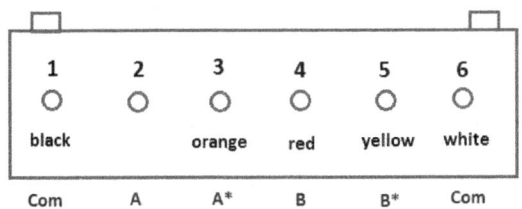

Algorithm:
1. PORTD is dedicated for the stepper motor interface and makes it as an output port.
2. Declare and initialize the step sequences for both clockwise and anti-clockwise rotation.
3. Use FOR loops to send 200 steps to the stepper motor driver for 360 degrees clockwise rotation.
4. Wait for 2 seconds.
5. Use FOR loops to send 200 steps to the stepper motor driver for 360 degrees anti-clockwise rotation.

6. Wait for 2 seconds.
7. Stop the program execution.

Program:

```c
#pragma config FOSC = HS, WDTE = OFF, PWRTE = OFF, BOREN = OFF, LVP = OFF, CPD = OFF, WRT = OFF, CP = OFF
#include <xc.h>
#define _XTAL_FREQ 20000000
#define step PORTD


void main() {                           // Main Function
unsigned int i,j;
int cw[]={0x0C,0x06,0x03,0x09};
int ccw[]={0x09,0x03,0x06,0x0C};
TRISD = 0x00;

// for 360 clk-wise rotation, 360/1.8 = 200 steps to the stepper motor
for (i=0; i<50; i++)                    // Loop count 50 x inner loop count 4
{
        for(j=0; j<4; j++)              // 4 step sequence
        {
        step = cw[j];                   // Move each step to the stepper motor
        __delay_ms(15);                 // 15 ms delay between steps
        }
}
__delay_ms (2000);                      // Hold rotation for 2 sec

// for 360 Anti-clk-wise rotation, 360/1.8 = 200 steps to the stepper motor
for (i=0; i<50; i++)                    // Loop count 50 x inner loop count 4
{
        for(j=0; j<4; j++)              // 4 step sequence
        {
        step = ccw[j];                  // Move each step to the stepper motor
        __delay_ms(15);                 // 15 ms delay between steps
```

        }
}
__delay_ms (2000);   // Hold rotation for 2 sec
while(1);
}

Circuit Diagram:

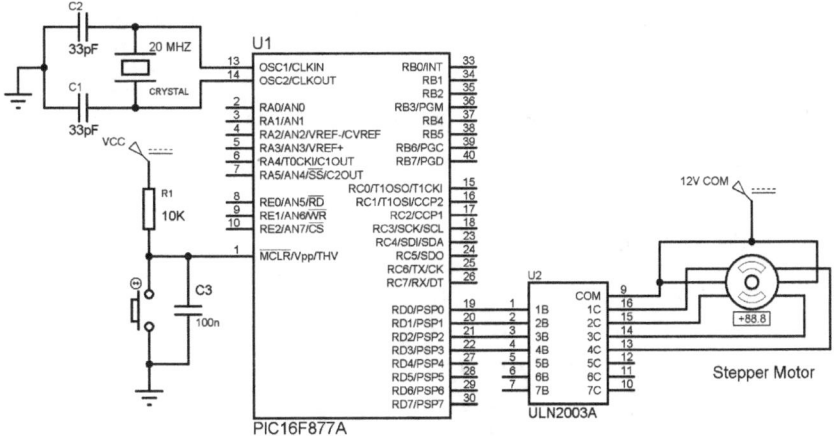

Conclusion:

Thus the stepper motor has been interfaced with PIC16F877A Microcontroller and executed the Embedded C Program for 360-degree clock-wise and 360-degree anti-clockwise rotation.

36.	**INTERFACING PROXIMITY SENSOR USING INTERRUPT**

Aim:

Write an Embedded C Program to interface a proximity sensor with PIC16F877A/887 Microcontroller using an external hardware interrupt.

Hardware and Software Used:
- o PIC16F877A Microcontroller Development Board, Proximity Sensor, Buzzer, LED and resistor

- MPLAB X IDE v6.05 & Compiler XC8 v2.40

Theory:

Hardware and Software Interrupts

PIC Microcontroller consists of both Hardware and Software Interrupts. If the interrupts are generated by external hardware at certain pins of the microcontroller, or by inbuilt devices like timer, they are called Hardware Interrupts. While Software interrupts are generated by a piece of code in the Program.

PIC 16F877A has the following 14 interrupt sources:

- Timer 0   - T0I
- External   - INT
- RB Port Change   - RBI
- Timer 1   - TMR1I
- TMR2 to PR2 Match   - TMR2I
- Parallel Slave Port Read/Write   - PSPI
- A/D Converter   - ADI
- USART Receive   - RCI
- USART Transmit   - TXI
- Synchronous Serial Port   - SSPI
- CCP1 (Capture, Compare, PWM)   - CCP1I
- CCP2 (Capture, Compare, PWM)   - CCP2I
- EEPROM Write Operation   - EEI
- Bus Collision   - BCLI

The 5 registers that used to control the operation of Interrupts in PIC 16F877A Microcontroller:

- INTCON   - Interrupt Control Register
- PIE1   - Peripheral Interrupt Enable Register 1
- PIR1   - Peripheral Interrupt Flag Register 1
- PIE2   - Peripheral Interrupt Enable Register 2
- PIR2   - Peripheral Interrupt Flag Register 2

In general, each interrupt source has the following related bits.

- Enable Bit - It can be used to enable/disable the related interrupt. When set to '1' it enables the interrupt.
- Flag Bit - It is set automatically by the related hardware when the interrupt condition occurs. When it is set to '1' we know that interrupt has occurred.

The following bits are used to control the interrupts globally,
- GIE – Global Interrupt Enable, enables/disables interrupts globally.
- PEIE – Enable/disable all peripheral interrupts.

Interrupt Vector

It is the address where the CPU jumps when an interrupt occurs. The RESET vector is at 0000h and the interrupt vector is at 0004h.

Algorithm:

Main Program: (Flashing an LED)
1. PORTB0 is an interrupt pin and it is configured as an input port.
2. PORTD is configured as an output port and clear it.
3. Interrupt settings:
    - Enable global interrupt (GIE) = 1.
    - Enable INT pin interrupt (INTE) = 1'
    - Disable peripheral interrupts (PEIE) = 0.
    - Select raising edge as interrupt event (INTEDG) = 1;
4. Clear RD0 (LED).
5. Wait for 300 ms.
6. Set RD0 (LED).
7. Wait for 300 ms.
8. Repeat steps from step 4.

ISR: (Sound Buzzer for 100 ms)
1. Check the INTE and INTF are set. If yes, continue the next step.
2. Clear INTE.
3. Set RD7 (Buzzer).
4. Make a 100 ms delay.
5. Clear RD7 (Buzzer).

Program:

```c
#pragma config FOSC = HS, WDTE = OFF, PWRTE = OFF, BOREN = OFF, LVP = OFF, CPD = OFF, WRT = OFF, CP = OFF
#include <xc.h>
#define _XTAL_FREQ 20000000


void __interrupt() isr (void)      // Interrupt Service Routine
{
if (INTE && INTF)                  // Check the occurrence of Ext. Hardware interrupt
{
INTF = 0;                          // Clear external interrupt flag
RD7 = 1;                           // Turn-on the buzzer
__delay_ms(100);                   // Make 100 ms delay
RD7 = 0;                           // Turn-off the buzzer
}
}


void main(void)
{
TRISB = 0x01;         // Set RB0/INTI as input port (Ext. int)
TRISD = 0x00;         // Set PORTD as output port
PORTD = 0x00;         // Clear PORTD
GIE = 1;              // Enable Global Interrupt
INTE = 1;             // Enable RB0/INT external hardware Interrupt
PEIE = 0;             // Disable peripheral interrupt
INTEDG = 1;           // Interrupt on raising edge
while(1)
{
RD0 =0;               // main program – flashing of LED at RD0.
__delay_ms(300);
RD0 =1;
__delay_ms(300);
}
}
```

Circuit Diagram:

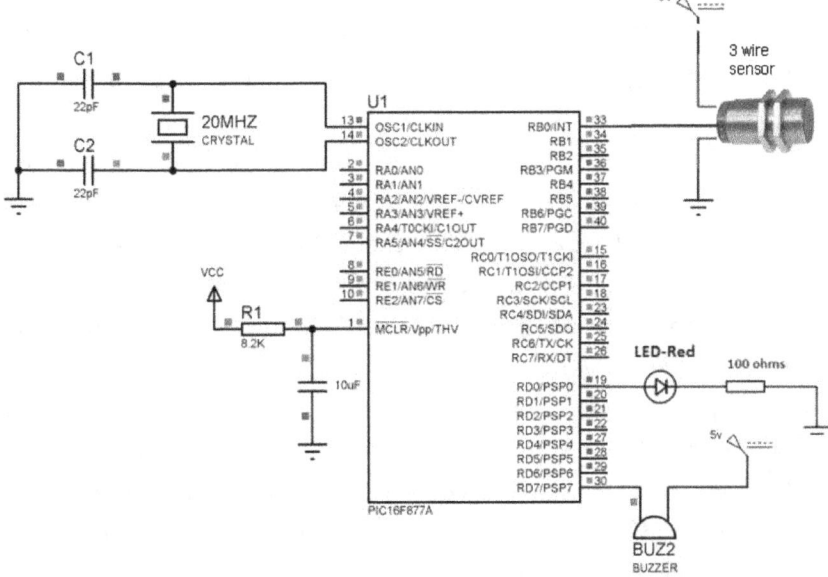

Conclusion:

Thus the proximity sensor has been interfaced with the PIC16F877A Microcontroller using the external hardware interrupt and tested the output.

37.	FLASHING LED USING ON-CHIP TIMER

Aim:

Write and execute an Embedded C Program to flash the LED using on-chip timer of PIC16F877A/887 Microcontroller.

Hardware and Software Used:
- PIC16F877A Microcontroller Development Board, LED and resistor
- MPLAB X IDE v6.05 & Compiler XC8 v2.40

Theory:

The PIC 16F877 has three independent hardware timers that are used to carry out the timing and counting operations. Timer0 is an 8-bit register, TMR0, file register address 01. Its output is an overflow flag, T0IF, bit 2 in the Interrupt Control Register INTCON, address 0B. Timer1 can be enabled/ disabled by setting/clearing TMR1ON bit (T1CON). TMR1 register is a pair of TMR1H and TMR1L, its value increments from 0000h to FFFFh, and rolls over to 0000h. The TMR1 interrupt, if enabled, is generated on overflow which is latched in interrupt flag bit, TMR1IF (PIR1). This interrupt can be enabled/ disabled by setting/clearing TMR1 interrupt enable bit, TMR1IE (PIE1).

The timer register is incremented by clock input which is derived either from the Microcontroller oscillator (FOSC) or an external pulse train at RA4. The timer clock time will be (4/FOSC)*Prescaler. The register counts from 0 to 0xff and then rolls over to 00 again. When the register goes from FF to 00, T0IF is set.

Timer	Size	Control Register	Count Register	Min Delay	Max Delay
TIMER0	8-bit	OPTION_REG	TMR0	0.2usec	13.107ms
TIMER1	16-bit	T1CON	TMR1H, TMR1L	0.2usec	104.857ms
TIMER2	8-bit	T2CON	TMR2	0.2usec	819usec

The formula of all three Timers for time delay calculation:

Timer	Size	Formula for delay calculation
TIMER0	8-bit	*Timer0_Reg* = 256 - ((Delay * Fosc)/(Prescaler*4))
TIMER1	16-bit	*Timer1_Reg* = 65536 - ((Delay * Fosc)/(Prescaler*4))
TIMER2	8-bit	*Timer2_Reg* = 256 - ((Delay * Fosc)/(Prescaler*4))

TIMER0 Delay Calculations for 10ms @20Mhz with Prescaler as 256,
TIMER0_Reg   = 256 - (Delay * Fosc)/(Prescaler*4))

$$= 256 - ((10ms * 20Mhz)/(256*4))$$
$$= 256 - 195$$
$$= 61$$

The steps to configure the Timer0 for delay generation:
1. Calculate the timer0 register value for the required delay. (TIMER0_Reg).
2. Clear the PSA bit for using the Prescaler. (PSA =0).
3. Set the Prescaler bits in OPTION_REG as per the delay calculations. (PS2:PS0).
4. Select the Clock Source which is Internal/External using TOCS bit. (T0CS=0 for internal & T0CS=1 for external).
5. Load the timer0 register value (calculated in step 1) into the TMR0 register.
6. Clear timer0 interrupt flag (TMR0IF = 0).
7. Enable/ disable the Timer0 Interrupt by setting/ clearing TMR0IE bit.
8. Enable/ disable the Global and Peripheral interrupts by setting/ clearing GIE and PIE bits.

PS2:PS0: Prescaler Rate Select bits

Bit Value	TMR0 Rate	WDT Rate
000	1 : 2	1 : 1
001	1 : 4	1 : 2
010	1 : 8	1 : 4
011	1 : 16	1 : 8
100	1 : 32	1 : 16
101	1 : 64	1 : 32
110	1 : 128	1 : 64
111	1 : 256	1 : 128

T1CKPS1:T1CKPS0:
Timer1 Prescale Select bits
11 = 1:8 prescale value
10 = 1:4 prescale value
01 = 1:2 prescale value
00 = 1:1 prescale value

TIMER1 Delay Calculations for 100ms @20Mhz with Prescaler as 8:
TMR1 Register = 65536 - (Delay * Fosc)/(Prescaler*4))
$$= 65536 - ((100ms * 20Mhz)/(8*4))$$
$$= 3036 = 0x0BDC$$

The steps for configuring and using the Timer1 for delay generation:
1. Calculate the Timer value for the required delay.
2. Set the Prescaler bits in T1CON as per the delay calculations.
   T1CKPS0=1;   for Prescaler value 1: 8, set to "11"
   T1CKPS1=1;

3. Select the Clock Source Internal/External using TMR1CS bit.
   TMR1CS=0;   for internal clock source
4. Load the timer value into TMR1H, TMR1L registers.
5. Clear timer1 interrupt flag (TMR1IF = 0)
6. Enable/disable the Timer1 Interrupt by setting/ clearing TMRIE bit
7. Enable/disable the Global and Peripheral interrupts by setting/ clearing GIE and PIE bits
8. Finally, start the timer by setting TMR1ON bit

Algorithm:

Main Program:
1. PORTD0 is configured as an output port.
2. Timer 1 Settings
   Set internal clock source by TMR1CS = 0.
   Set Prescaler 1:8 by T1CKPS0 = 1 & T1CKPS1 = 1.
   Clear Timer1 flag by TMR1IF = 0.
3. Clear RD0.
4. Time delay for 200 ms using on-chip Timer 1.
5. Set RD0.
6. Time delay for 200 ms using on-chip Timer 1.

Subroutine: timer1_100ms (2):
1. Clear Timer 1 flag (TMR1IF = 0).
2. Load TMR1 register by 0x0BDC for 100 ms.
   Repeat the steps from step 3 to step 5 for argument value.
3. Enable Timer 1.
4. Wait until the Timer 1 flag is set.
5. Clear Timer 1.
6. Disable Timer 1.

Program:
#pragma config FOSC = XT, WDTE = OFF, PWRTE = OFF, BOREN = OFF, LVP = OFF, CPD = OFF, WRT = OFF, CP = OFF
#include <xc.h>

```c
void timer1_100ms (unsigned int value)
{
    unsigned int i;                 // Initializing the local variable
    TMR1IF = 0;                     // Clear TIMER1 flag
    for (i=0; i<value; i++)         // for loop to increase time delay
    {
        TMR1 = 0x0BDC;              // TMR1 Register value for 100ms
        TMR1ON = 1;                 // Enable Timer1
        while(TMR1IF == 0);         // Wait for Timer 1 flag
        TMR1IF = 0;                 // Clear Timer 1 flag
    }
    TMR1ON = 0;                     // Disable Timer1
}

void main()
{
    TRISD0 = 0;                     // PORTD as output port
    TMR1CS = 0;                     // Set internal clock source for Timer 1
    T1CKPS0 = 1;                    // Prescaler is 1:8, set "11"
    T1CKPS1 = 1;
    TMR1IF = 0;                     // Clear TIMER1 flag

    while(1)
    {
        RD0 = 0;                    // Clear RD0
        timer1_100ms (2);           // 100 ms * 2 = 200 ms
        RD0 = 1;                    // Set RD1
        timer1_100ms (2);           // 100 ms * 2 = 200 ms
    }
}
```

Circuit Diagram:

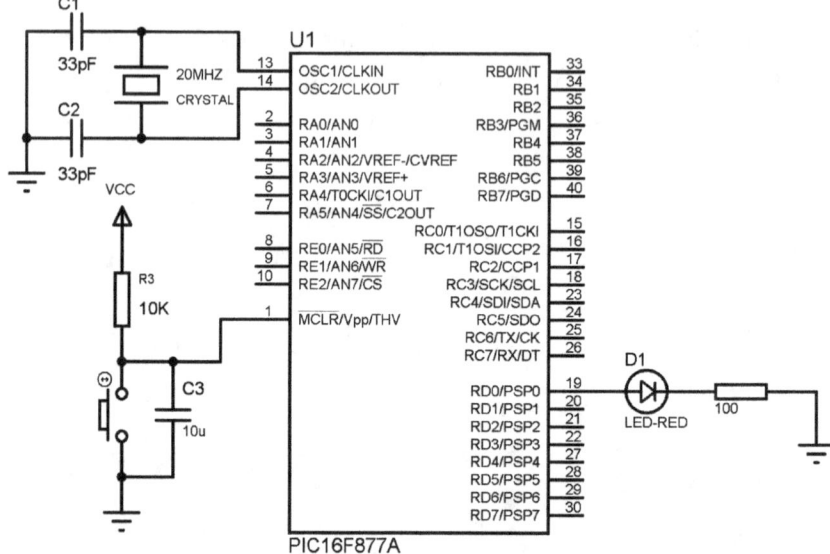

Conclusion:

Thus the Embedded C Program for flashing LED has been written and executed using the on-chip timer of PIC16F877A Microcontroller.

38. SPEED CONTROL OF DC MOTOR USING PWM

Aim:

Write and execute an Embedded C Program to control the speed of DC motor using PWM of PIC16F877A/887 Microcontroller.

Hardware and Software Used:

- o PIC16F877A Microcontroller Development Board, L293D driver, DC motor, Pushbuttons and resistors
- o MPLAB X IDE v6.05 & Compiler XC8 v2.40

Theory:
CCP – PWM Module

PWM signal can be generated in PIC Microcontroller by using the CCP (Compare Capture PWM) module. The PIC 16F877A microcontroller has two CCP modules, named as CCP1 and CCP2. The resolution of the PWM signal is 10-bit. The 8-MSB bits are stored in CCPRxL and the remaining 2-bits in the CCPxCON register. PIC uses TIMER2 for generating the PWM signal.

The following registers are used to generate PWM signal in CCP1:
- CCP1CON (CCP1 control Register)
- T2CON (Timer 2 Control Register)
- PR2 (Timer 2 Period Register)
- CCPR1L (CCP Register 1 Low)

PWM Period:

PR2 register is used to specify the PWM Period. The PWM period can be calculated using the following formula.

PWM Period = [(PR2) + 1] * 4 * TOSC * (TMR2 Prescale Value)

Therefore, PR2 = (_XTAL_FREQ / (PWM_Freq *4 * TMR2PRESCALE)) - 1;

Duty Cycle:

The percentage of ON time over the period of a signal. The PWM duty cycle is determined by the value in the CCPR1L and CCP1CON<5:4> registers.

CCPR1L+CCP1CON<5:4> = PR2 * DutyCycle %

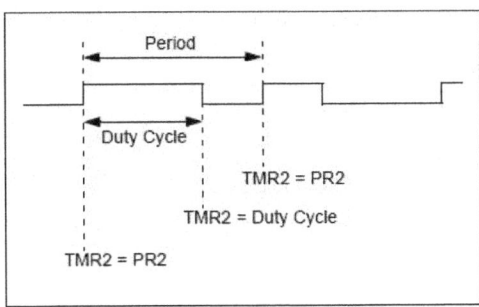

Setup for PWM Operation:
1. Set the PWM period by writing to the PR2 register.
2. Set the PWM duty cycle by writing to the CCPR1L register and CCP1CON<5:4> bits.
3. Make the CCP1/RC2 pin an output by clearing the TRISC<2> bit.
4. Set the TMR2 prescale value and enable Timer2 by writing to T2CON.
5. Configure the CCP1 module for PWM operation.

Algorithm:

Main Program:
1. Write the PR2 register for the defined PWM frequency.
2. Write Duty Cycle register.
3. Make RC2/CCP1 pin as output port and clear it.
4. Configure Timer 2 with 1:16 prescaler.
5. Configure CCP1 module for the PWM output.
6. If UP key is pressed, increment the Duty Cycle value by 5 and update it in the DutyCycle register. Do not allow the Duty Cycle value above the PR2.
7. If DOWN key is pressed, decrement the Duty Cycle value by 5 and update it in the DutyCycle register. The Duty Cycle value should not be negative.

Subroutine: PWM_DCycle():
1. Local variable declaration.
2. Calculate the Duty Cycle value.
3. Write the Duty Cycle value to the DutyCycle register.

Program:

```
#pragma config FOSC = XT, WDTE = OFF, PWRTE = OFF, BOREN = OFF, LVP = OFF, CPD = OFF, WRT = OFF, CP = OFF
#include <xc.h>
#include <math.h>
#define _XTAL_FREQ 20000000        // XTAL frequency 20 MHz
#define TMR2PRESCALE 16            // Timer 2 Prescaler 1:16
```

```c
#define PWM_Freq 2000        // PWM output frequency
#define UP RD0               // Control key to increase the speed
#define DOWN RD1             // Control key to decrease the speed
#define PER 0.01             // Percentage
unsigned int DCycle=0;       // Global variable
PWM_DCycle()                 // Function to write DutyCycle register
{
unsigned int n;
// CCPR1L+CCP1CON<5:4> = PR2 * DutyCycle %
n = PR2 * DCycle * PER;
CCP1X = n & 0x02;            // Store 1st bit
CCP1Y = n & 0x01;            // Store 0th bit
CCPR1L = n >> 2;             // Store remaining 8 MSB bits
}

void main (void)
{
// Writing to the PR2 register
PR2 = (_XTAL_FREQ /(PWM_Freq *4 * TMR2PRESCALE)) - 1;
PWM_DCycle();                // Function to write the DutyCycle reg.
TRISC2 = 0;                  // Configure RC2/CCP1 pin as output port
RC2=0;                       // Clear RC2
T2CON = 0x07;                // Configure Timer 2 with 1:16 Prescaler
CCP1CON = 0x0F;              //Configure CCP1 module for PWM output
while (1)                    // Forever loop
  {
  if (!UP)                   // if UP key is pressed
  {
  __delay_ms(50);            // Debounce delay
  while(!UP);                // Wait for key release
  DCycle = DCycle + 5;       // Increment % of duty cycle by 5
    if (DCycle > PR2){       // DutyCycle is <= Period
    DCycle = PR2;
    }
```

```
    PWM_DCycle();              // Function to write the DutyCycle reg.
}

if (!DOWN)                     // if UP key is pressed
{
__delay_ms(50);                // Debounce delay
while(!DOWN);
DCycle = DCycle - 5;           // Decrement % of duty cycle by 5
  if (DCycle < -1){            // DutyCycle should not be negative
  DCycle = 0;
  }
  PWM_DCycle();                // Function to write the DutyCycle reg.
  }
 }
}
```

Circuit Diagram:

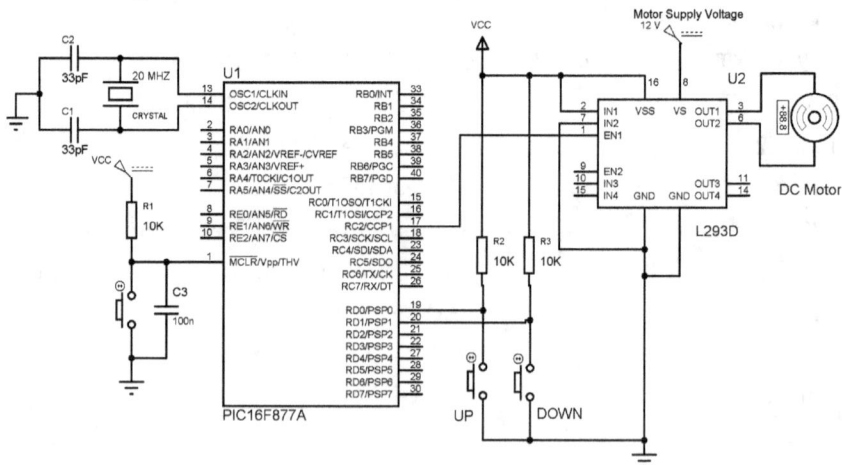

Conclusion:

Thus the Embedded C Program for speed control of DC motor using PWM has been written and executed using the PIC16F877A Microcontroller.

39. SERVO MOTOR CONTROL USING PWM

Aim:

Write an Embedded C Program to interface servo motor with PIC16F877A/887 Microcontroller and control the angle of rotation using the PWM pulses.

Hardware and Software Used:
- o   PIC16F877A Microcontroller Development Board and Servo motor
- o   MPLAB X IDE v6.05 & Compiler XC8 v2.40

Theory:

A servo motor consists of a DC motor, reduction gearbox, positional feedback device and some form of error correction circuits. Servo motor is an automatic closed loop control system. The device is controlled by a feedback signal generated by comparing output signal and reference input signal. The error detection amplifier looks at the input signal and compare it with the feedback signal from the motor output shaft and determine if the shaft is in correct position or not. If not, the controller makes appropriate correction either speeding up the motor or slowing it down. It will turn the servo motor to desired location. Normally a servo motor is used to control an angular motion between 0 and 180 degrees. Servomotors are used in applications such as robotics, CNC machinery or automated manufacturing.

Servo motor Control:

Servos are controlled by sending an electrical pulse of variable width, or pulse width modulation (PWM), through the control wire. The frequency of the control signal should be 50Hz or a pulse should occur every 20ms. The width of pulse determines angular position of the servo motor shaft. A servo motor can usually turn 90° in either direction for a total of 180° movement.

For example, a 1.5ms pulse will make the motor turn to the 90° position.

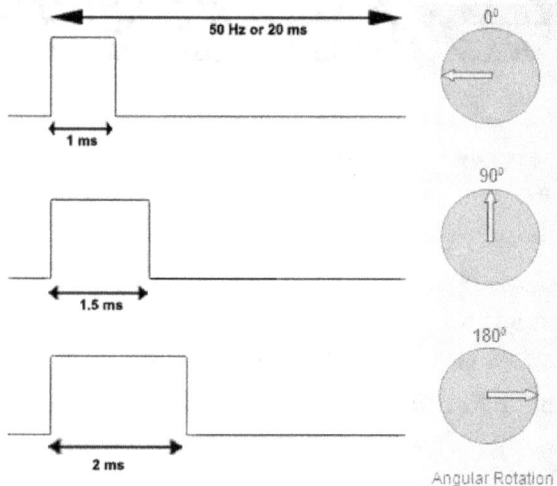

Servo Motors have three wires, two are power terminals and the third terminal is used to give the control signal. Program the MCU to send PWM signals to the signal wire of the Servo motor. There is a control circuitry inside the servo motor which reads the duty cycle of the PWM signal and position the servo motors shaft in the respective place.

The duty cycle time of SG90 servo motor for the angle of rotation from 0° to 180°.

At ~0.8 ms (4% duty cycle), get shaft position at 0° of its rotation.
At ~1.4 ms (7% duty cycle), get shaft position at 90° of its rotation.
At ~2.2 ms (11% duty cycle), get shaft position at 180° of its rotation.

CCP1 in Compare mode to generate PWM signal:

The lowest frequency from timer2 is 1220.7 Hz (assuming for 20MHz crystal oscillator = 20000000 / (4 * 16 * 256) = 1220.7 Hz). Thus we cannot generate the 50 Hz signal using the CCP1 as PWM. Therefore, the timer1 can be used to generate a 50 Hz PWM signal in the Compare mode of CCP1.

The 16-bit CCPR1 register is compared with the TMR1. When they match, one of the following actions occurs on the CCP1 pin:

1. Driven high
2. Driven low
3. Remains unchanged

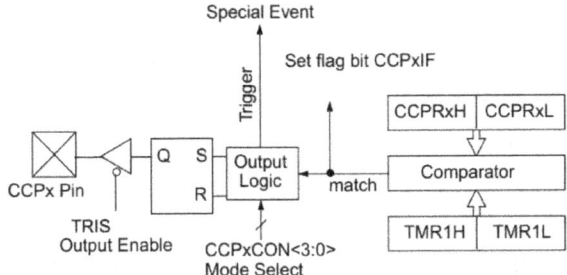

The required settings are
1. CCP1 (RC2): It should be an output port.
2. T1CON: Enable Timer 1 with 1:8 prescale (0x31)
   o TCY = 4/FOSC = 4/20MHz = 0.2 us.
   o Timer increments every 0.2 us * prescaler = 0.2 us * 8 = 1.6 us.
   o Number of ticks that corresponds to 20 ms PWM period = 20 ms/1.6 ms = 12500
3. CCP1CON: Configure CCP1 in compare mode
   o 1000 = Compare mode, set output on match (CCP1IF bit is set)
   o 1001 = Compare mode, clear output on match (CCP1IF bit is set)
4. Load CCPR1 Register
5. Wait for CCP1IF
6. Disable CCP1

Algorithm:
1. Initialize DutyCycle value for 0.8 ms, 1.5 ms, and 2.2 ms in an array variable.
2. PORTC2 is the CCP1 pin and it is configured as an output port. Clear RC2.
3. Enable Timer 1 with 1:8 Prescaler.
4. Clear Timer 1 register.
5. Clear CCP1IF.
6. Assign DutyCycle value [index number] to CCP1 register.
7. Enable CCP1 in compare mode (clear RC2 on the match).
8. Wait for CCP1IF.
9. Clear CCP1IF.

10. CCP1 register = 12500 - DutyCycle value [index number].
11. Enable CCP1 in compare mode (set RC2 on the match).
12. Wait for CCP1IF.
13. Clear CCP1IF.
14. Disable CCP1.
15. Repeat steps 50 times from step 3.
16. Make a delay for 3 sec.
17. Repeat steps from step 3.

Program:

```c
#pragma config FOSC = XT, WDTE = OFF, PWRTE = OFF, BOREN = OFF, LVP = OFF, CPD = OFF, WRT = OFF, CP = OFF
#include <xc.h>
#define _XTAL_FREQ 20000000        // XTAL frequency 20 MHz

void main (void)
{
// Initialize DutyCycle value for 0.8 ms, 1.5 ms and 2.2 ms
unsigned int i, j, DCycle[3]={0x1F4, 0x3A9, 0x55F};
TRISC2 = 0;                 // Set RC2/CCP1 as output
RC2 = 0;                    // Clear RC2

while (1)
{
for (i=0; i<3; i++){
    for (j=0; j<50; j++){          // Sending 50 pulses to the servo motor
    T1CON = 0x31;                  // Enable timer1 use 1:8 prescaler
    TMR1 = 0;                      // Clear timer1 register
    CCP1IF = 0;                    // Clear CCP1 flag
    CCPR1 = DCycle[i];             // Assign DutyCycle value to CCPR1
    CCP1CON = 0x09;                // Compare mode, clear output on match
    while(CCP1IF == 0);            // Wait for CCP1 flag
    CCP1IF = 0;                    // Clear CCP1 flag
    CCPR1 = 12500 - DCycle[i];     // Assign TOFF value to CCPR1
```

```
CCP1CON = 0x08;        // Compare mode, set output on match
while(CCP1IF == 0);    // Wait for CCP1 flag
CCP1IF = 0;            // Clear CCP1 flag
CCP1CON = 0x00;        // Disable CCP1 module
}
_delay_ms(3000);       // Wait for 3 sec
}
}
}
```

Circuit Diagram:

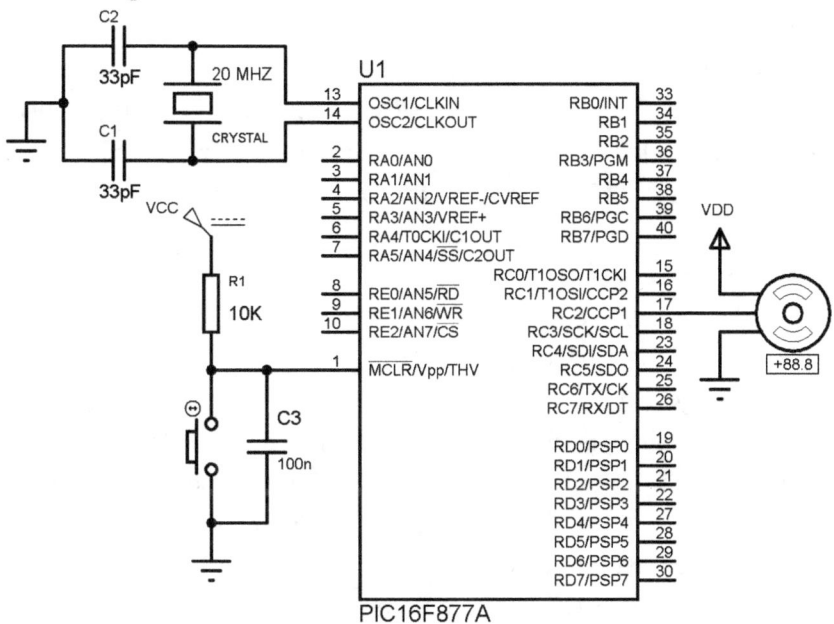

Conclusion:

Thus the Servo motor has been interfaced with PIC16F877A Microcontroller and controlled its angle of rotation using the PWM signal.

40. FREQUENCY MEASUREMENT

Aim:

Design the frequency meter using the PIC16F877A/887 Microcontroller using capture mode and verify its output with the function generator.

Hardware and Software Used:
- PIC16F877A Microcontroller Development Board, 16x2 LCD and function generator
- MPLAB X IDE v6.05 & Compiler XC8 v2.40

Theory:

Capture Mode

In Capture Mode, the 16-Bit CCPR1 (CCPR1H:CCPR1L) register captures the 16-bit value of the TMR1 register when an event occurs on the CCP1 pin (RC2). The event that fires a capture signal can be one of the following 4-options:

- Every rising edge
- Every falling edge
- Every 4th rising edge
- Every 16th rising edge

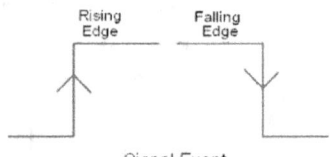

Signal Event

The programmers choose which event is going to fire the capture signal. The base timer for capture mode is Timer 1. The timer module is set to operate in timer or counter mode and its register's value (TMR1) starts incrementing for every event occurring.

T1CKPS1:T1CKPS0: Timer1 Input Clock Prescaler Select bits

　　11 = 1:8 prescaler value
　　10 = 1:4 prescaler value
　　01 = 1:2 prescaler value
　　00 = 1:1 prescaler value

The CCP module should be configured to operate in capture mode with a selectable trigger event via the **CCP1CON** register.

CCP1M3: CCP1M0: CCP1 Mode Select bits

0100 = Capture mode is selected for every falling edge detected.
0101 = Capture mode is selected for every rising edge detected.
0110 = Capture mode is selected for every 4th rising edge detected.
0111 = Capture mode is selected for every 16th rising edge detected.

Configuring CCP1 Module for Capture Mode:
1) RC2/CCP1 pin should be configured as an input
2) Set Timer1 module to operate in timer/counter mode
3) Set CCP1 module to operate in Capture Mode (using CCP1CON register) - Choose the event on which capture occurs (CCP1Mx Bits)
4) Clear the flag bits, CCP1IF & TMR1IF
5) Clear TMR1 register (start counting from 0) and CCPR1 register (capture count register) initially
6) Turn ON Timer1 module

Algorithm:
1. Assign RS and EN of LCD to the RC6 and RC7 respectively. Assign the Databus (D0-D7) of LCD for PORTD.
2. Include the lcd.h header file (same header file which is used in LCD interface experiment).

Main function:
1. Local declarations of variables for start, stop, TimerCount, frequency, period, d1, d2, d3, d4, d5.
2. Make CCP1 pin as input port and PORTD as an output port.
3. Initialize 16x2 LCD for 4-bit mode.
4. Display "Signal Frequency" on line1 of 16x2 LCD and Hz in line2 from 0xCA.
5. Set timer 1 for 16-bit mode and choose internal clock source for timer operation. The Prescaler is not assigned.
6. Clear CCP1 interrupt flag and Timer 1 flag.
7. Clear CCP1 register and Timer 1 register.
8. Set CCP1CON for capture mode and capture in every rising of event.
9. Turn-on Timer 1.

10. Wait for CCP1IF to set.
11. Clear CCP1IF.
12. Copy TimerCount of 1st rising edge at CCP1 register and move it to start variable.
13. Wait for CCP1IF to set.
14. Clear CCP1IF.
15. Copy TimerCount of 2nd rising edge at CCP1 register and move it to stop variable.
16. Turn-off the CCP1 module and the Timer 1 module.
17. Calculate frequency from the time duration between the start and stop variable.
18. Display the frequency value on line2 of the LCD screen.
19. Repeat the steps from step 6.

lcd.h() header file: (see the 16x2 LCD interface experiment)

Program:

```
/*Frequency Measurement using Capture Mode in CCP1 of PIC16F877A/887 */
#pragma config FOSC = HS, WDTE = OFF, PWRTE = OFF, BOREN = OFF,
LVP = OFF, CPD = OFF, WRT = OFF, CP = OFF
#include <xc.h>
#define _XTAL_FREQ  20000000
#define tick 0.0000002       // timer1 clock time = 0.2us (for 20MHZ with 1:1 prescaler)
#define RS      RD2          // RD2 is named as RS
#define EN      RD3          // RD3 is named as EN
#define D4      RD4          // 4-bit mode (RD4-D4, RD5-D5
#define D5      RD5          // RD6-D6, RD7-D7)
#define D6      RD6
#define D7      RD7
#include "lcd4bit_head.h"    // Include header file - lcd4bit_head.h

void main ()
{
unsigned long start, stop, TimerCount, frequency;
```

```c
float period;
unsigned int d1, d2, d3, d4, d5;
TRISC = 0x0F;                       // RC2/CCP1 is input pin
TRISD = 0x00;
lcd_init ();                        // LCD initialization
lcd_cmd (0x80);                     // Display the message on LCD screen
lcd_display ("Signal Frequency");
lcd_cmd (0xca);
lcd_data ('H');
lcd_data ('z');

// setting Timer1
TMR1CS = 0;
T1CKPS0 = 0;
T1CKPS1 = 0;
T1SYNC = 1;

while(1)
{
//clear flags
   CCP1IF = 0;
   TMR1IF = 0;
//clear registers
   TMR1 = 0;
   CCPR1 = 0;
//setting CCP1
   CCP1CON = 0x05;
//Turn ON Timer1
   TMR1ON = 1;

   while (!(CCP1IF));               //Wait for first rising edge of a signal
   CCP1IF = 0;
   start = CCPR1;                   //Copy TimerCount of 1st rising edge detected
```

```c
    while (!(CCP1IF));          //Wait for second rising edge of a signal
    CCP1IF = 0;
    stop = CCPR1;               //Copy TimerCount of 2nd rising edge detected
    CCP1CON = 0x00;             //Turn-off CCP1 and Timer 1
    TMR1ON = 0;

    //Calculation for Frequency Measurement
    TimerCount = stop - start;
    period = (float)(tick * TimerCount);
    frequency = (float)(1/period);

    // Display numbers on LCD display
    d1= (frequency /10000) + 48;
    d2= ((frequency /1000) % 10) + 48;
    d3= ((frequency /100) % 10) + 48;
    d4= ((frequency /10) % 10) + 48;
    d5= (frequency % 10) + 48;
    lcd_cmd (0xC4);
    lcd_data (d1);
    lcd_data (d2);
    lcd_data (d3);
    lcd_data (d4);
    lcd_data (d5);
    __delay_ms(500);
    }
}
```

//Header file:
Ref: 16x2 LCD interface in 4-bit mode with PIC16F877A experiment

Circuit Diagram:

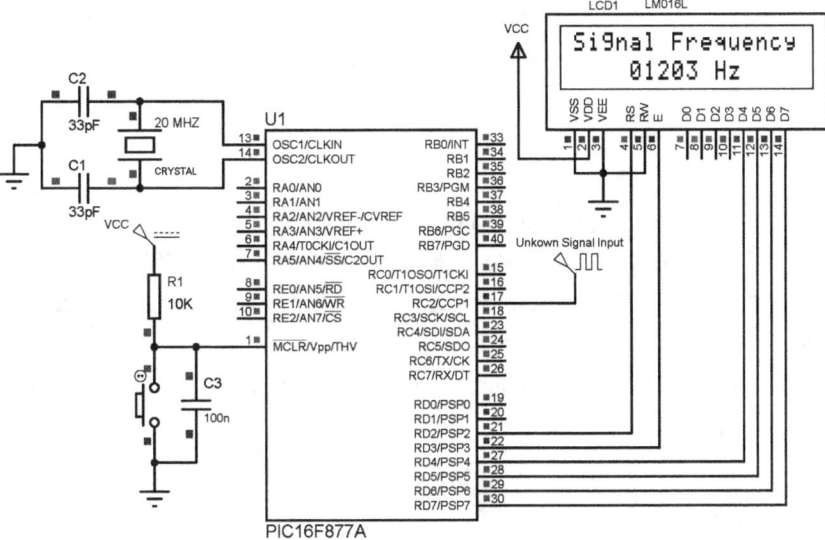

Conclusion:

Thus the frequency meter using the PIC16F877A Microcontroller has been successfully tested.

41. ANALOG TO DIGITAL CONVERSION

Aim:

Write and execute the Embedded C Program to verify the operation of on-chip analog to digital converter of PIC16F877A/887 Microcontroller.

Hardware and Software Used:
- PIC16F877A Microcontroller Development Board, LEDs and resistors
- MPLAB X IDE v6.05 & Compiler XC8 v2.40

Theory:
- PIC 16F877A microcontroller has 8 ADC inputs and it will convert analog inputs to a corresponding 10-bit digital number.
- ADC lower reference as 0V and higher reference as 5V.
    Vref- = 0V
    Vref+ = 5V
- Number of digital output bits (n) = 10-bits
- Resolution = (Vref+ − Vref-)/(2^n − 1) = 5/1023 = 0.00488V
    ADC resolution is 4.88mV, which is the minimum required voltage to change a bit.
- The analog input voltage of 3.65v will be represented by decimal number 748 or by binary number 1011101100.

$$\begin{cases} 5V \rightarrow 1024 \\ 3.65V \rightarrow X \end{cases} \rightarrow X = \frac{1024 * 3.65}{5} = 747.52 \approx 748$$

PIC 16F877A ADC module has four 8-bit registers:
- ADCON0 - A/D Control Register 0
- ADCON1 - A/D Control Register 1
- ADRESH - A/D Result High Register
- ADRESL - A/D Result Low Register

ADCON0 REGISTER (ADDRESS 1Fh)

R/W-0	R/W-0	R/W-0	R/W-0	R/W-0	R/W-0	U-0	R/W-0
ADCS1	ADCS0	CHS2	CHS1	CHS0	GO/DONE	—	ADON
bit 7							bit 0

ADCS1:ADCS0: A/D Conversion Clock Select bits
CHS2:CHS0: Analog Channel Select bits
GO/DONE: A/D Conversion Status bit
ADON: A/D On bit

ADCON1 REGISTER (ADDRESS 9Fh)

R/W-0	R/W-0	U-0	U-0	R/W-0	R/W-0	R/W-0	R/W-0
ADFM	ADCS2	—	—	PCFG3	PCFG2	PCFG1	PCFG0
bit 7							bit 0

ADFM: A/D Result Format Select bit

ADCS2: A/D Conversion Clock Select bit
PCFG3:PCFG0: A/D Port Configuration Control bits

The following steps to be used for the A/D Conversion:
1. Configure the A/D module
   - Select A/D input channel (ADCON0)
   - Select A/D conversion clock (ADCON0 (2-LSBs) & ADCON1 (1-- MSB))
   - Turn on A/D module (ADCON0)
   - Configure analog pins with a voltage reference and result justification (ADCON1)
2. Configure A/D interrupt (if desired):
   - Clear ADIF bit
   - Set ADIE bit
   - Set PEIE bit
   - Set GIE bit
3. Wait the required acquisition time (19.72µs).
4. Start conversion:
   - Set GO/nDONE bit (ADCON0)
5. Wait for A/D conversion to complete, by either:
   - GO/nDONE bit to be cleared; OR
   - A/D interrupt flag to be set
6. Read the A/D result register pair (ADRESH: ADRESL) and clear ADIF.

Algorithm:
1. Configure PORTA as an input port, and PORTB and PORTC as output ports.
2. Clear PORTB and PORTC.
3. Configure ADC by ADCON0 and ADCON1 register. Analog channel AN0, ADC clock FOSC/64, Right justified result, VDD, and VSS as reference inputs and Turn on ADC.
4. Set GO bit for the start of conversion.
5. Wait for DONE bit.

6. Move the result of ADC to PORTB and PORTC.
7. Wait for 100 ms.
8. Repeat the steps from step 3.

Program:

```c
#pragma config FOSC = HS, WDTE = OFF, PWRTE = OFF, BOREN = OFF, LVP = OFF, CPD = OFF, WRT = OFF, CP = OFF
#include <xc.h>
#define _XTAL_FREQ 20000000

void main()
{
TRISA = 0x01;              // Analog pin AN0 as Input port
TRISB = 0x00;              // Port B as Output port
TRISC = 0x00;              // Port C as Output port
PORTB = 0x00;              // Port B as Output port
PORTC = 0x00;              // Port C as Output port

while(1) {
   ADCON0 = 0x81;          // Channel AN0, ADC Clock FOSC/64 &
                           // Turn ON ADC
   ADCON1 = 0xCE;          // Right justified, AN0 Analog port &
                           // VDD and VSS references
   __delay_ms(1);          // Wait for acquisition time

   GO_nDONE = 1;           // Start A/D conversion
   while(GO_nDONE);        // Waiting for conversion to complete
   ADIF = 0;               // Clear ADC interrupt flag
   PORTB = ADRESL;         // Write Lower 8-bits(7-0) to PORTB
   PORTC = ADRESH;         // Write Higher 2-bits(9,8) to PORTC
   __delay_ms(100);
   }
}
```

Circuit Diagram:

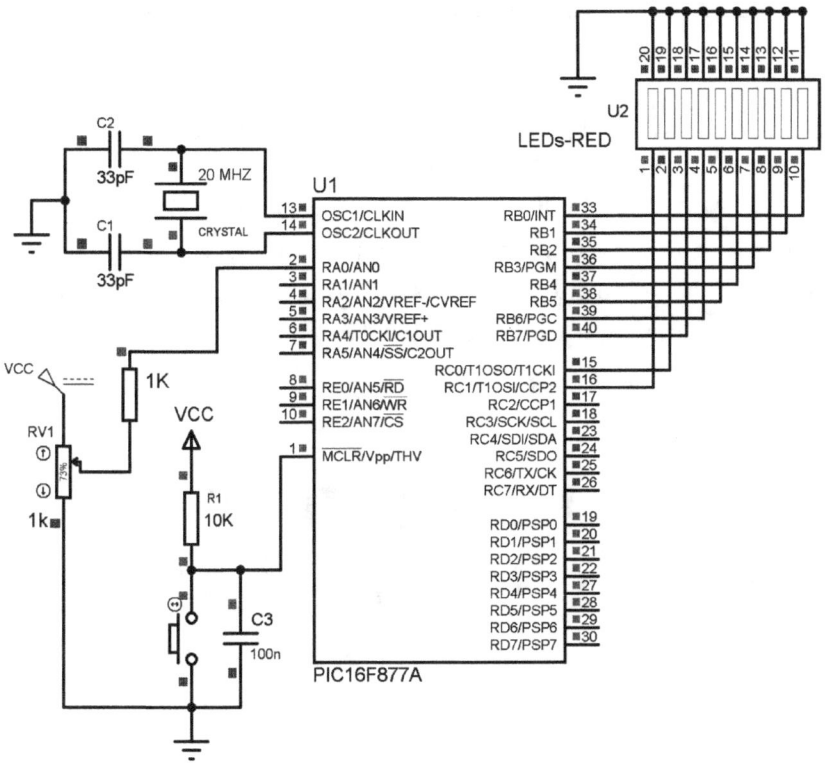

Conclusion:

Thus the operation of on-chip analog to digital converter in PIC16F877A Microcontroller has been verified.

42.	TEMPERATURE MONITOR USING ON-CHIP ADC

Aim:
Write and execute an Embedded C Program to monitor the temperature using the PIC16F877A/887 Microcontroller.

Hardware and Software Used:
- PIC16F877A Microcontroller Development Board, LM35 sensor and

- 16x2 LCD
  - MPLAB X IDE v6.05 & Compiler XC8 v2.40

Theory:

LM35 is an analog temperature sensing device. It provides output voltage in Centigrade (Celsius). The sensitivity of LM35 is 10 mV/degree Celsius. It does not require any additional calibration circuitry. As the temperature increases, the output voltage also increases. E.g. 275 mV means 27.5 °C. It is a 3-terminal sensor used to measure the surrounding temperature ranging from -55 °C to 150 °C.

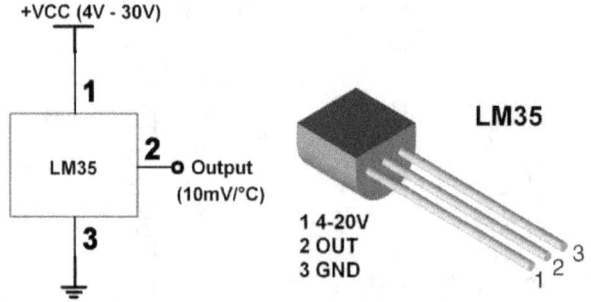

Algorithm:
1. Assign RS and EN of LCD to the RB6 and RB7 respectively. Assign the Databus (D0-D7) of LCD to PORTD.
2. Include the lcd4bit_head.h header file (same header file which is used in LCD interface experiment).

Main Program:
1. Local variable declaration.
2. Configure PORTB and PORTD are output ports.
3. Initialize 16x2 LCD in 4-bit mode.
4. Display "TEMPERATURE" on line1 of LCD.
5. Read an analog value from AN0 and store it in the adc_res variable.
6. Convert adc_res value into temperature equivalent and display it on line2 of LCD
7. Wait for 1 sec.

8. Repeat the steps from step 5.

float adc_ch0() function:
1. Configure on-chip ADC module: select AN0, ADC clock FOSC/64, Right justified result, VDD, and VSS as reference inputs and turn-on ADC.
2. Wait 20 ms for acquisition time 19.72µs.
3. Set GO bit for the start of conversion.
4. Wait for DONE bit.
5. Convert 16-bit binary into decimal.
6. Turn-off ADC
7. Adjust the decimal result into 100 along with the input span of ADC and return it to the main function.

lcd_num(int n) function:
1. Get the 10th digit position number from the argument value and convert it into an ASCII value. Then send it to the LCD screen.
2. Get the 1st digit position number from the argument value and convert it into an ASCII value. Then send it to the LCD screen.

Program:

Main Source File:
```
#pragma config FOSC = HS, WDTE = OFF, PWRTE = OFF, BOREN = OFF, LVP = OFF, CPD = OFF, WRT = OFF, CP = OFF
#include <xc.h>
#define _XTAL_FREQ 20000000

#define RS      RD2           // RD2 is named as RS
#define EN      RD3           // RD3 is named as EN
#define D4      RD4           // 4-bit mode (RD4-D4, RD5-D5
#define D5      RD5           // RD6-D6, RD7-D7)
#define D6      RD6
#define D7      RD7
#include "lcd4bit_head.h"     // Include header file - lcd4bit_head.h
```

```c
float adc_ch0(){
    unsigned int a;
    TRISA = 0x01;                           // Analog pin AN0 as Input port
    ADCON0 = 0x81;                          // Channel AN0, ADC Clock FOSC/64 & Turn ON ADC
    ADCON1 = 0xCE;                          // Right justified, AN0 Analog port & VDD and VSS references
    __delay_ms(1);                          // Wait for acquisition time
    GO_nDONE = 1;                           // Start A/D conversion
    while(GO_nDONE);                        // Waiting for conversion to complete
    ADIF = 0;                               // Clear ADC interrupt flag
    a = ((ADRESH*256) + ADRESL);            // Assign the ADC result to the variable 'a'
    ADON=0;                                 // Turn-off ADC
    return (a *(5.0/1023)*100);             // Return the ADC result out off 100
}

void lcd_num(int n)
{
    lcd_data((n/10)+48);    // n=12.45 --> n/10 = 1+48 (+48 for ASCII value in decimal)
    lcd_data((n%10)+48);    // n%10 --> 2 (modules) + 48
}

void main() {                               // Main function
    float adc_res;                          // Variable declaration
    TRISD = 0x00;                           // set PORT D as output ports
    lcd_init ();                            // Call lcd_init() function
    lcd_cmd(0x80);                          // cursor position at 0th addr of line1
    lcd_display("  TEMPERATURE  ");         // Call lcd_display() function
    while (1) {                             // Forever loop
        adc_res = adc_ch0();                // Read the analog value from AN0
        lcd_cmd(0xc4);                      // LCD cursor at C4
        lcd_num( (int) adc_res);            // Write the 1s and 10s digits
        lcd_cmd(0xC6);                      // Put decimal point at C6
        lcd_data('.');
        lcd_cmd(0xc7);                      // Write the .1th and 0.1th digits
        lcd_num(( adc_res - (int) adc_res)*100);
```

```c
        lcd_cmd(0xCA);              // LCD cursor at CA
        lcd_data(0xdf);             // 0xdf for degree symbol
        lcd_data('C');              // C for Celsius
        __delay_ms(1000);           // Make 1 sec delay for next cycle
    }
}
```

//*Header file:*

Ref: 16x2 LCD interface in 4-bit mode with PIC16F877A experiment

Circuit Diagram:

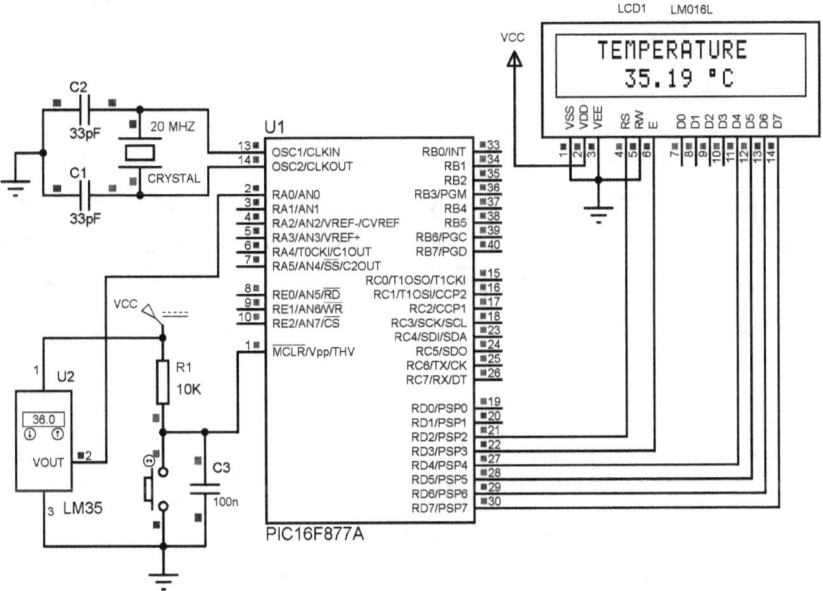

Conclusion:

Thus the Embedded C Program for temperature measurement using the PIC16F877A Microcontroller has been written and tested.

43. DATA TRANSFER USING USART

Aim:

Write an Embedded C Program to receive and re-transmit the characters between PIC16F877A/887 Microcontroller and PC through RS serial port at 9600 baud rate.

Hardware and Software Used:
- PIC16F877A Microcontroller Development Board, MAX-232-line driver and RS232 male to female DB9 connector
- MPLAB X IDE v6.05 & Compiler XC8 v2.40 and any serial window software

Theory:

USART stands for Universal Synchronous and Asynchronous Receiver / Transmitter. The Asynchronous mode provides Full Duplex communication between two devices. It uses two data lines for sending (TX) and receiving (RX) data. The ground of both devices should be made common. The popular asynchronous communication protocol is the RS232 standard.

USART Registers:

The registers associated with USART in PIC16F877A/887,

TXSTA	- Transmit Status and Control Register
RCSTA	- Receive Status and Control Register
SPBRG	- USART Baud Rate Generator
TXREG	- USART Transmit Register. Holds the data to be transmitted
RCREG	- USART Receive Register. Holds the received data

TXSTA – Transmit Status and Control Register:

R/W-0	R/W-0	R/W-0	R/W-0	U-0	R/W-0	R-1	R/W-0
CSRC	TX9	TXEN	SYNC	—	BRGH	TRMT	TX9D
bit 7							bit 0

- **TX9D**: This is the 9th bit of data in the 9-bit transmission mode which is commonly used as a Parity Bit.
- **TRMT**: This is the Transmit Shift Register (TSR) status bit. This can be used to check whether the data written to the transmit register is transmitted or not. When the TRS is empty this bit is set and when the TSR is full this bit will be 0.
- **BRGH**: This is the High Baud Rate Select bit for Asynchronous mode operation and is unused in Synchronous mode.
- **SYNC**: This is the USART Mode select bit. Setting this bit selects Synchronous mode while clearing this bit selects Asynchronous mode.
- **TXEN**: Setting this bit enables the transmission.
- **TX9**: Setting this bit enables the 9-bit transmission otherwise 8-bit transmission is used.
- **CSRC**: Clock Source Select Bit, this bit has no application in the Asynchronous mode. It is used to select master or slave mode in Synchronous mode operation.

RCSTA – Receive Status and Control Register

R/W-0	R/W-0	R/W-0	R/W-0	R/W-0	R-0	R-0	R-x
SPEN	RX9	SREN	CREN	ADDEN	FERR	OERR	RX9D
bit 7							bit 0

- **RX9D**: This is the 9th bit of Received Data and is commonly used as Parity Bit.
- **OERR**: Overrun Error bit. 1 at this bit indicates that Overrun error has occurred.
- **FERR**: Framing Error bit. 1 at this bit stands for Framing Error has occurred.
- **ADDEN**: Address Detect Enable bit. This bit is applicable only in Asynchronous 9-bit mode. Setting this bit enables the Address Detect.
- **CREN**: Continuous Receive Enable bit. Setting this bit will enable Continuous Receive. In the Synchronous Mode, CREN overrides SREN.

- **SREN**: Setting this bit will enable Single Receive. This bit will be cleared after the reception is complete.
- **RX9**: Setting this bit enables 9-bit reception otherwise it will be in 8-bit reception mode.
- **SPEN**: Serial Port Enable bit. Setting this bit enables the serial port and configures RC7, RC6 as serial port pins.

USART Baud Rate Generator (BRG):

Baud Rate Generator provides the required clock for the data transmission and reception. USART module has a dedicated 8-bit baud rate generator which supports both Synchronous and Asynchronous modes. In Asynchronous mode BRGH, 2nd bit of the TXSTA register also controls the generated baud rate but in Synchronous mode, it is ignored. Baud Rate can be calculated from the following equations, where FOSC is the clock frequency of the microcontroller.

SYNC	BRGH = 0 (Low Speed)	BRGH = 1 (High Speed)
0	(Asynchronous) Baud Rate = FOSC/(64 (X + 1))	Baud Rate = FOSC/(16 (X + 1))
1	(Synchronous) Baud Rate = FOSC/(4 (X + 1))	N/A

Legend: X = value in SPBRG (0 to 255)

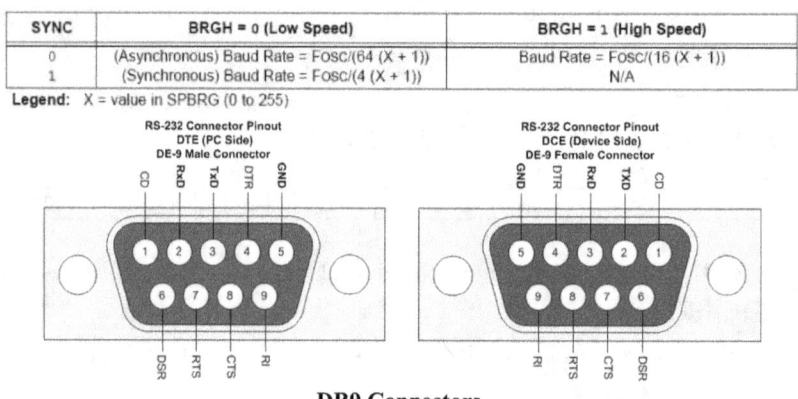

DB9 Connectors

Once the TXREG register transfers the data to the TSR register (occurs in one TCY), the TXREG register is empty and flag bit TXIF (PIR1<4>) is set. TRMT (TXSTA<1>), shows the status of the TSR register. The status bit TRMT is set when the TSR register is empty. At that point, transfer the TXREG register to TSR.

The received data in the RSR is transferred to the RCREG register (if it is empty). If the transfer is complete, flag bit RCIF (PIR1<5>) is set.

Algorithm:

Main program:
1. Declaration of local variables.
2. Configure the RC7 (Rx) pin as input port and RC6 (Tx) pin as an output port.
3. Configure the transmission and reception of USART in an asynchronous mode by TXSTA and RCSTA registers.
4. Set 9600 baudrate using the SPBRG register.
5. Wait for 100 ms.
6. Transmit the "Welcome to USART" characters on serial port.
7. Receive serial data through Rx port.
8. Transmit the received character to the Tx port.
9. Repeat steps from step 7.

trans(char t) function:
1. Load argument value in TXREG.
2. Wait for the transmit flag (TXIF) to send the character.
3. Clear Transmit flag.

char rec() function:
1. Check the OERR error flag, clear and set CREN bit if the OERR flag bit is set.
2. Wait for receive flag (RCIF) bit.
3. Clear RCIF.
4. Return RCREG value.

Program:
```
#pragma config FOSC = HS, WDTE = OFF, PWRTE = OFF, BOREN = OFF, LVP = OFF, CPD = OFF, WRT = OFF, CP = OFF
#include <xc.h>
#define _XTAL_FREQ 20000000
#define baudrate 9600

void trans(char t)                    // function for transmitting character
```

```c
{
    TXREG=t;                        // Load data to be transmit in TXREG
    while(TXIF==0);                 // wait for transmission over
    while(TRMT==0);                 // Wait for TRMT
    TXIF=0;                         // Clear TXIF
}
char rec()                          // function for receiving character
{
    if(OERR)                        // If overrun error occurred
    {
        CREN = 0;                   // Re-do the enabling of continuous reception
        CREN = 1;
    }
    while(RCIF==0);                 // Wait for data reception
    RCIF=0;                         // Clear RCIF
    return RCREG;                   // Return the received data
}

void main()                         // Main function
{
    char ch, i;                     // variable declarations
    char d[] = {"Welcome to USART: "};
    // Setting Baud rate 9600 at SPBRG for 20 MHz crystal
    SPBRG = (_XTAL_FREQ / (long)(64UL * baudrate)) - 1;
    TRISC = 0X80;                   // RC7 Rx pin (input) & RC6 Tx pin (output)
    TXSTA = 0X20;                   // Enable transmission & High speed baud rate
    RCSTA = 0X90;                   // Enable USART & Continuous reception
    __delay_ms(100);                // Wait for serial port stable
    for (i=0; i<d[i]!='\0'; i++){   // Transmit characters over Tx pin
        trans(d[i]);
    }
    while(1)                        // forever loop
    {
        ch = rec();                 // receive character from Rx
```

```
        trans(ch);          // retransmit the same character
    }
}
```

Circuit Diagram:

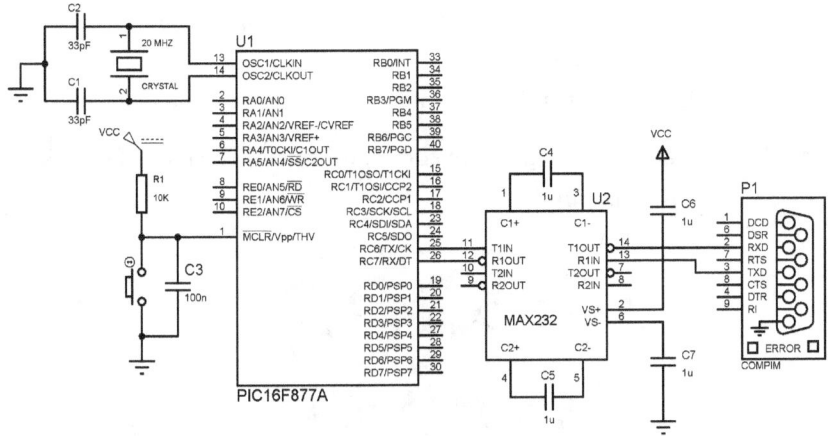

Conclusion:

Thus the Embedded C Program for asynchronous serial communication using USART in PIC16F877A Microcontroller has been written and tested.

44. BLUETOOTH CONTROLLED SYSTEM

Aim:

Write an Embedded C Program to interface HC-05 Bluetooth module with PIC16F877A/887 Microcontroller and control the LED ON/OFF through Smartphone.

Hardware and Software Used:
- PIC16F877A Microcontroller Development Board, HC-05 Bluetooth module, LED and resistor
- MPLAB X IDE v6.05 & Compiler XC8 v2.40

Theory:

HC-05 is a Bluetooth module that is used for wireless communication. It works on universal asynchronous receiver transmitter (UART) serial communication. The device can be operated in two modes; command mode and data mode.

- o The command mode is used for changing the settings of the Bluetooth module.
- o The data mode is used for data transfer between devices.

AT commands are required in command mode. The module works on 5V or 3.3V. It has six pins,

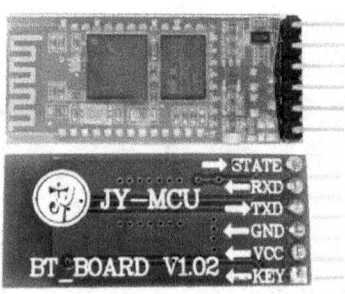

1. KEY   : if set to HIGH, the module goes into command mode
2. Vcc   : 5V supply
3. GND   : Ground
4. TXD   : TXD signal line
5. RXD   : RXD signal line
6. State   : Not connected

Step by step procedure:
- o Install a Bluetooth application in Smartphone from the play store.
- o After installation, pair the Bluetooth HC-05 module with Smartphone. The default pairing code is 1234.
- o Upload below program into the PIC microcontroller.
- o From the Smartphone, turn ON the LED which is connected with MCU port by sending the character 'N' from the Bluetooth app and similarly turn OFF the LED by sending the character 'F' from the Bluetooth app.

Algorithm:

Main Program:
1. Declaration of local variables.
2. Configure the RC7 (Rx) pin as input port and RC6 (Tx) pin as an output port.
3. Configure the transmission and reception of USART in an asynchronous mode by TXSTA and RCSTA registers.
4. Set 9600 baudrate using the SPBRG register.
5. Wait for 100 ms.
6. Transmit the "Welcome to USART" characters on line1 of the LCD screen.
7. Receive serial data through Rx port and store it in the 'ch' variable.
8. Transmit 'ch' value to the Tx port.
9. Check the 'ch' value if it is equal to 'N' then turn-on the LED connected at RD0.
10. Check the 'ch' value if it is equal to 'F' then turn-off the LED connected at RD0.
11. Repeat the steps from step 7.

trans(char t) function:
1. Load argument value in TXREG.
2. Wait for the transmit flag (TXIF) to send the character.
3. Clear Transmit flag.

char rec() function:
1. Check the OERR error flag, clear and set CREN bit if the OERR flag bit is set.
2. Wait for receive flag (RCIF) bit.
3. Clear RCIF.
4. Return RCREG value.

Program:
```
#pragma config FOSC = HS, WDTE = OFF, PWRTE = OFF, BOREN = OFF, LVP = OFF, CPD = OFF, WRT = OFF, CP = OFF
#include <xc.h>
```

```c
#define _XTAL_FREQ 20000000
#define baudrate 9600
#define LED     RD0

void trans(char t) {            // function for transmitting character
    TXREG=t;                    // Load data to be transmit in TXREG
    while(TXIF==0);             // wait for transmission over
    while(TRMT==0);             // Wait for TRMT
    TXIF=0;                     // Clear TXIF
}

char rec() {                    // function for receiving character
    if(OERR)                    // If overrun error occurred
    {
    CREN = 0;                   // Re-do the enabling of continuous reception
    CREN = 1;
    }
    while(RCIF==0);             // Wait for data reception
    RCIF=0;                     // Clear RCIF
    return RCREG;               // Return the received data
}

void main() {                   // Main function
    char ch, i;                 // variable declarations
    char d[] = {"Welcome to USART: "};
    TRISD = 0x00;               // RD0 is LED port (output)
    // Setting Baud rate 9600 at SPBRG for 20 MHz crystal
    SPBRG = (_XTAL_FREQ / (long)(64UL * baudrate)) - 1;
    TRISC = 0X80;               // RC7 Rx pin (input) & RC6 Tx pin (output)
    TXSTA = 0X20;               // Enable transmission & High speed baud rate
    RCSTA = 0X90;               // Enable USART & Continuous reception
    TXIF = 0;                   // Clear transmit flag
    RCIF = 0;                   // Clear receive flag
    __delay_ms(100);            // Wait for serial port stable
    for (i=0; i<d[i]!='\0'; i++){   // Transmit characters over Tx pin
```

```c
    trans(d[i]);
}
while(1) {                          // forever loop
    ch = rec();                     //receive serial data from HC-05 module
    trans(ch);                      // transmit the received character
    if(ch=='N') {                   // if a received char is 'N', turn-on the LED
        LED = 1;
        __delay_ms (500);           // wait for 500 ms
    }
    if(ch=='F') {                   // if a received char is 'F', turn-off the LED
        LED = 0;
        __delay_ms (500);           // wait for 500 ms
    }
} }
```

Circuit Diagram:

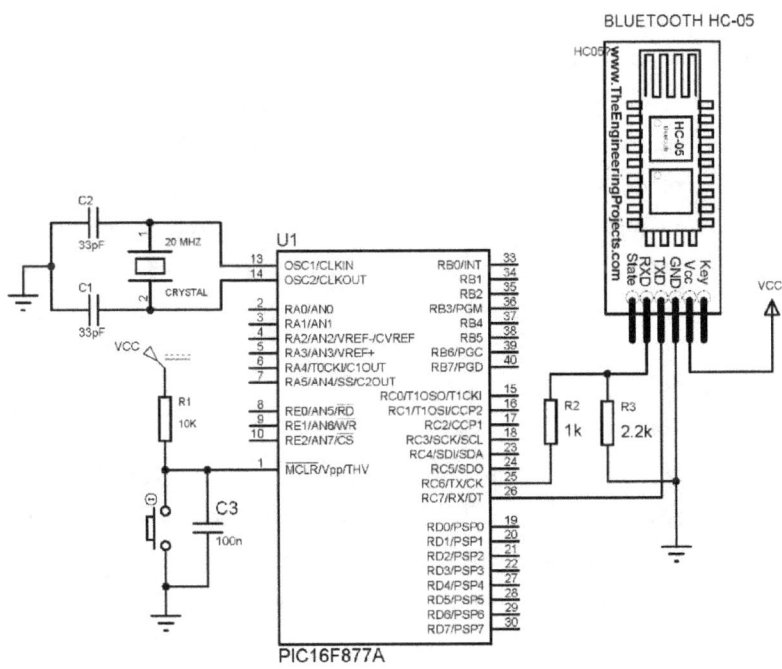

Conclusion:

Thus the HC-05 Bluetooth module has been interfaced with PIC16F877A Microcontroller and controlled the LED through Smartphone.

45. OBSTACLE DETECTOR USING ULTRASONIC SENSOR

Aim:

Write an Embedded C Program to detect the obstacle using the PIC16F877A/887 Microcontroller and ultrasonic sensor.

Hardware and Software Used:
- PIC16F877A Microcontroller Development Board, HC-SR04 Ultrasonic Sensor, 16x2 LCD, Buzzer, NPN transistor and resistor
- MPLAB X IDE v6.05 & Compiler XC8 v2.40

Theory:

HC-SR04 is an ultrasonic range sensor module designed to measure the distance between the sensor and target, ranging from 2cm to 500cm. The sensor module sends an ultrasonic burst signal to the object and then picks up its echo. The time taken by the ultrasonic signal from the sensor to the target and the target to the sensor will be used to measure the distance of the target. The microcontroller is used to perform necessary processing and displays the corresponding distance on the LCD. The obstacle can be detected with the specified distance. The HC-SR04 has four pins namely Vcc, Trigger, Echo, GND.

1) Vcc: 5V DC is connected to this pin.
2) Trigger: The trigger signal must be a pulse with 10uS ON time. Once the module receives a valid trigger signal, it generates 8 pulses of 40 kHz ultrasonic sound from the transmitter.
3) Echo: The status of this pin goes high when the module transmitted the pulses and it goes low when the receiver receives an echo signal from the target.

4) GND: Ground.

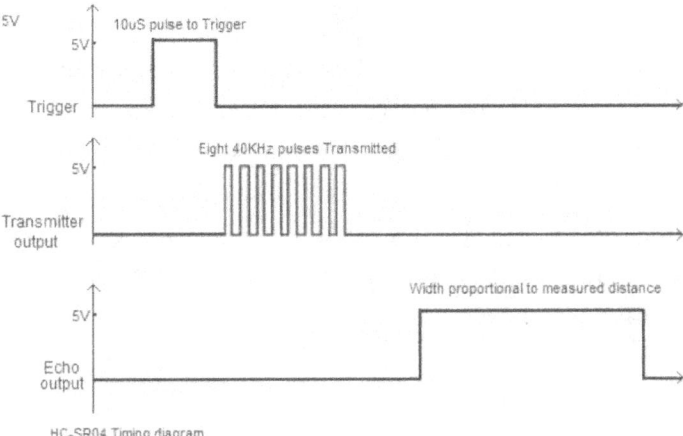

HC-SR04 Timing diagram

Working with the Ultrasonic sensor step by step:

Step 1: Make the "Trig" pin of the sensor high for 10μs.

Step 2: 8 pulses of 40 kHz ultrasonic signal will be generated by the sensor and the Echo pin goes high.

Step 3: 40 kHz sound wave will bounce off the target and return to the sensor.

Step 4: When the sensor detects the reflected wave (Echo), the Echo pin goes low.

Step 5: The distance between the target object and the sensor can be calculated from the length of the high status of the Echo pin.

Step 6: If there is no object, the Echo pin will stay high for *38 ms* and then goes low.

Algorithm:
1. Assign RS and EN of LCD to the RC6 and RC7 respectively. Assign Databus (D0-D7) of LCD to PORTD.
2. Assign Trig and Echo pins of Ultrasonic sensor for RB0 and RB1 ports respectively.
3. Include the lcd4bit_head.h header file (same header file which is used in LCD interface experiment).

Main Program:
1. Local variable declarations – TimerCount, dist as unsigned long int variables and d1, d2, d3 as char variables.
2. Configure PORTC and PORTD are output ports.
3. Configure RB0 as output port and RB1 as the input port.
4. Initialize 16x2 LCD in 4-bit mode.
5. Configure Timer 1 – Set the internal clock source for a timer with 1:8 Prescaler.
6. Clear TMR1.
7. Clear TMR1IF flag.
8. Turn-off Buzzer.
9. Clear the TimerCounter and dist variables.
10. Display "Distance   cm" on line1 of 16x2 LCD.
11. Clear Trig pin.
12. Wait for 10 ms to stable the ultrasonic sensor.
13. Set Trig pin.
14. Wait for 10 us to generate 8 cycles of 40 kHz ultrasonic waves.
15. Clear Trig pin.
16. Enable Timer 1 and wait for Echo to clear.
17. Disable Timer 1.
18. Calculate the time duration of the ultrasonic signal traveled between the sensor and the target object.
19. Display the distance in cm on LCD.
20. If the target object distance is less than or equal to 50 cm, display "Target Detected" on LCD and turn-on buzzer for 1 sec.
21. Repeat the steps from step 6.

Program:

```c
#pragma config FOSC = HS, WDTE = OFF, PWRTE = OFF, BOREN = OFF, LVP = OFF, CPD = OFF, WRT = OFF, CP = OFF
#include <xc.h>
#define _XTAL_FREQ 20000000
#define Trig RB0            // Trigger pin is connected with RB0
#define Echo RB1            // Echo pin is connected with RB1
#define Buzzer RC0          // Buzzer circuit is connected with RC0
#define RS    RC6           // RC6 is named as RS
#define EN    RC7           // RC7 is named as EN
#define D4    RD4           // 4-bit mode (RD4-D4, RD5-D5
#define D5    RD5           // RD6-D6, RD7-D7)
#define D6    RD6
#define D7    RD7
#include "lcd4bit_head.h"   // Include header file - lcd4bit_head.h

void main() {                               // Main function
    unsigned long int TimerCount, dist;     // local variables declarations
    unsigned char d1, d2, d3;
    TRISB = 0x02;                           // Trig pin is output and Echo pin is input
    TRISC = 0x00;                           // set PORT C as output port
    TRISD = 0x00;                           // set PORT D as output port
    lcd_init ();                            // Call lcd_init() function to initialize 16x2 LCD
    TMR1CS = 0;                             // Set internal clock source for Timer 1
    T1CKPS0 = 1;                            // Prescaler is 1:8
    T1CKPS1 = 1;
    while (1) {                             // Forever loop
        TMR1 = 0;                           // Clear TMR1 Register value
        TMR1IF = 0;                         // Clear TIMER1 flag
        Buzzer = 0;                         // Turn-off buzzer
        TimerCount =dist=0;                 // clear variables
        lcd_cmd(0x80);                      // cursor position at 0th addr of line1
        lcd_display("Distance:    cm ");    // Call lcd_display() function
        Trig=0;                             // Clear Trig pin
```

```c
    __delay_ms (10);              // Wait for 10 ms
    Trig=1;                       // Make Trig pin '1' to send ultrasonic pulses for 10us
    __delay_us (10);
    Trig=0;                       // Clear Trig pin
    while(Echo==0);               // wait for sending 8 cycles of 40khz burst
    TMR1ON = 1;                   // Enable Timer1
    while(Echo==1);               // wait for echo signal ( if target present)
    TMR1ON = 0;                   // Disable Timer1
    TimerCount = (TMR1H*256) + TMR1L; // Get decimal value of 16-bit binary
    // Ultrasonic Sound Velocity = 34029 (in cm per second)
    // Timer gets incremented for every 1.085 us
    // Distance in cm
    dist = TimerCount * 0.01846;  // distance in cm
    d1 = (dist/100) + 48;         // Calculate ASCII value for each digit
    d2 = ((dist%100)/10) + 48;
    d3 = (dist%10) + 48;
    lcd_cmd(0x89);                // Sending distance value to LCD
    lcd_data(d1);
    lcd_data(d2);
    lcd_data(d3);
    if (dist <= 50)               // if obstacle with 50 cm
    {
       lcd_cmd(0xC0);             // cursor position at 0th addr of line2
       lcd_display("Target Detected "); // Display 'Target detected' in line 2
       Buzzer = 1;                // Turn-on Buzzer
       __delay_ms(1000);          // Make delay for 1000 ms
    }
       lcd_cmd(0x01);             // clear the screen
   }
}
```

//*Header file:*

Ref: 16x2 LCD interface in 4-bit mode with PIC16F877A experiment

Circuit Diagram:

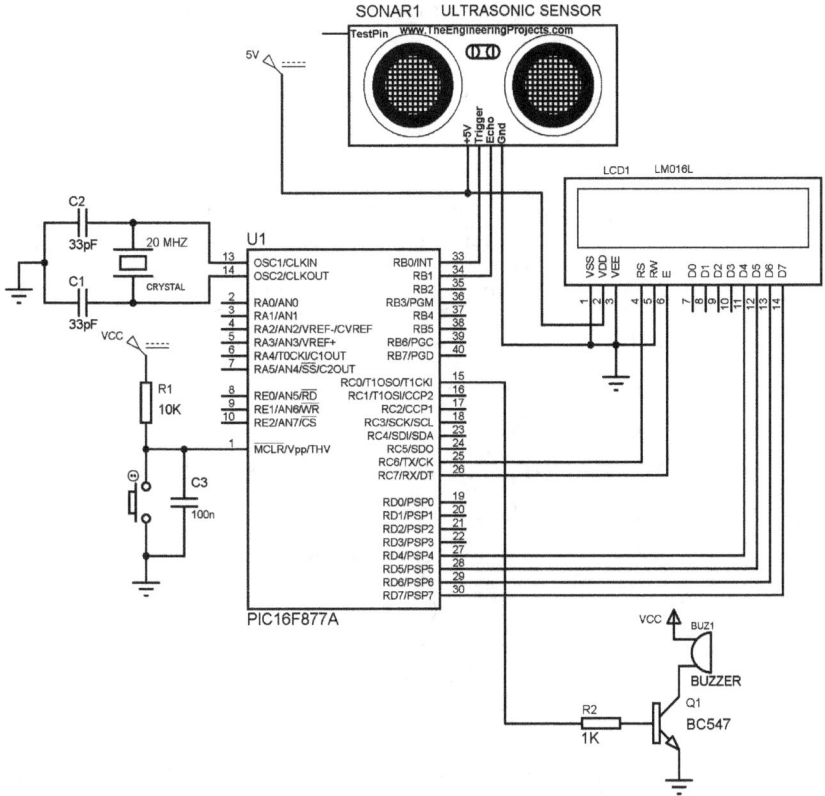

Conclusion:

Thus the Embedded C Program for obstacle detection using the PIC16F877A Microcontroller and the ultrasonic sensor has been written and tested.

46. SENDING SMS USING GSM MODULE

Aim:

Write an Embedded C Program for sending SMS using the SIM900 GSM module and the PIC16F877A/887 Microcontroller.

Hardware and Software Used:
- o PIC16F877 Microcontroller Development Board and GSM SIM900 module
- o MPLAB X IDE v6.05 & Compiler XC8 v2.40

Theory:

GSM (Global System for Mobile Communications) module is used to interact with the GSM network using a computer/MCU. GSM module only understands the AT commands. Some of them are,

- o AT+CSMS – Select message service.
- o AT+CMGF – Message format.
- o AT+CMGL – List messages.
- o AT+CMGR – Read the message.
- o AT+CMGS – Send the message.
- o AT+CMGD – Delete the message.
- o ATA   – Answer a call.
- o ATD   – Dial a number.
- o ATDL   – Dial the last outgoing number.
- o ATH   – Hang up the call.

GSM SIM900 is used for a GSM system that operates in 900 MHz. The 900 MHz band defined in the ETSI standard includes the primary GSM band (GSM-P) and the extension (E-GSM). The serial port of the microcontroller is used to communicate with the SIM900 module using RxD and TxD. The default baud rate of GSM SIM900 is 9600 bps.

Algorithm:

1. Initialize the on-chip USART for asynchronous mode with a 9600 baud rate.
2. Wait for a few seconds.
3. Send the AT command (AT+CMGF =1) to set SMS text mode.
4. Wait for a few seconds.
5. Send the AT command (AT+CMGS) to set receiver's mobile number and send SMS Message in Text Mode.
6. Wait for a few seconds.
7. Send the CTRL+Z character.
8. Wait for a few seconds.
9. Send the command AT.
10. Halt

String function:
1. Send the string data to TXREG using the pointer variable.
2. Wait until TXIF is set.
3. Clear the TXIF flag.

Tx_data function:
1. Send the character data to TXREG.
2. Wait until TXIF is set.
3. Clear the TXIF flag.

InitUSART function:
1. Load SPBRG register to set the baud rate for 9600.
2. Configure the TxD and RxD ports as an output and an input for serial communication respectively.
3. Load TXSTA and RCSTA register to configure serial transmission and reception.
4. Clear TXIF and RCIF flags.

Program:

```
#pragma config FOSC = HS, WDTE = OFF, PWRTE = OFF, BOREN =
OFF, LVP = OFF, CPD = OFF, WRT = OFF, CP = OFF
#include <xc.h>
```

```c
#define _XTAL_FREQ 20000000

void string (unsigned char *s)      // Function for sending string serially
{
while(*s!=0x0) {                    // Execute the block until null character in the string
TXREG=*s;                           // Move the character to TXREG pointed by 's'
while(TXIF==0);                     // Wait for TXIF
while(TRMT==0);                     // Wait for TRMT
TXIF=0;                             // Clear TXIF
s++;                                // Increment the pointer variable
}
}

void tx_data (unsigned char data1)  // Function for sending single character
{
    TXREG=data1;                    // Load data in TXREG
    while(TXIF==0);                 // Wait for TXIF
    while(TRMT==0);                 // Wait for TRMT
    TXIF=0;                         // Clear TXIF
}

void InitUSART (const long int baudrate)
{
SPBRG = (_XTAL_FREQ/(long)(64UL * baudrate)) - 1;
TRISC6 = 0;                         // Tx pin (output)
TRISC7 = 1;                         // Rx pin (input)
TXSTA = 0b00100000;                 // Setting UART for transmission
RCSTA = 0b10010000;                 // Setting UART for reception
__delay_ms(100);                    // Wait for serial port stable
TXIF=0;                             // Clear transmit flag
RCIF=0;                             // Clear receive flag
}

void main(void)                     // Main function
{
```

```
InitUSART(9600);                              // Initialize the USART
__delay_ms(2000);                             // Wait to get ready SIM900
string("AT\r\n");                             // Send AT
__delay_ms(1000);                             // wait for 1 sec
string("AT+CMGF=1\r\n");                      // Send AT+CMGF=1
__delay_ms(1000);                             // wait for 1 sec
// Send AT+CMGS =\"mobile number of receiver\"
string("AT+CMGS=\"0xxxxxxxxxx\";\r\n");
__delay_ms(2000);                             // wait for 2 sec
string("This is a test MESSAGE \r\n");        // Send "message block'
__delay_ms(1000); __delay_ms(1000);           // wait for 2 sec
tx_data(0x1A);                                // Send return character
__delay_ms(2000);                             // wait for 2 sec
string("AT\r\n");                             // Send AT
__delay_ms(1000);                             // wait for 1 sec
while(1);                                     // Halt
}
```

Circuit Diagram:

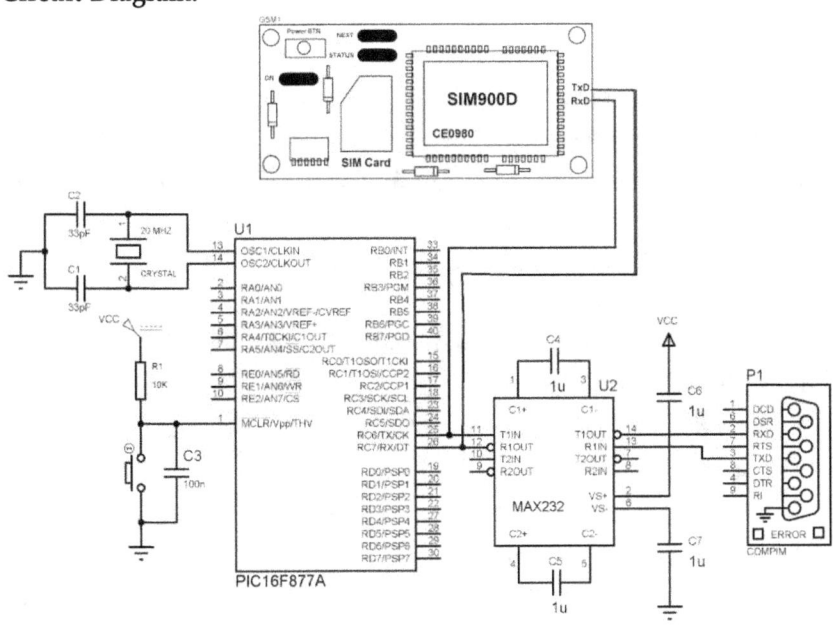

Conclusion:

Thus the Embedded C Program for sending SMS using the SIM900 GSM module and the PIC16F877A Microcontroller has been tested.

47. LED ON/OFF CONTROL USING GSM MODULE

Aim:

Write an Embedded C Program to control the LED ON/OFF through SMS using GSM SIM900 and PIC16F877A/887 Microcontroller.

Hardware and Software Used:

- PIC16F877A Microcontroller Development Board, SIM900 GSM module, LED and resistor
- MPLAB X IDE v6.05 & Compiler XC8 v2.40

Algorithm:

1. Initialize the on-chip USART for asynchronous mode with a 9600 baud rate.
2. Wait for a few seconds.
3. Send the AT command to turn off echo.
4. Wait for a few seconds.
5. Send the AT command to store the Current Configuration.
6. Wait for a few seconds.
7. Send the AT command to select text mode for SMS.
8. Wait for a few seconds.
9. Send the AT command for the notification of new SMS.
10. Wait for a few seconds.
11. Send the AT command to read SMS.
12. Wait for a few seconds.
13. Send the AT command to save settings.
14. Wait for a few seconds.
15. Check the message body which starts with '#' and end with '@'.
16. If the received message is ON, turn-on the LED.

17. If the received message is OFF, turn-off the LED.

String function:
1. Send the string data to TXREG using the pointer variable.
2. Wait until TXIF is set.
3. Clear the TXIF flag.

ISR function:
1. Checks overrun error and clear it.
2. Read the received character from RCREG.
3. Store the received character in msg[] array.
4. Clear RCIF.

InitUSART function:
1. Load SPBRG register to set the baud rate for 9600.
2. Configure the TxD and RxD ports as an output and an input for serial communication respectively.
3. Load TXSTA and RCSTA register to configure serial transmission and reception.
4. Clear TXIF and RCIF flags.

Program:
```
#pragma config FOSC = HS, WDTE = OFF, PWRTE = OFF, BOREN = OFF, LVP = OFF, CPD = OFF, WRT = OFF, CP = OFF
#include <xc.h>
#define _XTAL_FREQ 20000000
unsigned char msg[25]={0x0}, RDS = '\0', t = '\0';
unsigned int c;


void string (unsigned char *s)     // Function for sending string serially
{
while(*s!=0x0) {                   // Execute the block until null character in the string
TXREG=*s;                          // Move the character to TXREG pointed by 's'
while(TXIF==0);                    // Wait for TXIF
while(TRMT==0);                    // Wait for TRMT
TXIF=0;                            // Clear TXIF
s++;                               // Increment the pointer variable
```

```c
}
}

void __interrupt() serial1 (void)   // ISR for receive interrupt
{
if(RCIF==1){                        // Check if RCIF is set
if (OERR){                          // Checking overrun error
CREN=0;
CREN=1;
}
RDS = RCREG;                        // Read the received character from RCREG
if (t=='s'){                        // if t='s', store the received character in msg[] array
msg[c]=RDS;
c++;                                // Increment array index
} }
RCIF=0;                             // Clear RCIF
}

void InitUSART (const long int baudrate)
{
SPBRG = (_XTAL_FREQ/(long)(64UL * baudrate)) - 1;
TRISC6 = 0;                         // Tx pin (output)
TRISC7 = 1;                         // Rx pin (input)
TXSTA = 0b00100000;                 // Setting UART for transmission
RCSTA = 0b10010000;                 // Setting UART for reception
__delay_ms(100);                    // Wait for serial port stable
TXIF=0;                             // Clear transmit flag
RCIF=0;                             // Clear receive flag
}

void main (void)                    // Main function
{
InitUSART(9600);                    // Initialize the USART for asynchronous mode
TRISD2 = 0;                         // Configure PORTD2 as output port
```

```c
RD2 = 0;                            // Clear RD2
__delay_ms(1000);                   // Wait 2 sec to stabilize SIM900
__delay_ms(1000);
string("AT\r\n");                   // Send AT
__delay_ms(1000);
string( "ATE1\r");                  // Turn off echo
__delay_ms(1000);
string( "AT&W\r");                  // Stores Current Configuration
__delay_ms(1000);
string( "AT+CMGF=1\r");             // Select text mode for sms
__delay_ms(1000);
string( "AT+CNMI= 1,2,0,0,0\r");    // notification of new sms
__delay_ms(1000);
__delay_ms(1000);
string( "AT+CMGR=1\r");             // AT command to read sms
__delay_ms(1000);
string("AT+CSAS\r");                // Save settings
__delay_ms(1000); __delay_ms(1000);
__delay_ms(1000); __delay_ms(1000);
__delay_ms(1000); __delay_ms(1000);
string("AT\r\n");

INTCON|=0b11000000;                 // GIE=1; PEIE=1; RCIE = 1;
PIE1=0b00100000;
while(1){
   while(RDS != '*');               // Check message body (message start from '*'
   t='s';                           // Move character 's' to variable t
   while(RDS != '@');               // Check message end character '@'
   __delay_ms(1000);                // Wait for 1 sec
   string(msg);                     // Send received char to serial port
   if (msg[0]=='O' && msg[1]=='N' )    // If msg is 'ON'
   {
   RD2=1;                           // Turn-on LED
   }
```

```
if (msg[0]=='O' && msg[1]=='F' && msg[2]=='F' )        // If msg is 'OFF'
{
RD2=0;                          // Turn-off LED
}
c=0; RDS = '\0'; t='\0';        // Clear c, RDS and t
}
}
```

Circuit Diagram:

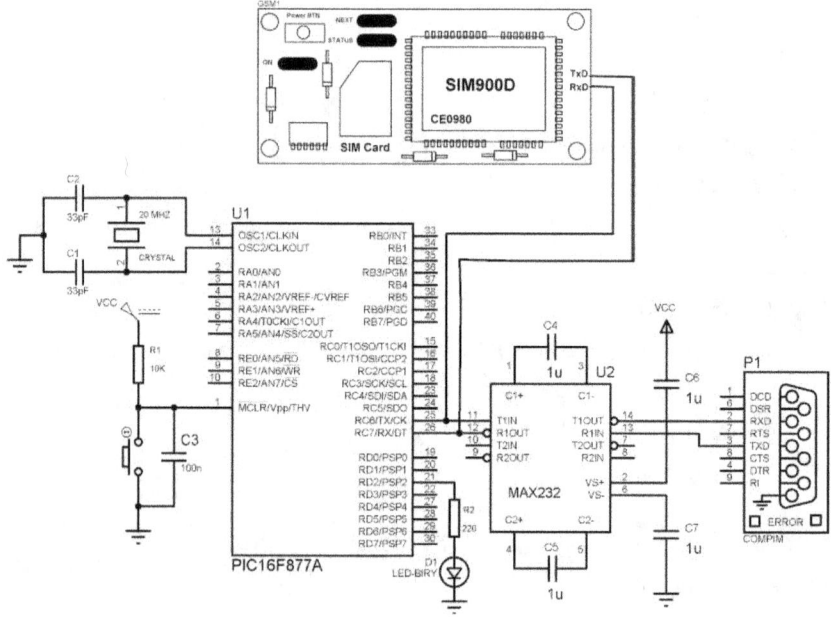

Conclusion:

Thus the SIM900 GSM module has been interfaced with the PIC16F877A Microcontroller. The turn-on and turn-off control of an LED has done by sending SMS from the mobile device.

48. GPS MODULE INTERFACE

Aim:
Write an Embedded C Program to receive the latitude and longitude values from GPS module using the PIC16F877A/887 Microcontroller and display it on the LCD.

Hardware and Software Used:
o   PIC16F877A Microcontroller Development Board
o   MPLAB X IDE v6.05 & Compiler XC8 v2.40

Theory:
Global Positioning System is based on satellite navigation technology. A GPS Receiver provides the location of an object in terms of latitude and longitude. GPS also provides time in GMT and a lot of geographical information for a particular object like a number of satellites view, Altitude, the direction of travel, etc. This information is assembled in a particular string format which is to be decoded by GPS modems. A GPS modem gives the serial output data in the following string format. It is called as NMEA Format.

$GPGGA,100908.00,**2604.7041778,N,07047.8466270,**
E,4,08,1.00,495.144,M,29.310,M,0.10,0000*40

1. A string always starts with a '$' sign
2. GPGGA: Global Positioning System Fix Data
3. ',' Comma indicates the separation between two values
4. 100908.00: GMT time as 10(hr):01(min):56(sec):000(ms)
5. 2604.7041778,N: Latitude 26(degree) 50(minutes) 9416(sec) North
6. 07047.8466270,E: Longitude 075(degree) 47(minutes) 8441(sec) East
7. 4: Fix Quantity 0= invalid data, 1= valid data, 2=DGPS fix, 4 = RTK Fix coordinate
8. 08: Number of satellites currently viewed
9. 1.00: HDOP
10. 495.144,M : Altitude (Height above sea level in meter)

11. 29.310,M : Geoids height
12. 0.10, the age of the correction (if any)
13. 0000 : the correction station ID (if any)
14. *40 : checksum

The heart of the module is a NEO-6M GPS chip from u-blox. It can track up to 22 satellites on 50 channels and achieves the industry's highest level of sensitivity. The GPS module gives output data in the RS232 logic level format. To convert the RS232 logic level into TTL using a line converter MAX232 with PIC16F877A/887. The latitude and longitude data are to be displayed on the 16x2 LCD.

First download and install the Windows PC debug/evaluation tool "u-center". Run the u-center software (ensure that the RS232 port of the GSP module is connected with RS232 port of PC). It can clearly display GPS data/information on the screen. We can check whether the NEO-6M GPS module is working properly or not. Identify the baud rate of the module, and change it in the program if it is not 9600 bps.

Algorithm:
1. Set the baud rate of USART in Asynchronous to 9600 bps.
2. Enable the SPEN and CREN bits (RCSTA register).
3. Receive the Serial data from the GPS module and compare it with the string '$GPGGA,' byte by byte.
4. Wait for comma (,) as the string gets matched.
5. Store the data which appears after the comma and before 'N' into an array variable which will be the Latitude.
6. After the next comma (,), store the data into another array variable which will be the Longitude.

7. Display both Latitude and Longitude value on LCD.
8. Repeat the steps from step 3 to update the current latitude and longitude of the GPS receiver.

Program:

```c
#pragma config FOSC = HS, WDTE = OFF, PWRTE = OFF, BOREN = OFF, LVP = OFF, CPD = OFF, WRT = OFF, CP = OFF
#include <xc.h>
#define _XTAL_FREQ 20000000
#define RS RB6              // RB6 is named as RS
#define EN RB7              // RB7 is named as EN
#define D4    RD4           // 4-bit mode (RD4-D4, RD5-D5
#define D5    RD5           // RD6-D6, RD7-D7)
#define D6    RD6
#define D7    RD7
#include "lcd4bit_head.h"   // Include header file - lcd4bit_head.h

unsigned char rx_data()
{
if (OERR){                  // Checking overrun error
CREN=0;
CREN=1;
}
while(RCIF==0);             // Wait until RCIF gets low
return RCREG;               // Return RCREG value
}
void InitUSART(const long int baudrate)
{
SPBRG = (_XTAL_FREQ/(long)(64UL * baudrate)) - 1;
TRISC6 = 0;                 // Tx pin (output)
TRISC7 = 1;                 // Rx pin (input)
TXSTA = 0b00100000;         // Setting UART for transmission
RCSTA = 0b10010000;         // Setting UART for reception
__delay_ms(100);            // Wait for serial port stable
```

```c
TXIF=0;                    // Clear transmit flag
RCIF=0;                    // Clear receive flag
}

void main(void)
{
unsigned char i, gps=0, lati_data[11], long_data[12];
TRISB = 0x00;              // set PORT B as output port
TRISD = 0x00;              // set PORT D as output port
InitUSART(9600);           // Initialize USART in asynchronous mode
lcd_init ();               // Call lcd_init() function to initialize 16x2 LCD

while(1){
gps=rx_data();             // Check the string '$GPGGA,'
if(gps=='$')
{
gps=rx_data();
if(gps=='G')
{
gps=rx_data();
if(gps=='P')
{
gps=rx_data();
if(gps=='G')
{
gps=rx_data();
if(gps=='G')
{
gps=rx_data();
if(gps=='A')
{
gps=rx_data();             // Check first comma
if(gps==',')
{
```

```c
gps=rx_data();
while(gps != ','){        // Check second comma
gps=rx_data();
}
for(i=0; gps != 'N'; i++){
gps=rx_data();
lati_data[i]=gps;         // Store the Latitude data
}
gps=rx_data();            // skip comma
for(i=0; gps != 'E'; i++){
gps=rx_data();
long_data[i]=gps;         // Store the Longitude data
}                         // End if cases
}}}}}}}

lcd_cmd(0x80);            // cursor position at 0th addr of line1
lcd_display("Lt ");       // Display 'Lt' for Latitude
for (i=0; i<11; i++) {
  lcd_data(lati_data[i]); // Display the Latitude data on LCD
}

lcd_cmd(0xC0);            // Cursor position at 0th addr of line2
lcd_display("Lg ");       // Display 'Lg' for Longitude
for (i=0; i<12; i++) {
  lcd_data(long_data[i]); // Display the Longitude data on LCD
}
__delay_ms(3000);         // Wait for 3 sec
lcd_cmd(0x01);            // Clear screen
}
}
```

//*Header file*:
Ref: 16x2 LCD interface in 4-bit mode with PIC16F877A experiment

Circuit Diagram:

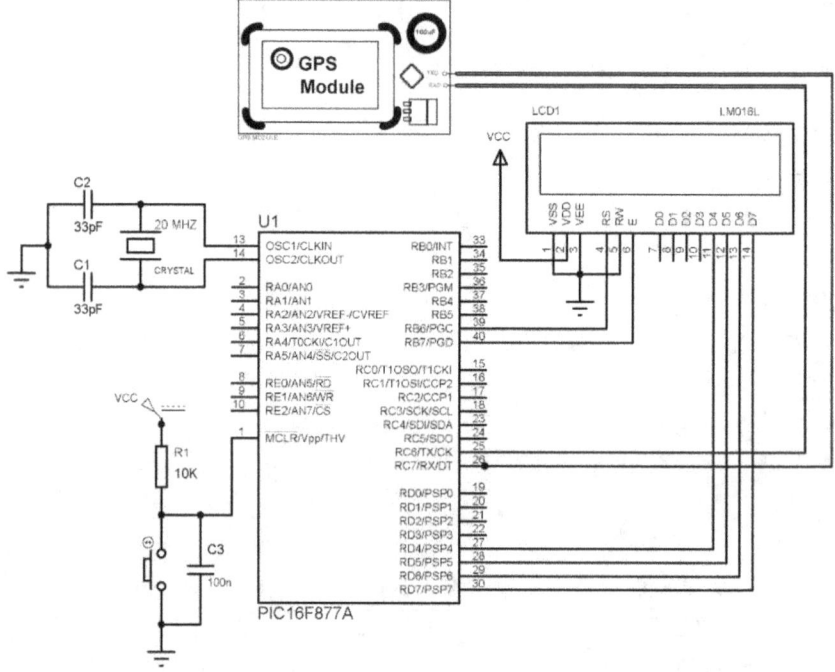

Conclusion:

Thus the GPS module has been interfaced with the PIC16F877A Microcontroller and the Latitude and Longitude values are displayed on the 16x2 LCD.

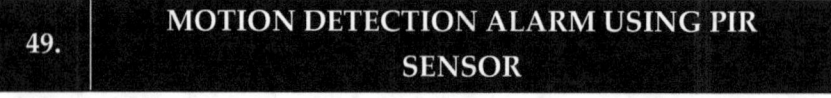

49. MOTION DETECTION ALARM USING PIR SENSOR

Aim:

Write an Embedded C Program to develop a motion detection alarm based on a Passive Infra-Red (PIR) sensor using the PIC16F877A/887 Microcontroller.

Hardware and Software Used:
- PIC16F877A Microcontroller Development Board, PIR sensor, NPN transistor and Buzzer
- MPLAB X IDE v6.05 & Compiler XC8 v2.40

Theory:

PIR sensor detects infrared (IR) heat radiations. Usually, a living body emits infrared radiation above absolute zero. The sensor responds to infrared radiation at the wavelength of 10μm. Therefore, the PIR sensor can be used to detect the presence of living things that can move. The PIR sensor having two slots and is connected to a differential amplifier. If a stationary object is present in front of the sensor, the two slots receive the same amount of radiation and the output is zero. If an object moving in front of the sensor, one of the slots receives more radiation than the other slot. This makes the output swing high or low. This change in output voltage is the result of the detection of motion.

The Fresnel lenses are most commonly used to enhance the sensing range about 10 meters and field of view less than 180 degrees. PIR sensor has three pins:
1. VDD: +3.3-5 v power supply
2. Output: Digital output pin
3. GND: Power supply ground

Algorithm:
1. Configure RB0 as an input port for the external interrupt.
2. Enable Global interrupt, Enable INT0 interrupt.
3. Select the raising edge of an interrupt event.
4. Halt the main function.

ISR:
1. Check the INTE and INTF bits; if they are set continue the next step.
2. Clear INTF.
3. Turn-on the buzzer.

4. Call the delay function for 500 ms.
5. Turn-off the buzzer.

Program:
```c
#pragma config FOSC = HS, WDTE = OFF, PWRTE = OFF, BOREN = OFF, LVP = OFF, CPD = OFF, WRT = OFF, CP = OFF
#include <xc.h>
#define _XTAL_FREQ 20000000
#define buzzer RB2
// RB0 (INT0) is connected with the output of PIR sensor

void __interrupt() isr (void)           // Interrupt Service Routine
{
if (INTE && INTF)                       // Check the occurrence of Ext. Hardware interrupt
{
INTF = 0;                               // Clear external interrupt flag
buzzer = 1;                             // Turn-on the buzzer
__delay_ms(500);                        // Make 100 ms delay
buzzer = 0;                             // Turn-off the buzzer
}
}

void main(void) {
TRISB = 0x01;                           // Set RB0/INTI as input port (Ext. int)
RB2 = 0;                                // Clear RB2
GIE = 1;                                // Enable Global Interrupt
INTE = 1;                               // Enable RB0/INT external hardware Interrupt
PEIE = 0;                               // Disable peripheral interrupt
INTEDG = 1;                             // Interrupt on raising edge
while(1);                               // wait for forever
}
```

Circuit Diagram:

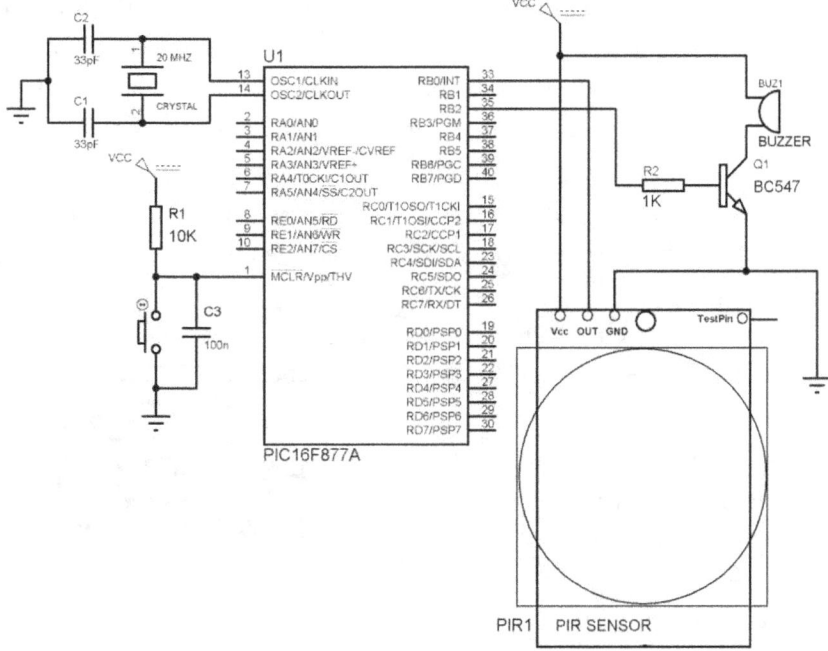

Conclusion:

Thus the motion detection alarm system has been designed using the PIR sensor and the PIC16F877A Microcontroller.

50.	ACCELEROMETER SENSOR INTERFACE

Aim:

Write an Embedded C Program to interface the accelerometer sensor with the PIC16F877A/887 Microcontroller.

Hardware and Software Used:
- PIC16F877A Microcontroller Development Board and ADXL 335 accelerometer
- MPLAB X IDE v6.05 & Compiler XC8 v2.40

Theory:

The Accelerometer is an electromechanical MEMS device that measures the force of acceleration in 3 axes. The popular three-axis analog accelerometer module is ADXL335. It gives analog voltage output proportional to the acceleration along X, Y, and Z axes. It can be converted to a digital value using on-chip ADC for various applications. It can be used for tilt sensing applications like automobiles, robots, drones, gaming applications, etc. The sensor has a full sensing range of +/-3g in the x, y, and z axes.

The ADXL 335 accelerometer consists of five pins which are,
1. VCC: 5V dc regulated power source
2. Ground
3. X-axis analog output
4. Y-axis analog output
5. Z-axis analog output

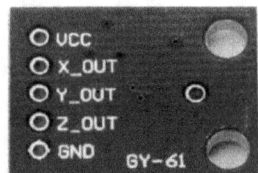

Angles using ADXL335:

The sensor outputs can be used to calculate the angle of inclination and angle of rotation. First, the 10-bit ADC value is converted into g unit. As per the ADXL335 datasheet, the maximum voltage level at 0g is 1.65V and sensitivity scale factor of 330mV/g.

The formula for acceleration value in g unit

$$A_{out} = \frac{ADCvalue * V_{ref} - VoltageLevel @ 0g}{SensitivityFactor}$$

Axout = (((X axis ADC value * Vref) / 1024) – 1.65) / 0.330
Ayout = (((Y axis ADC value * Vref) / 1024) – 1.65) / 0.330
Azout = (((Z axis ADC value * Vref) / 1024) – 1.65) / 0.330

Angle of Inclination:

The angle of inclination means by how much angle the device is tilted from its plane of the surface. It can be calculated as,

$$\theta(theta) = a\tan\left(\frac{A_{xout}}{\sqrt{A_{yout}^2 + A_{zout}^2}}\right)$$

$$\psi(psi) = a\tan\left(\frac{A_{yout}}{\sqrt{A_{xout}^2 + A_{zout}^2}}\right)$$

$$\phi(phi) = a\tan\left(\frac{\sqrt{A_{xout}^2 + A_{yout}^2}}{A_{zout}}\right)$$

The above equations give angles in radians. To get angles in degrees, multiply these values by ($180/\pi \approx 57.29577951$) within range of -90° to +90° each axis.

Angle of Rotation:

A complete angle of rotation from 0° to 360° around X, Y, Z axes are called,

Roll - Angle of rotation about the X-axis
Pitch - Angle of rotation about the Y-axis
Yaw - Angle of rotation about the Z-axis
It can be calculated as,
Roll = (atan2(Ayout, Azout)) *57.29577951+180
Pitch = (atan2(Azout, Axout)) *57.29577951+180
Yaw = (atan2(Axout, Ayout)) *57.29577951+180

Algorithm:
1. Declaration of variables: ADC_X, ADC_Y, and ADC_Z are as integers and Axout, Ayout and Azout are as double.
2. Configure AN0, AN1 and AN2 are analog ports.
3. Initialize the on-chip USART for asynchronous mode with a 9600 baud rate.
4. Configure ADCON0 for Channel AN0, ADC Clock FOSC/64 & Turn ON ADC.
5. Read the analog value for AN0 and store it in ADC_X.

6. Configure ADCON0 for Channel AN1, ADC Clock FOSC/64 & Turn ON ADC.
7. Read the analog value for AN1 and store it in ADC_Y.
8. Configure ADCON0 for Channel AN2, ADC Clock FOSC/64 & Turn ON ADC.
9. Read the analog value for AN2 and store it in ADC_Z.
10. Convert X, Y and Z values in g unit.
11. Print the X, Y and Z axes values in serial port.
12. Wait for 1 sec.
13. Repeat the steps from step 4.

String() function:
1. Send the string data to TXREG using the pointer variable.
2. Wait until TXIF is set.
3. Clear the TXIF flag.

Tx_data() function:
1. Send the character data to TXREG.
2. Wait until TXIF is set.
3. Clear the TXIF flag.

InitUSART() function:
1. Load SPBRG register to set the baud rate for 9600.
2. Configure the TxD and RxD ports as an output and an input for serial communication respectively.
3. Load TXSTA and RCSTA register to configure serial transmission and reception.
4. Clear TXIF and RCIF flags.

SerialPrint() function:
1. Declare the array variable buf[].
2. Convert the double into char and store it in buf[].
3. Print the string.
4. Print the buf[].
5. Wait for 10 ms.

adc_read() function:
1. Configure ADC Clock, right justified result, AN0-AN4 as Analog ports, VDD and VSS as references and Turn on ADC.
2. Wait for acquisition time (1 ms).
3. Set GO bit for the start of conversion.
4. Wait for DONE bit.
5. Move the result of ADC to adc_res.
6. Clear ADIF.
7. Return adc_res value.

Program:

```c
#pragma config FOSC = HS, WDTE = OFF, PWRTE = OFF, BOREN = OFF, LVP = OFF, CPD = OFF, WRT = OFF, CP = OFF
#include <xc.h>
#include <stdio.h>
#include <stdlib.h>
#include <math.h>
#define _XTAL_FREQ 20000000
```

void string (char *s)	// Function for sending string serially
{	
while(*s!=0x0) {	// Execute the block until null character in the string
TXREG=*s;	// Move the character to TXREG pointed by 's'
while(TXIF==0);	// Wait for TXIF
while(TRMT==0);	// Wait for TRMT
TXIF=0;	// Clear TXIF
s++;	// Increment the pointer variable
}	
}	
void tx_data (char data1)	// Function for sending single character
{	
TXREG=data1;	// Load data in TXREG
while(TXIF==0);	// Wait for TXIF

```c
    while(TRMT==0);              // Wait for TRMT
    TXIF=0;                      // Clear TXIF
}

void InitUSART (const long int baudrate)
{
SPBRG = (_XTAL_FREQ/(long)(64UL * baudrate)) - 1;
TRISC6 = 0;                      // Tx pin (output)
TRISC7 = 1;                      // Rx pin (input)
TXSTA = 0b00100000;              // Setting UART for transmission
RCSTA = 0b10010000;              // Setting UART for reception
__delay_ms(100);                 // Wait for serial port stable
TXIF=0;                          // Clear transmit flag
RCIF=0;                          // Clear receive flag
}

void SerialPrint (const char* str, double val, char unit)
{
        char buf[10];
        sprintf(buf,"%.2f",val);  // Convert double into string
        string(str);              // Send string
        string(buf);              // Send value
        tx_data(unit);            // Send unit char
        tx_data('\t');            // Send tab char
        __delay_ms(10);
}

int adc_read()
{
int adc_res;
// (1) ADC Clock, (1) Right justified, AN0-4 Analog ports & VDD and VSS references
ADCON1 = 0xC2;
__delay_ms(1);                   // Wait for acquisition time
GO_nDONE = 1;                    // Start A/D conversion
```

```c
while(GO_nDONE);              // Waiting for conversion to complete
adc_res = (ADRESH*256)+ ADRESL;  // ADC result in decimal
ADIF = 0;                     // Clear ADC interrupt flag
ADON=0;                       // Turn-off ADC
return adc_res;               // Return ADC result to main function
}

void main()
{
int ADC_X,ADC_Y,ADC_Z;
double Axout, Ayout, Azout;
TRISA = 0x07;                 // Analog pin AN0-2 as Input port
InitUSART(9600);

while(1) {
    ADCON0 = 0x81;    // Channel AN0, (10)ADC Clock FOSC/64 & Turn ON ADC
    ADC_X = adc_read();
    ADCON0 = 0x89;    // Channel AN1, (10)ADC Clock FOSC/64 & Turn ON ADC
    ADC_Y = adc_read();
    ADCON0 = 0x91;    // Channel AN2, (10)ADC Clock FOSC/64 & Turn ON ADC
    ADC_Z = adc_read();

    //Convert X, Y and Z values in g unit
        Axout = (((double)(ADC_X*5)/1.024)-1650.0)/330.0;
        Ayout = (((double)(ADC_Y*5)/1.024)-1650.0)/330.0;
        Azout = (((double)(ADC_Z*5)/1.024)-1650.0)/330.0;

    SerialPrint("Axout = ", Axout, 'g');   // Print X, Y, Z values in g unit
    SerialPrint("Ayout = ", Ayout, 'g');
    SerialPrint("Azout = ", Azout, 'g');
    string("\r\n");           // Carriage Return & Move cursor to the new line
    __delay_ms(1000);         // wait 1 sec for next cycle
    }
}
```

Circuit Diagram:

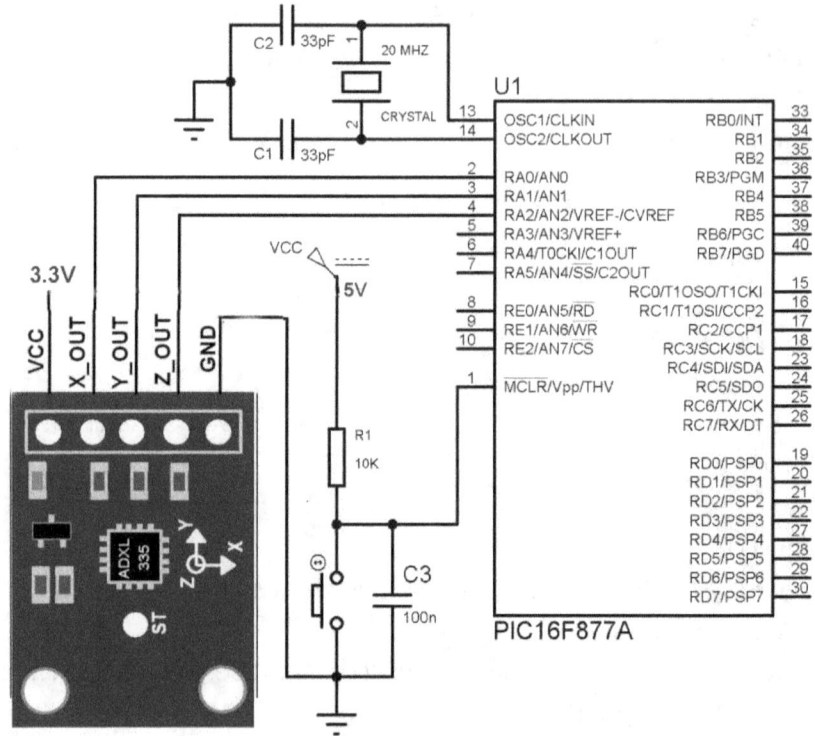

Conclusion:

Thus the accelerometer sensor has been interfaced with the PIC16F877A Microcontroller, and the acceleration value of X, Y, & Z axes in g unit have displayed on the serial monitor.

51. GRAPHICAL LCD INTERFACE

Aim:

Write an Embedded C Program to display the message on graphical LCD using the PIC16F877A/887 Microcontroller.

Hardware and Software Used:
- PIC16F877 Microcontroller Development Board and Graphical LCD
- MPLAB X IDE v6.05 & Compiler XC8 v2.40

Theory:

A graphical LCD is an electronic display unit that not only displays alphanumeric characters but also can display alphanumeric characters, images, fonts, and other structures. A graphical LCD has a resolution of 128×64 which means that it has 128 columns and 64 rows. It can display 8192 pixels on the screen. The LCD screen is divided equally in two halves. The first half from 1 to 64 columns is controlled by the first controller and this controller is capable of controlling 4096 dots. The second half from 64 to 128 columns is controlled by the second controller. Each half is further divided into 8 pages of equal sizes (64 rows/8) so that each page has 8 vertical dots. Each page size is 8 rows and 64 columns so that it contains 8x64=512 dots or 512/8=64 pixels. Each pixel contains vertical 8 dots.

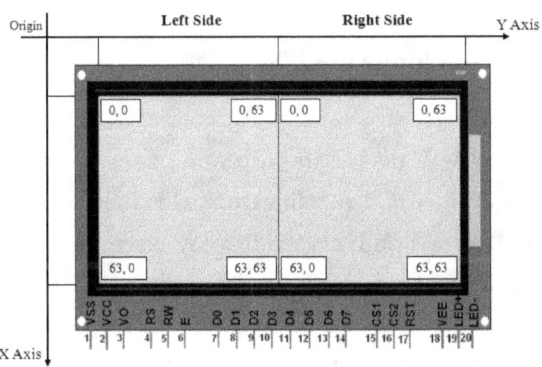

Page Selection (X address):

Page0 Address = 0xB8 (Separate X counter for both left and right half of the screen)
Page1 Address = 0xB9
Page2 Address = 0xBA
Page3 Address = 0xBB
Page4 Address = 0xBC
Page5 Address = 0xBD
Page6 Address = 0xBE
Page7 Address = 0xBF

Cursor/Char Position (Y address):

To set the cursor position (0-63), send the following address to GLCD. It is incremented by 1 automatically to read or write operations of display data.

Cursor Position 0 (Address = 0x40) (Left most pixel)
Cursor Position 1 (Address = 0x41)
.
.
.
Cursor Position 63 (Address = 0x7F)

Start Line (Z address):

The Z address will decide the top line of the liquid crystal display screen. It starts from 0xC0 (0th line) to 0xFF (63rd line). It is used for scrolling (y-axis) of the liquid crystal display screen.

KS0108/JHD12864E is a 20-pin GLCD module. It has 6 control & 8 data pins, and 6 power pins.

Pin No	Name	Function
1	VCC	Supply voltage (5V)
2	VSS	Ground
3	V0	Contrast adjustment (V0)
18	VEE	Negative voltage used along with VCC for brightness control
19	A	Backlight (+)
20	K	Backlight (-)
12	CS1	Chip select 1(enables left half)

13	CS2	Chip select 2 (enables right half)
14	RST	Reset
15	R/W	Read / Write (1/0)
16	D/I	Data/Instruction (1/0)
17	E	Enable

There are 4 modes of operation

D/I	R/W	Mode
0	0	Instruction write
0	1	Read the GLCD status
1	0	Data write to the RAM
1	1	Data read

Example: For displaying 'P' in the first line of GLCD. We will make a font of size 5x7 pixels by leaving the first two columns, 8th column and last row of the page for spacing.

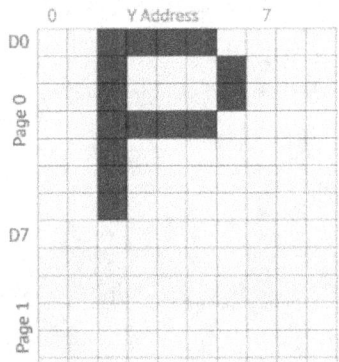

In order to display 'P', The following bytes to be transferred to the first page of the display by selecting left controller (CS1) in Y address from 0 to 7: 0x00, 0x00, 0x7F, 0x09, 0x09,0x09,0x06,0x00.

Initialize the display:
Send 0x3E - Display OFF command
Send 0x40 - Y address (Start address)
Send 0xB8 - X address (Page0)
Send 0xC0 - Z address (Start line)

Send 0x3F - Display ON command

Command Write:

Send command on data pins.

Make RS = 0 (Select Command Register) and RW = 0 (Write Operation).

Make High to Low transition on Enable pin(>1us).

Data Write:

Send Data on data pins.

Make RS = 1 (Select Data Register) and RW = 0 (Write Operation).

Make High to Low transition on Enable pin (>1us).

Algorithm:
1. Initialize GLCD – Use PORTC and PORTD as output ports, configure both left and right half of the display, Set the x, y, and z addresses.
2. Clear display.
3. Select the left half and set the addresses.
4. Display "ECS" on page 0.
5. Select the right half and set the addresses.
6. Display "DEPT" on page 0.
7. Halt

Program:

```
#pragma config FOSC = HS, WDTE = OFF, PWRTE = OFF, BOREN = OFF, LVP = OFF, CPD = OFF, WRT = OFF, CP = OFF
#include <xc.h>
#define _XTAL_FREQ 20000000
#define GLCD_DataBus    PORTD
#define EN      RC0
#define RW      RC1
#define RS      RC2
#define CS2     RC3
#define CS1     RC4
char A[]={0x7e, 0x11, 0x11, 0x11, 0x7e, 0x00}; // 41 A
char B[]={0x7f, 0x49, 0x49, 0x49, 0x36, 0x00}; // 42 B
```

```c
char C[]={0x3e, 0x41, 0x41, 0x41, 0x22, 0x00}; // 43 C
char D[]={0x7f, 0x41, 0x41, 0x22, 0x1c, 0x00}; // 44 D
char E[]={0x7f, 0x49, 0x49, 0x49, 0x41, 0x00}; // 45 E
char F[]={0x7f, 0x09, 0x09, 0x09, 0x01, 0x00}; // 46 F
char G[]={0x3e, 0x41, 0x49, 0x49, 0x7a, 0x00}; // 47 G
char H[]={0x7f, 0x08, 0x08, 0x08, 0x7f, 0x00}; // 48 H
char I[]={0x00, 0x41, 0x7f, 0x41, 0x00, 0x00}; // 49 I
char J[]={0x20, 0x40, 0x41, 0x3f, 0x01, 0x00}; // 4a J
char K[]={0x7f, 0x08, 0x14, 0x22, 0x41, 0x00}; // 4b K
char L[]={0x7f, 0x40, 0x40, 0x40, 0x40, 0x00}; // 4c L
char M[]={0x7f, 0x02, 0x0c, 0x02, 0x7f, 0x00}; // 4d M
char N[]={0x7f, 0x04, 0x08, 0x10, 0x7f, 0x00}; // 4e N
char O[]={0x3e, 0x41, 0x41, 0x41, 0x3e, 0x00}; // 4f O
char P[]={0x7f, 0x09, 0x09, 0x09, 0x06, 0x00}; // 50 P
char Q[]={0x3e, 0x41, 0x51, 0x21, 0x5e, 0x00}; // 51 Q
char R[]={0x7f, 0x09, 0x19, 0x29, 0x46, 0x00}; // 52 R
char S[]={0x46, 0x49, 0x49, 0x49, 0x31, 0x00}; // 53 S
char T[]={0x01, 0x01, 0x7f, 0x01, 0x01, 0x00}; // 54 T
char U[]={0x3f, 0x40, 0x40, 0x40, 0x3f, 0x00}; // 55 U
char V[]={0x1f, 0x20, 0x40, 0x20, 0x1f, 0x00}; // 56 V
char W[]={0x3f, 0x40, 0x38, 0x40, 0x3f, 0x00}; // 57 W
char X[]={0x63, 0x14, 0x08, 0x14, 0x63, 0x00}; // 58 X
char Y[]={0x07, 0x08, 0x70, 0x08, 0x07, 0x00}; // 59 Y
char Z[]={0x61, 0x51, 0x49, 0x45, 0x43, 0x00}; // 5a Z

void GLCD_LeftHalf()        // Select left half of GLCD screen
{
   CS1=0;
   CS2=1;
}
void GLCD_RightHalf()       // Select right half of GLCD screen
{
   CS1=1;
   CS2=0;
```

```c
}
void GLCD_Cmd(char cmd)
{
    GLCD_DataBus = cmd;       //Send the Command to LCD
    RS = 0;                   // Make LOW RS pin for selecting Command register
    RW = 0;                   // Make LOW RW pin for Write operation
    EN = 1;                   // Generate a High-to-low pulse on EN pin
    __delay_us(10);
    EN = 0;
    __delay_us(10);
}
void GLCD_Data(char dat)
{
    GLCD_DataBus = dat;       //Send the Data to LCD
    RS = 1;                   // Make HIGH RS pin for selecting Command register
    RW = 0;                   // Make LOW RW pin for Write operation
    EN = 1;                   // Generate a High-to-low pulse on EN pin
    __delay_us(10);
    EN = 0;
    __delay_us(10);
}
LCD_Char(char *pa)            // Sending Char to the LCD
{
    int i,s;
    for(i=0;i<6;i++) {        // 5x7 font, 1 char + 1 blank space
        GLCD_Data(pa[i]);
        __delay_us(5);
    }}
void GLCD_Init()              // GLCD initialization function
{
    TRISC = 0x00;             // Make PORTC and PORTD as output ports
    TRISD = 0x00;
    CS1=0;                    // Select both left & right half of display
    CS2=0;
```

```c
    __delay_ms(5);
    GLCD_Cmd(0x3E);             // Display OFF
    GLCD_Cmd(0x40);             // Set Y address (column=0)
    GLCD_Cmd(0xB8);             // Set x address (page=0)
    GLCD_Cmd(0xC0);             // Set z address (start line=0)
    GLCD_Cmd(0x3F);             // Display ON
}
void GLCD_ClearAll()            // GLCD all display clear function
{
    int i,j;
    CS1=0;                      // Select both left & right half of display
    CS2=0;
    for(i = 0; i <8; i++)       // Total pages are 8
    {
    GLCD_Cmd((0xB8) + i);       // Increment page
    for(j = 0; j < 64; j++)     // Total columns are 64
    {
    GLCD_Data(0x00);            // Write zeros to all 64 columns
    }
    }
    GLCD_Cmd(0x40);             // Set Y address (column=0)
    GLCD_Cmd(0xB8);             // Set X address (page=0)
}

void main(){
    GLCD_Init();                // Initialize GLCD
    GLCD_ClearAll();            // Clear all pixels in GLCD
    GLCD_LeftHalf();            // Select Left Half
    GLCD_Cmd(0x3F);             // Display on
    GLCD_Cmd(0x40);             // Setting Y-address, Column 0
    GLCD_Cmd(0xB8);             // Setting X-address, Page 0
    GLCD_Cmd(0xC0);             // Setting Z-address, start line
    __delay_ms(1);              // Wait for 1 ms
    LCD_Char(E);                // Display " ECS " on left half in page 0
```

```c
LCD_Char(C);
LCD_Char(S);
GLCD_RightHalf();
GLCD_Cmd(0x3F);         // Display on
GLCD_Cmd(0x40);         // Setting Y-address, Column 0
GLCD_Cmd(0xB8);         // Setting X-address, Page 0
GLCD_Cmd(0xC0);         // Setting Z-address, start line
__delay_ms(1);          // Wait for 1 ms
LCD_Char(D);            // Display " DEPT" on right half in page 0
LCD_Char(E);
LCD_Char(P);
LCD_Char(T);
while(1);               // Remain forever here
}
```

Circuit Diagram:

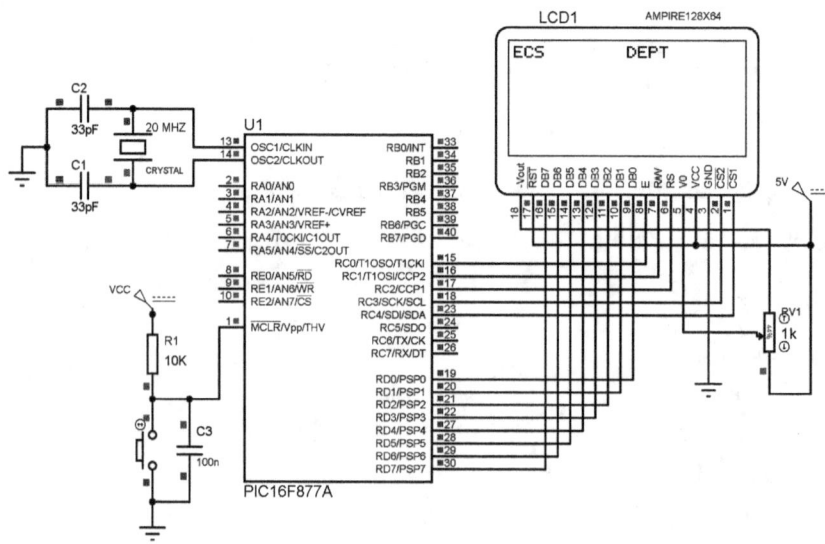

Conclusion:

Thus the graphical LCD has interfaced with the PIC16F877A Microcontroller and displayed the message on the LCD screen.

52. I2C COMMUNICATION

Aim:

Write an Embedded C Program to transfer the data between two PIC16F877A/887 Microcontrollers using I2C communication.

Hardware and Software Used:
- PIC16F877A Microcontroller Development Board
- MPLAB X IDE v6.05 & Compiler XC8 v2.40

Theory:

I2C (Inter Integrated Circuit):

The I2C bus is a bi-directional two-wire serial bus that provides a communication link between integrated circuits (ICs). I2C is a synchronous protocol that allows a master device to initiate communication with a slave device. Data is exchanged between these devices. It provides half duplex mode communication. It was first introduced by the Philips semiconductors in 1982. The I2C bus consists of various data transfer speeds such as standard, fast-mode and high-speed-mode. Bidirectional data transfers can be made at up to 100 kbit/s in the Standard-mode, up to 400 kbit/s in the Fast-mode, up to 1 Mbit/s in Fast-mode plus, or up to 3.4 Mbit/s in the High-speed mode. Unidirectional data transfers up to 5 Mbit/s in Ultra-Fast-mode. The I2C bus supports 7-bit and 10-bit addressing. The I2C bus consisting of two signal lines: SCL and SDL. The SCL is a 'serial clock line' and SDL is a 'serial data line',

SCL and SDL lines are in open-drain state and these terminals are connected to VCC thorough pull-up resistors for the communication. Only a Master can initiate a data transfer and Slaves respond to the Master. It is possible to have multiple Masters on a common bus, but only one could be active at a time. The SCL clock line is always driven by the master. Slaves can never initiate a data transfer but they can transfer data over the I2C bus, and that is always controlled by the Master.

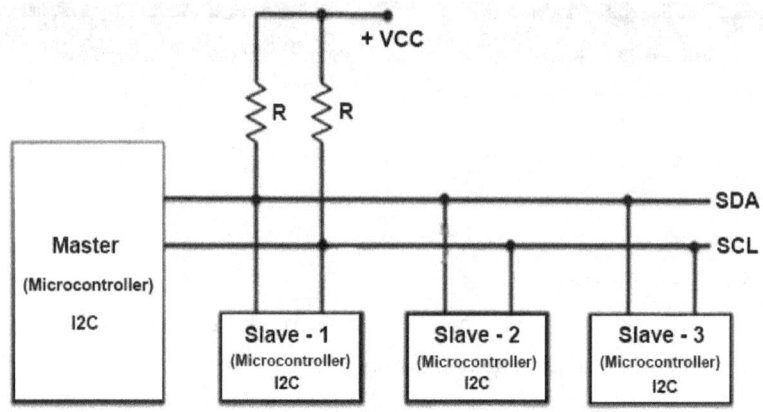

An I2C data transfer consists of the following fundamental signal components/elements:
- Start (S)
- Stop (P)
- Repeated start (R)
- Data
- Acknowledge (A)

A start condition indicates that a device would like to transfer data on the I2C bus. Start condition is represented by the SDA line going low when the clock (SCL) signal is high.

A stop condition indicates that a device wants to release the I2C bus. Then, other master devices may use the bus to transfer data. Stop condition is represented by the SDA signal going high when the clock (SCL) signal is high.

A restart condition indicates that a device would like to transfer more data, for that no need to release the bus. It is similar to Start condition. The data block represents the transfer of eight bits of information. The data is sent on the SDA line, whereas clock pulses are carried on the SCL line.

The data transfer in the I2C protocol needs to be acknowledged either positively (A) or negatively (NACK). A device can acknowledge (A) the transfer of each byte by bringing the SDA line low during the 9th clock pulse of SCL. A "NACK" is when the SDA line floats high during the 9th clock pulse. It is the opposite of an ACK.

I2C masters may read or write to slave devices. This is indicated with a single bit transmitted after the address bits. A 1 means it is a read, and a 0 means it is a write.

The data transfer formats for 7-bit addressing:

Master Transmitter to Slave Receiver

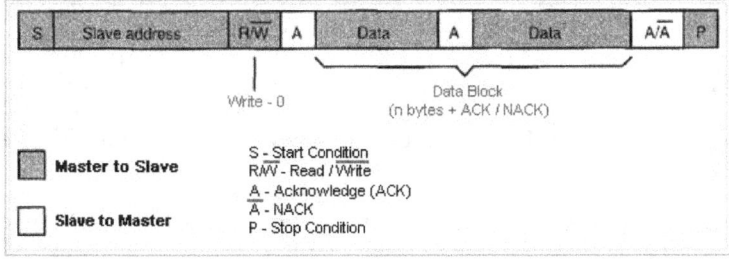

Master Receiver from Slave Transmitter

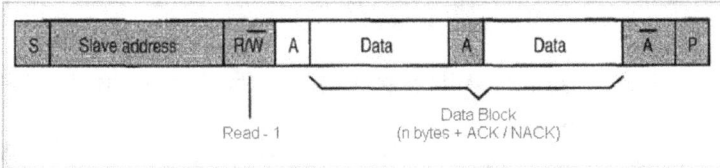

Algorithm:

Master Device:
1. The user generates a Start condition by setting the Start Enable bit, SEN (SSPCON2<0>).
2. SSPIF is set. The MSSP module will wait the required start time before any other operation takes place.
3. The user loads the SSPBUF with the slave address to transmit.
4. The address is shifted out the SDA pin until all eight bits are transmitted.
5. The MSSP module shifts in the ACK bit from the slave device and writes its value into the SSPCON2 register (SSPCON2<6>).
6. The MSSP module generates an interrupt at the end of the ninth clock cycle by setting the SSPIF bit.
7. The user loads the SSPBUF with eight bits of data.
8. Data is shifted out the SDA pin until all eight bits are transmitted.

9. The MSSP module shifts in the ACK bit from the slave device and writes its value into the SSPCON2 register (SSPCON2<6>).
10. The MSSP module generates an interrupt at the end of the ninth clock cycle by setting the SSPIF bit.
11. The user generates a Stop condition by setting the Stop Enable bit, PEN (SSPCON2<2>).

Slave Device:
1. Set the I2C Pins to input mode (High-Impedance). Both SCL, SDA are set to input.
2. Set the address of slave unit by writing it to the SSPADD register.
3. Disable Slew Rate control (For standard mode operation).
4. Select and Enable I2C Slave mode operation for the MSSP module.
5. Enable The SSP Interrupts Signals.

ISR:
1. Check the overflow and write collusion flag bits. If they are set, clear the flags.
2. Release the clock and write the SSPBUF value into the PORT register for display if R_nW bit is reset.
3. If R_nW bit is set, write the PORT register value into the SSPBUF register for the transmission.
4. The Buffer Full bit, BF, is set.
5. Clear the SSPIF.

Program:
// *Transfer data from the Master device to Slave device*
// *Master Transmitter:*
```
#pragma config FOSC = HS, WDTE = OFF, PWRTE = OFF, BOREN = OFF, LVP = OFF, CPD = OFF, WRT = OFF, CP = OFF
#include <xc.h>
#define _XTAL_FREQ 20000000
#define I2C_BaudRate 100000         // I2C Baud Rate = 100 Kbps
void I2C_Master_Init(void);         // Function declarations
void I2C_Wait(void);
```

```c
void I2C_Start(void);
void I2C_Stop(void);
void I2C_Restart(void);
void I2C_ACK(void);
void I2C_NACK(void);
I2C_Write(unsigned char Data);

void main()                        // Main function
{
  unsigned char i=0;
  TRISD3 = 0;                      // RD3 as output port
  RD3 = 0;                         // Clear RD3
  I2C_Master_Init();               // Calling Master_Init function
  while(1)
  {
    I2C_Start();                   // Releasing I2C Start Condition
    I2C_Write(0x40);               // Writing I2C Slave Device Address + Write mode (0)
    I2C_Write(i++);                // Sending data
    I2C_NACK();                    // Releasing I2C NACK Condition
    I2C_Stop();                    // Releasing I2C Stop Condition
    __delay_ms(200);
    RD3 = ~RD3;                    // Toggle LED at RD3
  }
}
void I2C_Master_Init()             // I2C master initialization
{
  // SSPM3:SSPM0: 1000 = I2C Master mode, clock = FOSC/(4 * (SSPADD + 1))
  SSPCON = 0x28;                   // Enable SSP & set SSPM3:SSPM0 bits
  SSPCON2 = 0x00;                  // Clear all I2C signal conditions
  SSPSTAT = 0x80;                  // Slew rate disabled
  SSPADD = ((_XTAL_FREQ/4)/I2C_BaudRate) - 1;
  TRISC3 = 1;                      // SCL and SDA are configured as inputs
  TRISC4 = 1;
  SSPIF = 0;                       // Clear SSPIF
```

```c
}
void I2C_Idle()
{
   while ((SSPSTAT & 0x04) || (SSPCON2 & 0x1F));
}
void I2C_Start()                    // Releasing I2C Start Condition
{
   I2C_Idle();
   SEN = 1;
   while(SEN);
}
void I2C_Stop()                     // Releasing I2C Stop Condition
{
   I2C_Idle();
   PEN = 1;
   while(PEN);
}
void I2C_Restart()                  // Releasing I2C Restart Condition
{
   I2C_Idle();
   RSEN = 1;
   while(RSEN);
}
void I2C_ACK(void)                  // Releasing ACK Condition
{
   I2C_Idle();
   ACKDT = 0;
   ACKEN = 1;
}
void I2C_NACK(void)                 // Releasing NACK Condition
{
   I2C_Idle();
   ACKDT = 1;
   ACKEN = 1;
```

}
```
I2C_Write(unsigned char Data)    // Sending Data
{
   I2C_Idle();
   SSPBUF = Data;
   while(!SSPIF);                 // wait until SSPIF
   SSPIF = 0;
}
unsigned char I2C_Read(unsigned char Data)    // Read Data
{
   RCEN = 1;
   while(!BF);
   SSPIF = 0;
   return SSPBUF;                 // Return received data
}
```

// *Slave Receiver:*
```
#pragma config FOSC = HS, WDTE = OFF, PWRTE = OFF, BOREN = OFF, LVP = OFF, CPD = OFF, WRT = OFF, CP = OFF
#include <xc.h>
#define _XTAL_FREQ 20000000
#define ReceivedData    PORTD
#define DataToTX        PORTC
void I2C_Slave_Init(unsigned char);

void main(void) {                 // Main function
   TRISD = 0x00;                  // Configure PORTD as output
   ReceivedData = 0x00;
   I2C_Slave_Init(0x40);          // Initiate I2C Slave with slave address 0x40
   while(1);                      // End
}
void __interrupt() I2C_Slave(void)    // ISR for Slave Read operation
{
unsigned char Dmy;
```

```c
    if(SSPIF)                          // Check SSPIF is set
    {
      CKP = 0;                         // Hold clock
      if(SSPOV || WCOL)                //Overflow OR Write Collision Check
      {
        SSPOV = 0;                     // Clear Overflow flag
        WCOL = 0;                      // Clear WCOL
        CKP = 1;                       // Release Clock
      }
      if(!D_nA && !R_nW)               // Check valid data & Slave receive
      {
        Dmy = SSPBUF;                  // Dummy Read
        while(!BF);                    // Wait until receive complete
        ReceivedData = SSPBUF;         // Read the Buffer data
        CKP = 1;                       // Release Clock
      }
      else if (!D_nA && R_nW){
        Dmy = SSPBUF;                  // Read the last byte to Clear the Buffer
        BF = 0;                        // Clear BF flag
        SSPBUF = DataToTX;             // Write Data to Buffer
        CKP = 1;                       // Release Clock
        while(BF);                     // wait to write data on I2C bus
      }
    SSPIF = 0;
    }
}

void I2C_Slave_Init(unsigned char Address)
{
    SSPADD = Address;                  // Set the I2C Slave Device Address
    SSPSTAT = 0x80;                    // 1 = Slew rate control disabled
    // Serial Port Enable & Release clock & 0110 = I2C Slave mode, 7-bit address
    SSPCON = 0x36;
    SSPCON2 = 0x01;                    // 1 = Clock stretching is enabled
```

```
TRISC3 = 1;            // SCL Set to Input
TRISC4 = 1;            // SDA Set to Input
GIE = 1;               // Enable Interrupts
PEIE = 1;
SSPIF = 0;
SSPIE = 1;
}
```

Circuit Diagram:

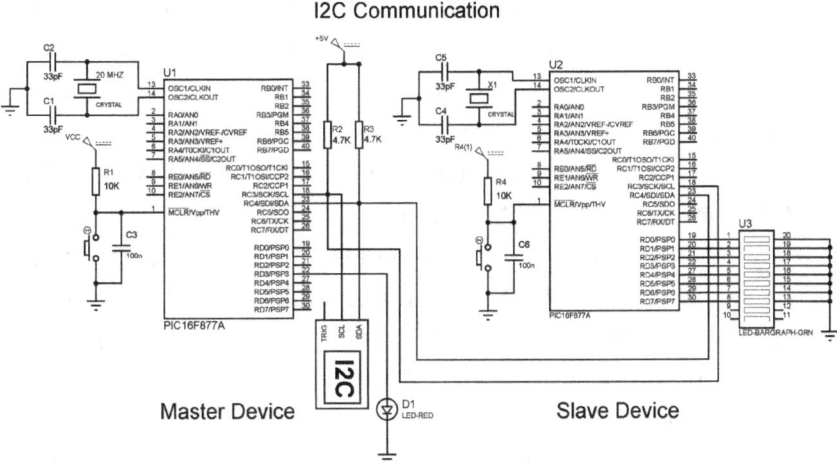

I2C Communication

Master Device — Slave Device

Conclusion:

Thus the two PIC16F877A Microcontrollers have been interfacing using I2C protocol and sent the data from master device to slave device.

53. INTERFACING RTC USING I2C PROTOCOL

Aim:

Write an Embedded C Program to interface RTC with the PIC16F877A/887 Microcontroller using I2C protocol and display the time and date on LCD.

Hardware and Software Used:
- PIC16F877 Microcontroller Development Board, RTC DS3231 Module and LCD module
- MPLAB X IDE v6.05 & Compiler XC8 v2.40

Theory:

RTC DS3231 Module:

Real Time Clock or RTC is a timekeeping device in the form of an Integrated Circuit. The DS3231 is Precise Real-Time Clock IC developed by Maxim Integrated. The DS3231 RTC Module is a low-cost, extremely accurate I²C real-time clock with an integrated temperature-compensated crystal oscillator (TCXO) and crystal so no need to connect an external crystal. The device incorporates a battery input and maintains accurate timekeeping when main power to the device is interrupted. Almost all the modules having 24C32N IC, it is an EEPROM IC of 32Kb size. Both RTC and EEPROM ICs are interfaced through I2C Protocol; both I2C Devices can act as slaves. A 3V CR2032 Lithium Battery is connected to the RTC IC to keep the clock ticking. In the DS3231 Module, there is a provision to connect a battery on the back.

The RTC provides seconds, minutes, hours, day, date, month, and year information. The date at the end of the month is automatically adjusted for months with fewer than 31 days, including corrections for leap year. The clock operates in either the 24-hour or 12-hour format with an AM/PM indicator. The internal registers are accessible though I2C bus interfaces. The bus must be controlled by a master device that generates the serial clock (SCL), controls the bus access, and generates the START and STOP conditions. The DS3231 operates as a slave on the I2C bus.

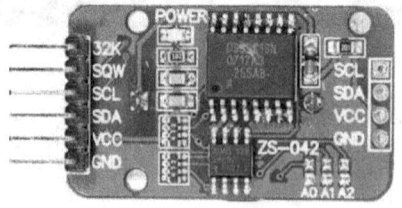

DS3231 is a six terminal device,
VCC   - Connected to positive of power source (+5V).
GND   - Connected to ground.
SDA   - Serial Data pin (I2C interface)
SCL   - Serial Clock pin (I2C interface)
SQW   - Square Wave output pin
32K   - 32K oscillator output

The DS3231 requires four connections: SDA, SCL, VCC and GND.
DS3231 RTC
- The write address is 11010000 (0xD0)
- The read address is 11010001 (0xD1)

AT24C32 EEPROM
- The write address is 10101110 (0xAE)
- The read address is 10101111 (0xAF)

The I2C bus conditions are:

Bus not busy: Both data and clock lines remain high.

START data transfer: A change in the state of the data line from high to low, while the clock line is high, defines a START condition.

STOP data transfer: A change in the state of the data line from low to high, while the clock line is high, defines a STOP condition.

Data valid: The state of the data line represents valid data when, after a START condition, the data line is stable for the duration of the high period of the clock signal. The data on the line must be changed during the low period of the clock signal. There is one clock pulse per bit of data.

Acknowledge: Each receiving device, when addressed, is obliged to generate acknowledge after the reception of each byte. The master device must generate an extra clock pulse, which is associated with this acknowledge bit. A device that acknowledges must pull down the SDA line during the acknowledge clock pulse.

Data transfer from a master transmitter to a slave receiver:

The first byte transmitted by the master is the slave address. Next follows a number of data bytes. The slave returns an acknowledge bit after each received byte. Data is transferred with the most significant bit (MSB) first. The master generates the START condition and then release the slave address byte 0xD0. The 7-bit slave address (1101000) followed by the direction bit (R/W), which is **0** for a write. The DS3231 slave decodes it and releases acknowledge condition on SDA. After the DS3231's acknowledgement, the master transmits a word address to the DS3231. The word-address sets the register pointer on the DS3231. For the seconds, it is 0x00 for without alarm and 0x07 for with alarm. The register pointer increment after each data byte is transferred. The master generates a STOP condition to terminate the data write.

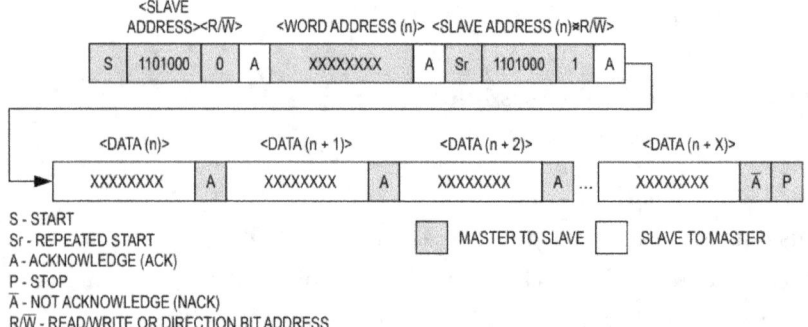

Data transfer from a slave transmitter to a master receiver:

The first byte (the slave address) is transmitted by the master. The slave then returns an acknowledge bit. Next follows a number of data bytes transmitted by the slave to the master. The master returns an acknowledge bit after received byte. At the end of the last received byte, a not acknowledge is returned. After start condition or repeat start condition, the master will release the slave address to read data from slave DS3231. The 7-bit slave address (1101000), followed by the direction bit (R/W), which is 1 for a read. It is 0xD1. After decoding the slave address byte, the DS3231 release an acknowledgement on SDA. Then DS3231 begins to transmit data starting with the register pointer.

Algorithm:

Step 1:

Initially, set the clock and calendar values, then RTC always keeps updating this clock and calendar values. The steps to set clock and calendar values of RTC DS3231 are as follows,

- Initialize PIC16F877A MCU as a master device for I2C communication.
- Master device generates start condition on I2C bus.
- Master device place the DS3231 RTC's device address 0xD0 for master transmitter.
- Master device needs to wait for slave acknowledgement.
- Then, Send the DS3231's register address of Seconds which is 0x00, after the slave acknowledgement master device sends the value of seconds to write in RTC. RTC address gets auto incremented, accordingly master sends the next values of minutes, hours, day, date, month and year to the slave.
- Finally, master device generates stop condition to release the I2C bus.

Step2:

To read the Time and Date value from RTC DS1307,

- Start the I2C communication by releasing start condition on I2C bus, followed by the master device release the slave device address. It is 0xD0 to set master as a transmitter.
- Master device needs to wait for slave acknowledgement.
- Then write the DS1307's register pointer from where we have to read the data ('0x00' to get data from seconds register).
- Master device needs to wait for slave acknowledgement.
- Then master device releases the repeat start condition with slave address. Now it is 0xD1 to set slave as a transmitter.
- Now master device read the DS1307's data with acknowledgment from location 0x00.
- The last location always read with the negative acknowledgment, the master device will understand this is the last data to read from the DS1307.
- Finally, master device generates stop condition to release the I2C bus.

Program:

```c
#pragma config FOSC = HS, WDTE = OFF, PWRTE = OFF, BOREN = OFF, LVP = OFF, CPD = OFF, WRT = OFF, CP = OFF
#include <xc.h>
#define _XTAL_FREQ 20000000
#define RS RD2              //Define the LCD pins
#define EN RD3
#define D4 RD4
#define D5 RD5
#define D6 RD6
#define D7 RD7
//Set the current value of date and time variables
unsigned char sec = 00;
unsigned char min = 30;
unsigned char hour = 01;
unsigned char date = 14;
unsigned char month = 05;
unsigned char year = 20;
#include "lcd4bit_head.h"    // Include header files
#include "I2C.h"
#include "DS3231.h"

void main()                  // Main function
{
unsigned char sec_0, sec_1, min_0, min_1, hour_0, hour_1, date_0, date_1, month_0, month_1, year_0, year_1;
TRISD = 0x00;                // Make Port D as output port for LCD
lcd_init();                  // To initialize 16x2 LCD in 4-bit mode
I2C_init(100);               // To initialize I2C Master with 100KHz clock
Set_Time_Date();             //set time and date on the RTC module
while(1)
{
sec_0 = sec%10;              //Split the character for the LCD
sec_1 = (sec/10);
```

```c
min_0 = min%10;
min_1 = min/10;
hour_0 = hour%10;
hour_1 = hour/10;
date_0 = date%10;
date_1 = date/10;
month_0 = month%10;
month_1 = month/10;
year_0 = year%10;
year_1 = year/10;

//Read the current date and time from RTC module
Update_Current_Date_Time();
lcd_cmd(0x01);                    //Display the Time on the LCD screen at line 1
lcd_cmd(0x80);
lcd_display("TIME: ");
lcd_data(hour_1+'0');
lcd_data(hour_0+'0');
lcd_data(':');
lcd_data(min_1+'0');
lcd_data(min_0+'0');
lcd_data(':');
lcd_data(sec_1+'0');
lcd_data(sec_0+'0');
lcd_cmd(0xC0);                    //Display the Date on the LCD screen at line 2
lcd_display("DATE: ");
lcd_data(date_1+'0');
lcd_data(date_0+'0');
lcd_data(':');
lcd_data(month_1+'0');
lcd_data(month_0+'0');
lcd_data(':');
lcd_data(year_1+'0');
lcd_data(year_0+'0');
```

```c
    __delay_ms(50);
  }
}
```

`//#include "I2C.h"`   // *Header for I2C protocol*

```c
void I2C_init(const unsigned long MasClk)        //Begin IIC as master
{
  TRISC3 = 1;                   //Set SDA and SCL lines as input ports
  TRISC4 = 1;
  //SSPEN=1: Enable synchronous serial port & SSPM0-SSPM3: 1000 for master mode
  SSPCON  = 0b00101000;
  SSPCON2 = 0x00;               // Clear all I2C conditions
  //Setting Clock Speed
  SSPADD = (_XTAL_FREQ/(4*MasClk*100))-1;
  SSPSTAT = 0x00;               //Clear MSSP Status Register
}

void I2C_MasterWait()
{
//Transmission in progress
  while (  (SSPCON2 & 0b00011111)  ||  (SSPSTAT & 0b00000100)  ) ;
}

void I2C_StartCondition()
{
  I2C_MasterWait ();             // Check I2C bus free
  SEN = 1;                       // Initiate start condition
}

void I2C_StopCondition()
{
  I2C_MasterWait ();
  PEN = 1;                       //Initiate stop condition
}
```

```c
void I2C_MasterWrite(unsigned data)
{
  I2C_MasterWait ();
  SSPBUF = data;                // Write data to SSPBUF
}

unsigned short I2C_MasterRead(unsigned short ak)
{
  unsigned short t1;
  I2C_MasterWait ();
  RCEN = 1;                     // Receive enable
   I2C_MasterWait ();
  t1 = SSPBUF;                  // Read data from SSPBUF
  I2C_MasterWait ();
  ACKDT = (ak) ? 0 : 1;         //check if acknowledge bit received
  ACKEN = 1;                    // Acknowledge sequence
  return t1;
}
```

```c
//#include "DS3231.h"            //Header for DS3231 RTC module

int  BCD_2_DEC(int c1)           // Convert BCD to Decimal
{
  return (c1 >> 4) * 10 + (c1 & 0x0F);
}

int DEC_2_BCD (int c2)           // Convert Decimal to BCD
{
  return ((c2 / 10) << 4) + (c2 % 10);
}

void Set_Time_Date()             // Setting Time and Date
{
  I2C_StartCondition ();         // Release start condition
  I2C_MasterWrite (0xD0);        // Write slave address for master transmitter
```

```c
    I2C_MasterWrite (0);                    // Register pointer for seconds
    I2C_MasterWrite (DEC_2_BCD(sec));       //update sec
    I2C_MasterWrite (DEC_2_BCD(min));       //update min
    I2C_MasterWrite (DEC_2_BCD(hour));      //update hour
    I2C_MasterWrite (1);
    I2C_MasterWrite (DEC_2_BCD(date));      //update date
    I2C_MasterWrite (DEC_2_BCD(month));     //update month
    I2C_MasterWrite (DEC_2_BCD(year));      //update year
    I2C_StopCondition();
}

void Update_Current_Date_Time()
{
    I2C_StartCondition ();                  // Start condition with slave select
    I2C_MasterWrite (0xD0);
    I2C_MasterWrite (0);
    I2C_StopCondition();
    //Read Slave data bytes
    I2C_StartCondition ();
    I2C_MasterWrite (0xD1);                 // Initialize master receiver
    sec = BCD_2_DEC(I2C_MasterRead (1));    // Read Time registers
    min = BCD_2_DEC(I2C_MasterRead (1));
    hour = BCD_2_DEC(I2C_MasterRead (1));
    I2C_MasterRead (1);
    date = BCD_2_DEC(I2C_MasterRead (1));   // Read Date registers
    month = BCD_2_DEC(I2C_MasterRead (1));
    year = BCD_2_DEC(I2C_MasterRead (1));
    I2C_StopCondition();
    I2C_StartCondition ();                  //END Reading
    I2C_MasterWrite (0xD1);
    I2C_MasterRead (1);
    I2C_StopCondition();
}
```

Circuit Diagram:

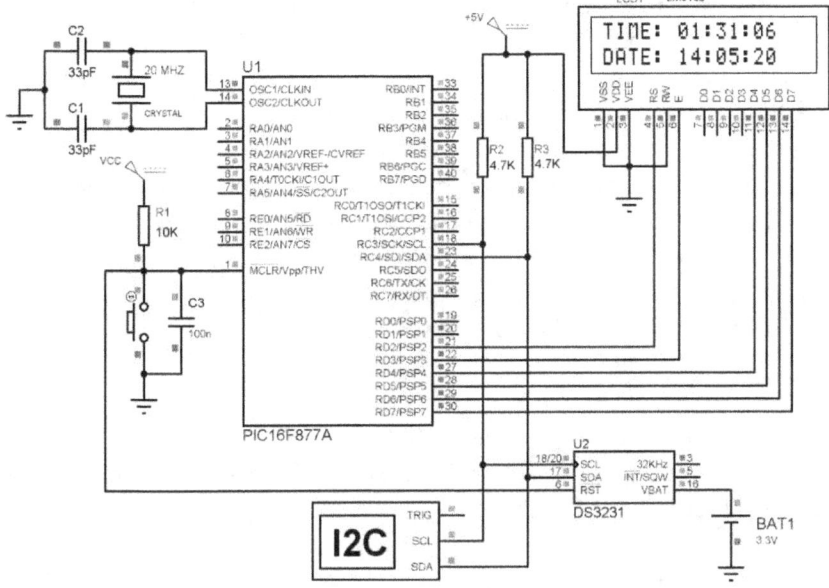

Conclusion:

Thus the RTC module has interfaced with the PIC16F877A Microcontroller using I2C protocol and displayed the time and date on LCD.

54.	SPI COMMUNICATION

Aim:

Write an Embedded C Program to transfer the data between two PIC16F877A/887 Microcontrollers using SPI protocol.

Hardware and Software Used:
- PIC16F877A Microcontroller Development Board
- MPLAB X IDE v6.05 & Compiler XC8 v2.40

Theory:

SPI communication is serial peripheral interface protocol. SPI protocol was developed and proposed by Motorola in the 1970s. In this system, one device acts as the master and other devices in the network as slaves. The master device will initiate the communication and also provide the clock signal to the slave devices. The Master Synchronous Serial Port (MSSP) on-chip module is dedicated for the synchronous protocols: SPI and I2C.

SPI is 4-wire full duplex synchronous serial communication whereas I2C protocol is half duplex (2-wire protocol). To accomplish communication, typically four lines are used:
- Serial Clock (SCK) – RC3/SCK/SCL
- Serial Data In (SDI) – RC4/SDI/SDA
- Serial Data Out (SDO) – RC5/SDO
- Slave Select (SS) – RA5/AN4/SS/C2OUT

The MSSP registers used in PIC16F877A for the SPI communication are SSPSTAT and the SSPCON.

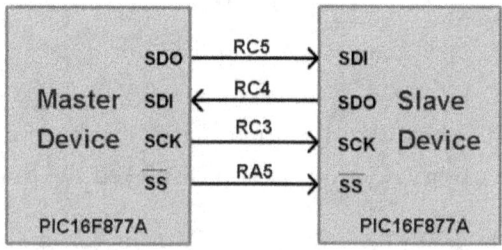

SPI allows 8 bit of data to be synchronously transmitted and received simultaneously. The data transmission is done through SDO (serial data output) line and the data reception is done through the SDI (serial data input) line. A clock (SCK) is generated by the master device using one the four options.

0011 = SPI Master mode, clock = TMR2 output/2
0010 = SPI Master mode, clock = FOSC/64
0001 = SPI Master mode, clock = FOSC/16
0000 = SPI Master mode, clock = FOSC/4

It controls the data transfer rate between the master and slave devices. Master selects the slave device using SS (slave select) line. When multiple slaves are used, GPIO pins of master device are used to select slave devices. The SSPSR shifts the data in and out of the device, MSB first.

Master Transmitter and Slave Receiver:

Master Device Initialization
1. Configure the IO pins for SPI Master Mode.
   TRISC3 = 0;   // SCK -> 0 in master mode
   TRISC4 = 1;   // SDI -> Input
   TRISC5 = 0;   // SDO -> Output
   ADCON1 = 0x07;   // Set PORTA as digital port
   TRISA5 = 0;   // SS as a output
2. Set the SPI master mode and Set the desired Clock Rate FOSC/64 = 312.5 KBs
   SSPM3 = 0; SSPM2 = 0; SSPM1 = 1; SSPM0 = 0;
3. Enable the Synchronous Serial Port and disable slave select (active low)
   SSPEN = 1;
   RA5 = 1;   // Disable slave select
4. Configure the Serial Clock Polarity (Rising edge)
   CKP = 0;   // 0 = Idle state for clock is a low level
   CKE = 0;   // 0 = Transmit occurs on transition from Idle to active clock state
5. Configure when the input data is sampled at the Middle
   SMP = 0;   // 0 = Input data sampled at middle of data output time
6. Enable SPI Transmission Interrupts (if needed)
   SSPIE = 1;   PEIE = 1;   GIE = 1;

Slave Device Initialization
1. Configure the IO pins for SPI Master Mode.
   TRISC3 = 1;   // SCK -> 1 in slave mode
   TRISC4 = 1;   // SDI -> Input
   TRISC5 = 0;   // SDO -> Output
   ADCON1 = 0x07;   // Set PORTA as digital port
   TRISA5 = 1;   // SS as a input
2. Set the MSSP module in SPI Slave Mode
   // 0100 = SPI Slave mode, clock = SCK pin. SS pin control enabled.
   SSPM3 = 0;   SSPM2 = 1;   SSPM1 = 0;   SSPM0 = 0;
2. Enable the Synchronous Serial Port and disable slave select
   SSPEN = 1;
   RA5 = 1;
3. Configure the Serial Clock Polarity (Rising Edge)
   CKP = 0;   CKE = 0;
4. Clear the SMP Bit

SMP = 0;
5. Enable SPI Reception Interrupts (Recommended)
SSPIE = 1;   PEIE = 1;   GIE = 1;

Algorithm:

// *For the Master Transmitter*
1. Configure the PIC16F877A as a master device.
2. Enable slave select using RA5.
3. Write the data on SPI bus.
4. Call delay for 500 ms.
5. Disable slave select using RA5.
6. Repeat the steps from step 2.

// *For the Slave Receiver*
1. Configure the PIC16F877A as a slave device.
2. Set PORTB as output port.
3. Read SPI bus and move the received data to PORTB.
4. Repeat the step 3.

// *Header file: "spi1.h"*
SPI_Master_Init()
1. Configure the IO pins for SPI Master Mode.
2. Set the SPI master mode and Set the desired Clock Rate FOSC/64 = 312.5 KBs.
3. Enable the Synchronous Serial Port and disable slave select (active low).
4. Configure the Serial Clock Polarity (Rising edge).
5. Configure when the input data is sampled at the Middle.
6. Enable SPI Transmission Interrupts (if needed).

SPI_Slave_Init()
1. Configure the IO pins for SPI Slave Mode.
2. Set the MSSP module in SPI Slave Mode.
3. Enable the Synchronous Serial Port and disable slave select.

4. Configure the Serial Clock Polarity (Rising Edge).
5. Enable SPI Reception Interrupts (Recommended).

SPI_Write(unsigned char)
1. Clear write collision detect flag.
2. Clear flag.
3. Load Buffer Register.
4. Wait until set SSPIF.

SPI_ReceiveWait()
Wait for 1 = Receive complete.

SPI_Read()
1. Copy flush data in SSBUF.
2. Wait until the all bits receive.
3. Return the received data from the buffer.

Program:
// *Master Transmitter*
```
#pragma config FOSC = HS, WDTE = OFF, PWRTE = OFF, BOREN = OFF, LVP = OFF, CPD = OFF, WRT = OFF, CP = OFF
#include <xc.h>
#define _XTAL_FREQ 20000000
#include "spi1.h"                  // Include header file
void main() {                      // Main function
    unsigned char i;
    SPI_Master_Init();             // Initializing master device for SPI
    while (1) {                    // Forever loop
        RA5 = 0;                   // Enable slave select
        for(i=0; i<16; i++){
            SPI_Write(i);          // Write data on SPI bus
            __delay_ms(500);
        }
        RA5 = 1;                   // Disable slave select
```

```c
    }
}
```

// *Slave Receiver*
```c
#pragma config FOSC = HS, WDTE = OFF, PWRTE = OFF, BOREN = OFF, LVP = OFF, CPD = OFF, WRT = OFF, CP = OFF
#include <xc.h>
#define _XTAL_FREQ 20000000
#define output PORTB
#include "spi1.h"                  // Include header file
void main() {                      // Main function
    SPI_Slave_Init();              // Initializing slave device for SPI
    TRISB = 0x00;
    while (1) {                    // Forever loop
        output = SPI_Read();       // Read SPI bus and display it in PORTB
    }
}
```

// *Header file: "spi1.h"*
```c
void SPI_Master_Init()
{
//Configure the IO pins for SPI Master Mode.
TRISC3 = 0;          // SCK -> 0 in master mode
TRISC4 = 1;          // SDI -> Input
TRISC5 = 0;          // SDO -> Output
ADCON1 = 0x07;       // Set PORTA as digital port
TRISA5 = 0;          // SS as a output
//Set the SPI master mode and Set the desired Clock Rate FOSC/64 = 312.5 KBs
SSPM3 = 0; SSPM2 = 0; SSPM1 = 1; SSPM0 = 0;
//Enable the Synchronous Serial Port and disable slave select (active low)
SSPEN = 1;
RA5 = 1;             // Disable slave select
//Configure the Serial Clock Polarity (Rising edge)
CKP = 0;             // 0 = Idle state for clock is a low level
```

```c
CKE = 0;         // 0 = Transmit occurs on transition from Idle to active clock state
//Configure when the input data is sampled at the Middle
SMP = 0;         // 0 = Input data sampled at middle of data output time
//Enable SPI Transmission Interrupts (if needed)
// SSPIE = 1;    PEIE = 1;       GIE = 1;
__delay_ms(100);
}


void SPI_Slave_Init()
{
//Configure the IO pins for SPI Slave Mode.
TRISC3 = 1;                  // SCK -> 1 in slave mode
TRISC4 = 1;                  // SDI -> Input
TRISC5 = 0;                  // SDO -> Output
ADCON1 = 0x07;               // Set PORTA as digital port
TRISA5 = 1;                  // SS as a input
//Set the MSSP module in SPI Slave Mode
// 0100 = SPI Slave mode, clock = SCK pin. SS pin control enabled.
SSPM3 = 0;     SSPM2 = 1;     SSPM1 = 0;     SSPM0 = 0;
//Enable the Synchronous Serial Port and disable slave select
SSPEN = 1;
RA5 = 1;
//Configure the Serial Clock Polarity (Rising Edge)
CKP = 0;       CKE = 0;
// Clear the SMP Bit
SMP = 0;
// Enable SPI Reception Interrupts (Recommended)
//SSPIE = 1;    PEIE = 1;       GIE = 1;
__delay_ms(100);
}


void SPI_Write(unsigned char Data1)
{
  if (WCOL == 1){              // Clear write collision detect flag
  WCOL = 0;
```

```
}
    SSPIF = 0;                    // Clear flag
    SSPBUF = Data1;               // Load Buffer Register
    while(!SSPIF);                // Wait until set SSPIF
}

static void SPI_ReceiveWait() {
    while ( !BF );                // Wait for 1 = Receive complete
}

char SPI_Read()
{
    SSPBUF=0xff;                  // Copy flush data in SSBUF
    SPI_ReceiveWait();            // wait until the all bits receive
    return(SSPBUF);               // Return the received data from the buffer
}
```

Circuit Diagram:

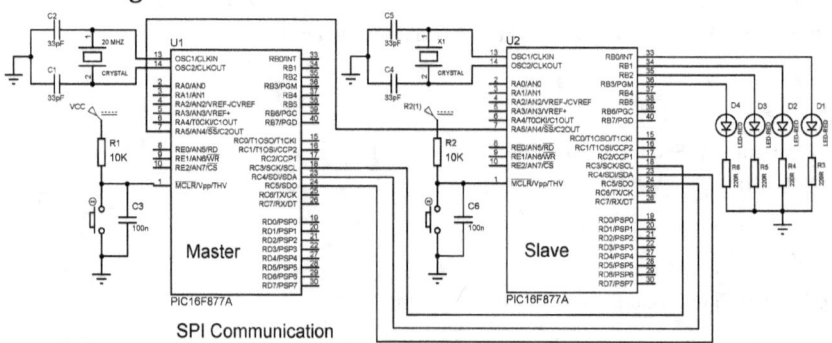

SPI Communication

Conclusion:

Thus the Embedded C program for SPI communication between two PIC16F877A Microcontrollers has been written and executed. The data transmitted by the master is received in slave and displayed it in PORTB.

55. INTERFACING ESP8266 WI-FI MODULE

Aim:

To design an IoT based temperature monitoring system using ESP8266 Wi-Fi Module and the PIC16F887 Microcontroller.

Hardware and Software Used:
- PIC16F887 Microcontroller Development Board, ESP8266 Wi-Fi Module, 16x2 LCD Module and LM35 Sensor
- MPLAB X IDE v6.05 & Compiler XC8 v2.40

Theory:

ESP8266 is a WiFi Module based on Cadence Tensilica L106 32-bit MCU manufactured by Espressif Systems. The ESP8266 SoC contains a fully functional Wi-Fi Stack and TCP/IP Stack that allows any Microcontroller to get connected to Wi-Fi Network. The ESP8266's on-chip Microcontroller can be directly programmed, without the need of external programmer.

The several third party manufacturers have designed the ESP8266 SoC based custom boards and one such manufacturer is Ai-Thinker. The Ai-Thinker's ESP-01 module is used in this experiment. It consists of 8 pins.

VCC:	3.3V power supply pin
GND:	Power ground pin
TX:	This pin transmits serial data to other device
RX:	This receives serial data from other device
RST:	It is an active low Reset pin
CH_PD:	This is an active high chip enable pin
GPIO0:	The General Purpose I/O 0 pin has dual functions – one for normal GPIO operation and other for enabling the programming mode of ESP8266
GPIO2:	The General Purpose I/O 2 pin

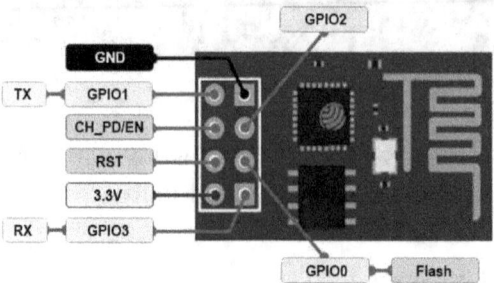

The ESP8266 runs on 3.3V while the PIC runs on 5 V. Therefore, the voltage level converter circuit (5V to 3.3V) need to be used in Rx line of ESP8266 module. This circuit need not to be used in Tx line because the PIC can recognize 3.3V as logic '1'.

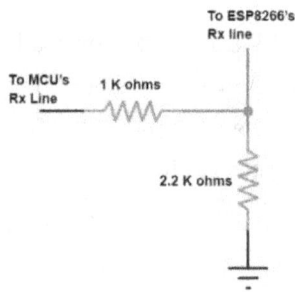

Establishing the PIC16F887 Internet Connection:

The ESP8266 modules comes with a default firmware, hence the module can be programmed using AT commands. These commands are send through a serial communication channel. The USART in the PIC microcontroller is used to establish serial communication between the PIC MCU and the ESP8266 module.

Commonly used AT Commands are,

AT	Test AT startup
AT+RST	Restart module
AT+RESTORE	Factory Reset
ATE	ATE0: Switch echo off
AT+UART_DEF=<baudrate>,<databits>,<stopbits>,<parity>,<flow control>	AT+UART_DEF=115200,8,1,0,0 to make it definite and get it saved in the flash memory

AT+CWMODE_DEF=3	Set the module to "SoftAP+Station mode"
AT+CWJAP_DEF=<ssid>,<pwd>	AT+CWJAP_DEF="abc","0123459"
AT+CWLIF	This command is used to get the IP of stations
AT+CWAUTOCONN	ESP8266 station will connect to AP automatically when power on
Enable/Disable DHCP and save to flash AT+CWDHCP_DEF=<mode>,<en>	AT+CWDHCP_DEF= 2, 1 2 : set both softAP and station 1 : Enable DHCP
Set IP address of ESP8266 station AT+CIPSTA=<IP>[,<gateway>,<netmask>]	AT+CIPSTA="192.168.6.100","192.168.6.1","255.255.255.0"
Set IP address of ESP8266 softAP, save to Flash AT+CIPAP_DEF=<IP>[,<gateway>,<netmask>]	AT+CIPAP_DEF="192.168.5.1","192.168.5.1","255.255.255.0"
Start SmartConfig AT+CWSTARTSMART	AT+CWMODE=1 AT+CWSTARTSMART
Stop SmartConfig AT+CWSTOPSMART	AT+CWSTOPSMART
AT-CIPMUX=0	Enables single connection mode
Establish TCP connection or register UDP port, start connection AT+CIPSTART=<type>,<remote IP>,<remote port>[,<UDP local port>,<UDP mode>][,<TCP keep alive>]	AT+CIPSTART="TCP","192.168.101.110",1000
Send data AT+CIPSEND=<length>	AT+CIPSEND=4 // set date length which will be sent, such as 4 bytes
Close TCP or UDP connection AT+CIPCLOSE=<link ID>	AT+CIPCLOSE=0 // Delete NO.0 connection.
Configure as TCP server AT+CIPSERVER=<mode>[,<port>]	AT+CIPSERVER=1,80 The '1' creates a server and listens to port 80.

ESP8266 Wi-Fi module is used here to connect MCU with Wi-Fi network and upload temperature data to ThingSpeak. ThingSpeak is an open source Internet of Things (IoT) application and API to store and retrieve data from things over the Internet. It enables to collect, store, analyze, and visualize the data. Sign in to www.thingspeak.com and then create own channel by creating a field. After saving the channel, we will get channel ID and two API keys - a write API key and a read API key (it is used to check the data from website)

The temperature data from LM35 sensor is fed to pin 2 (RA0) of PIC16F887 Microcontroller. This data is given to ESP8266 Wi-Fi module and it is transmitted to the ThingSpeak Cloud platform. The temperature data can be accessed on a remote device like a smartphone or laptop using ThingSpeak website. An LCD is also used as a user interface device to see circuit configuration status and temperature data.

ThingSpeak API – Keywords:

- Channel – The name for where data can be inserted or retrieved within the ThingSpeak API, identified by a numerical Channel ID
- Field – One of eight specific locations for data inside of a channel, identified by a number between 1 to 8 – A field can store numeric data from sensors or alphanumeric strings from serial devices or RFID readers
- Status – A short status message to augment the data stored in a channel
- Location – The latitude, longitude, and elevation of where data is being sent from
- Feed – The collective name for the data stored inside a channel, which may be any combination of field data, status updates, and location info
- Write API Key – A 16-digit code that allows an application to write data to a channel
- Read API Key – A 16-digit code that allows an application to read the data stored in a channel

ThingSpeak - Addresses and Locations:
- Regular URL: http://api.thingspeak.com
- Secure URL: https://api.thingspeak.com
- IP Address: http://184.106.153.149
- Cross-domain XML: http://api.thingspeak.com/crossdomain.xml

Algorithm:
1. Initialize the PORTD for 16x2 LCD.
2. Declare the lcd4bit_head.h (lcd header file).
3. Declare the global variables – value[50], pos, sec.
4. Define the delay (unsigned int) function.
5. Define the ISR for serial port Rx.
6. Define transmit (unsigned char) function (using serial data).
7. Define transmit2 (unsigned char) function (using pointer variable).
8. Define transmit_string (unsigned char) function.
9. Define the delay1sec() function.
10. Define the lcd_write function to display the string from the specified character address.

Main function:
1. Set the direction of PORTD as output port.
2. Set the direction for Tx and Rx using TRISC.
3. Enable serial port receive interrupt.
4. Configure USART for asynchronous communication.
5. Configure the ADC for analog read at AN0.
6. Initialize the 16x2 LCD in 4-bit mode.
7. Display "IOT TEMP monitor" on LCD screen.
8. Send command AT to ESP8266.
9. Check the return from ESP8266.
10. If ESP8266 returns OK, continue the next step otherwise go to previous step.
11. Send command ATE0 to ESP8266.
12. Check the return from ESP8266.
13. If ESP8266 returns OK, continue the next step otherwise go to

previous step.
14. Send command AT+CWMODE=3 to ESP8266.
15. Check the return from ESP8266.
16. If ESP8266 returns OK, continue the next step otherwise go to previous step.
17. Send command AT+CIPMUX=1 to ESP8266.
18. Check the return from ESP8266.
19. If ESP8266 returns OK, continue the next step otherwise go to previous step.
20. Send command AT+CWJAP="TP-LINK_A6A8","password" to ESP8266.
21. Check the return from ESP8266.
22. If ESP8266 returns OK, continue the next step otherwise go to previous step.
23. Start AD Conversion (LM35 sensor connected at RA0/AN0).
24. Wait until the conversion over.
25. Display the ADC result on LCD.
26. After 30 secs, clear the LCD screen and display "Uploading" on screen.
27. Send the IP Address of Thingspeak.com to the ESP8266 - 184.106.153.149
28. Check the return from ESP8266.
29. If ESP8266 returns OK, continue the next step otherwise go to previous step.
30. Set the data length which will be sent to Thingspeak.com.
31. Check the return from ESP8266.
32. If ESP8266 returns OK, continue the next step otherwise go to previous step.
33. Update Thingspeak Channel using Write API Key.
34. Transmit the ADC value to the Cloud.
35. Close the Channel.
36. Repeat the steps from step 23.

Program:
#pragma config FOSC = HS, WDTE = OFF, PWRTE = OFF, BOREN =

OFF, LVP = OFF, CPD = OFF, WRT = OFF, CP = OFF
#include <xc.h>
#define _XTAL_FREQ 20000000
#define RS   RD2   // RD2 is named as RS
#define EN   RD3   // RD3 is named as EN
#define D4   RD4   // 4-bit mode (RD4-D4, RD5-D5
#define D5   RD5   // RD6-D6, RD7-D7)
#define D6   RD6
#define D7   RD7
#include "lcd4bit_head.h"   // Include header file
#include<string.h>
unsigned char value[50], pos;
unsigned char sec;

void delay(unsigned int a) {   // Delay subroutine
    while(a--);
}

void __interrupt() Serial()   // ISR
{
if(RCIF==1&&pos<28)
{
value[pos]=RCREG;
pos++;
RCIF=0;
}
}

void transmit(unsigned char x) // Serial data transmit 1
{
TXREG=x;
while(TRMT==0);
}

```c
void transmit2(unsigned char *ptr)        // Serial data transmit 2
{
int i=0;
pos=0;
while(ptr[i]!='\0')
   {
   transmit(ptr[i]);
   i++; delay(100);
   }
delay(10000);
}

void transmit_string(unsigned char *ptr)  // Serial data transmit 2
{
int i=0;
pos=0;
transmit(0x0d);
transmit(0x0d);
while(ptr[i]!='\0')
   {
   transmit(ptr[i]);
   i++; delay(100);
   }
transmit(0x0d);
transmit(0x0a);
delay(60000);
}

void clearVAL() {                         // Clear the values
char i;
for(i=0;i<30;i++)
value[i]=' ';
}
```

```c
void delay1sec()                        // Delay function for 1 sec
{
char i;
for(i=0;i<20;i++)
{
TMR1H=0x3a;
TMR1L=0xbb;
TMR1ON=1;
while(TMR1IF==0);
TMR1ON=0;
TMR1IF=0;
}
sec++;
}

void lcd_write(char *p,unsigned char x)  // LCD write function
{
 int hj=0;
 if(x!='0')
 lcd_cmd(x);
   while(p[hj]!='\0')
     {
     lcd_data(p[hj]);
     hj++;
     }
}

void main()                  // Main function
{
char i,x,flag;
unsigned int adc_val;
TRISD=0x00;                  // Set PORTD as output port
T1CON=0x00;                  // Clear T1CON
TRISC=0X80;                  // Set the direction for Tx and Rx pins
```

```c
delay(60000);
GIE=1;                          // Enable serial receive interrupt
RCIE=1;
PEIE=1;
SPBRG=0x19;                     // Set Baudrate (9600)
TXSTA=0x26;                     // Configure USART for receive and transmit
RCSTA=0x90;
TRISA = 0x01;                   // Analog pin AN0 as Input port
ADCON0 = 0x81;                  // Channel AN0, ADC Clock FOSC/64 & Turn ON ADC
ADCON1 = 0xCE;                  // Right justified, AN0 Analog port & VDD and VSS Ref.
delay(1000);
lcd_init();                     // Initializing 16x2 LCD
delay(60000);
lcd_write("IoT TEMP Monitor",0x80);
delay(60000);
delay(60000);
delay(60000);
lcd_cmd(0x01);                  // Clear LCD screen
```

//*Sending at Commands*

```c
clearVAL();                     //AT
lcd_write("AT",0x80);
transmit_string("AT");
while(1) {
x=strstr(&value,"OK");          // Check the returns from ESP8266
if(x-32<0)
   { lcd_write("ERROR1",0xc3);}
else
   { lcd_write("OK1   ",0xc3); break; }
}
delay(60000);
clearVAL();                     //ATE0
lcd_write("ATE0",0x80);
transmit_string("ATE0");
```

```c
while(1) {
x=strstr(&value,"OK");              // Check the returns from ESP8266
if(x-32<0)
  { lcd_write("ERROR2",0xc3);}
else
  { lcd_write("OK2   ",0xc3); break; }
}
delay(60000);

clearVAL();                         //AT+CWMODE=3
lcd_write("AT+CWMODE=3",0x80);
transmit_string("AT+CWMODE=3");
while(1) {
x=strstr(&value,"OK");              // Check the returns from ESP8266
if(x-32<0)
  { lcd_write("ERROR3",0xc3);}
else
  { lcd_write("OK3   ",0xc3); break; }
}
delay(60000);

clearVAL();                         //AT+CIPMUX=1
lcd_write("AT+CIPMUX=1",0x80);
transmit_string("AT+CIPMUX=1");
while(1) {
x=strstr(&value,"OK");              // Check the returns from ESP8266
if(x-32<0)
  { lcd_write("ERROR4",0xc3);}
else
  { lcd_write("OK4   ",0xc3); break; }
}
delay(60000);
clearVAL();                         //AT+CWJAP
lcd_write("connecting...",0x80);
```

```c
value[0]='\0';
//Connect to WIFI network
strcat(value,"AT+CWJAP=\"TP-LINK_A6A8\",\"password\"");
transmit_string(&value);
while(1)  {
x=strstr(&value,"OK");                    // Check the returns from ESP8266
if(x-32<0)
   { lcd_write("ERROR/WAIT",0xc3);}
else
   { lcd_write("OK5   ",0xc3); break; }
}
delay(60000);
lcd_cmd(0x01);
delay(2000);
lcd_write("TEMP:-",0x80);                 // Send "TEMP" to line1 of LCD
lcd_write("Upload after:",0xc0);          // Send "Upload after" to LCD line2
sec=0;

while(1)                                  // forever loop
{
GO=1;                                     // Start AD conversion
while(GO==1);                             // Wait until the conversion over
adc_val=((ADRESH<<8)+ADRESL)*4.88;
lcd_cmd(0x87);                            // Display the ADC value on LCD
lcd_data((adc_val/1000)+48);
lcd_data(((adc_val%1000)/100)+48);
lcd_data(((adc_val%100)/10)+48);
lcd_data('.');
lcd_data((adc_val%10)+48);
lcd_data('C');
adc_val=adc_val/10;
delay(20000);
delay1sec();
lcd_cmd(0xce);
```

```c
lcd_data((30-sec)/10+48);
lcd_data(((30-sec)%10)+48);

if(sec==30)   {
   lcd_cmd(0x01);                        // Clear screen
   delay(1000);
   delay(60000);
   lcd_write("Uploading...",0x80);       // Display "Uploading" on LCD
   clearVAL();
   value[0]='\0';
   //IP Address: http://184.106.153.149 to Thingspeak.com
   strcat(value,"AT+CIPSTART=4,\"TCP\",\"184.106.153.149\",80");
   transmit_string(&value);
   sec=0;
   delay(60000);
   delay(60000);
   delay(60000);
   delay(60000);
   while(1)  {
     x=strstr(&value,"OK");              // Check the returns from ESP8266
     if(x-32<0)
        { lcd_write("Error",0xc3); flag=0; break;}
     else
        { lcd_write("OK6  ",0xc3);flag=1; break; }
   }
     delay(10000);

  if(flag==1)
  {
   clearVAL();
   value[0]='\0';
   //Send No. of characters
   strcat(value,"AT+CIPSEND=4,46");      //Set data length which will be sent
   transmit_string(&value);
```

```c
    delay(60000);
    delay(60000);
    delay(60000);
    while(1)  {
      x=strstr(&value,">");                    // Check the returns from ESP8266
      if(x-32<0)
         { lcd_write("ERROR",0xc3); flag=0; break;}
      else
         { lcd_write("OK7   ",0xc3);flag=1; break; }
      }
      delay(60000);
      delay(60000);

    if(flag==1)
    {
    clearVAL();
    value[0]='\0';
    lcd_write("GET DATA",0xc0);
    //Update Channel using Write API Key
    strcat(value,"GET /update?key=xxxxxxxxxxxx&field1=");
    transmit2(&value);lcd_data('1');
    transmit((adc_val/1000)+48); lcd_data('1');
    transmit(((adc_val%1000)/100)+48);lcd_data('1');
    transmit(((adc_val%100)/10)+48);lcd_data('1');
    transmit((adc_val%10)+48);lcd_data('1');
transmit(0x0d);
transmit(0x0a);
delay(40000);
lcd_data('1');
delay(10000);

lcd_cmd(0x01);
delay(2000);
lcd_write("CIPLCOSE",0x80);
```

```
clearVAL();   //AT+CIPCLOSE=0
value[0]='\0';
delay(3000);
strcat(value,"AT+CIPCLOSE");        //Close Channel
transmit_string(&value);
lcd_cmd(0x01);
delay(1000);
} }
lcd_cmd(0x01);
delay(1000);
lcd_write("TEMP:-",0x80);
lcd_write("Upload after:",0xc0);
sec=0;
} } }
```

Circuit Diagram:

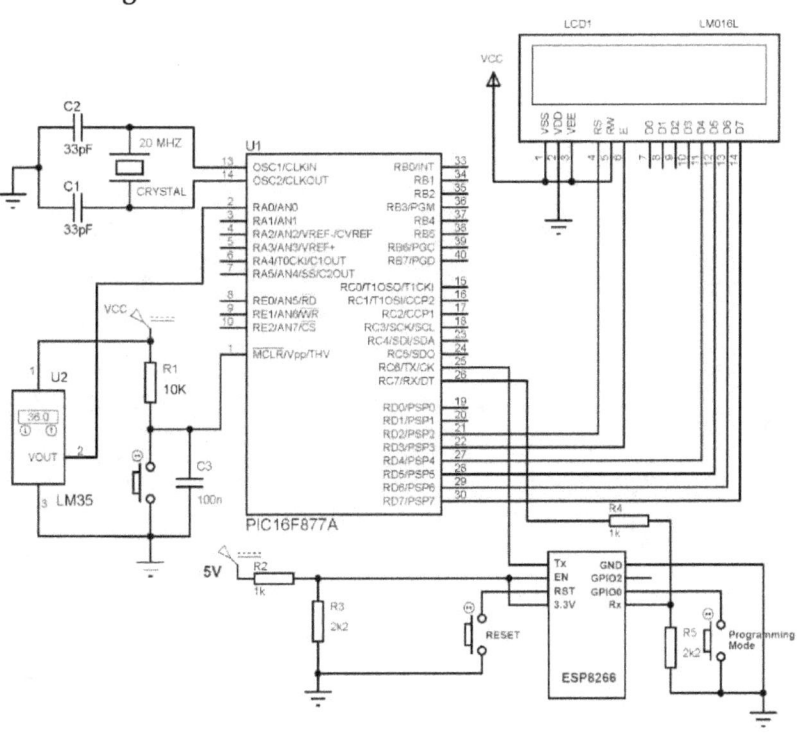

Conclusion:

Thus the IoT based temperature monitor system has designed using ESP8266 Wi-Fi module and the PIC16F887 Microcontroller and verified the output.

****

www.ingramcontent.com/pod-product-compliance
Lightning Source LLC
Chambersburg PA
CBHW071449220526
45472CB00003B/726